APPALACHIAN MOUNTAIN CLUB

Quiet Water

Canoe Guide

Massachusetts
Connecticut
Rhode Island

BEST PADDLING LAKES AND PONDS
FOR ALL AGES

Alex Wilson

APPALACHIAN MOUNTAIN CLUB BOOKS
BOSTON, MASSACHUSETTS

Cover Photograph: Hanson Carroll
Other Photographs: Alex Wilson
Cartography: Nadav Malin, West River Communications, Inc., Brattleboro, Vermont
All artwork copyright © 1993 Gordon Morrison. All rights reserved.
Book Design: Carol Bast Tyler

Distributed by The Globe Pequot Press, Inc., Guilford, CT

Library of Congress Cataloging-in-Publication Data

Wilson, Alex, 1955–
   Appalachian Mountain Club quiet water canoe guide: Massachusetts, Connecticut, Rhode Island: best paddling lakes and ponds for all ages / Alex Wilson.
      p. cm.
   Includes index.
   ISBN 1-878239-19-8: $12.95
   1. Canoes and canoeing—Massachusetts—Guidebooks. 2. Canoes and canoeing—Connecticut—Guidebooks. 3. Canoes and canoeing—Rhode Island—Guidebooks. 4. Massachusetts—Guidebooks. 5. Connecticut—Guidebooks. 6. Rhode Island—Guidebooks. I. Title. II. Title: Quiet Water canoe guide.
GV776.M4W55   1993
797.1'22'09744—dc20   93–21820
                                                                          CIP

**Due to changes in conditions, use of the
information in this book
is at the sole risk of the user.**

Printed in the United States of America.

⊛ Printed on recycled paper.

10 9 8 7   02 03 04

Contents

How to Use This Book

For each lake or pond included in this book, a short descriptive write-up and map have been provided. Most maps show the roads providing access to the body of water, as well as boat launch sites. Some launch sites have boat ramps, while others are unimproved and require a carry to the water. These types of launch sites are not differentiated on the maps.

The maps and write-ups included in this guide are designed to accompany conventional road maps. If you are not familiar with your destination, don't rely on just this book to get there; get a state highway map. Connecticut and Rhode Island have excellent official state highway maps that should provide adequate detail to get you where you're going. The Commonwealth of Massachusetts does not publish a highway map with a scale suitable to show all the bodies of water described in this book. Some privately published maps are better but still may not show all the detail you would like. For more detail, refer to the USGS topographic maps or detailed municipal road maps covering the area in question.

With many of the lakes and ponds, I've included information on nearby camping. If you're interested in more sophisticated lodging, check your local bookstore or library for guides to bed-and-breakfasts or country inns, many of which can be found near the lakes and ponds in this guide. You might also want to contact Chambers of Commerce to get more information on lodging, restaurants, and area attractions.

Several different terms are used throughout this book to identify a body of water—primarily lake, pond, and reservoir. Though there are some differences in these terms (a lake is usually bigger than a pond, and reservoirs are always man-made), they are often used interchangeably. I have tried to stick with the term most widely used in referring to each body of water, but confusion can arise.

Finally, while the book is about quiet water *canoeing,* the information applies equally well to kayaking. In fact, some of the tidal areas are better for sea kayaking than canoeing because of wakes and choppy water that can splash into an open boat. Some of the lakes and ponds included would be fine for sculling as well—though many do not have suitable access.

Legend

Tent site	
Lean-to	
Picnic area	
State or federal campground	
Private campground	
Boat access	
P	Parking area
Marsh	
Peak	
Interstate highway	
State highway	
Paved road	
Less-traveled road	
Rough dirt road	
Foot path	
River	
Stream	

} arrow indicates direction of flow

Locator Map

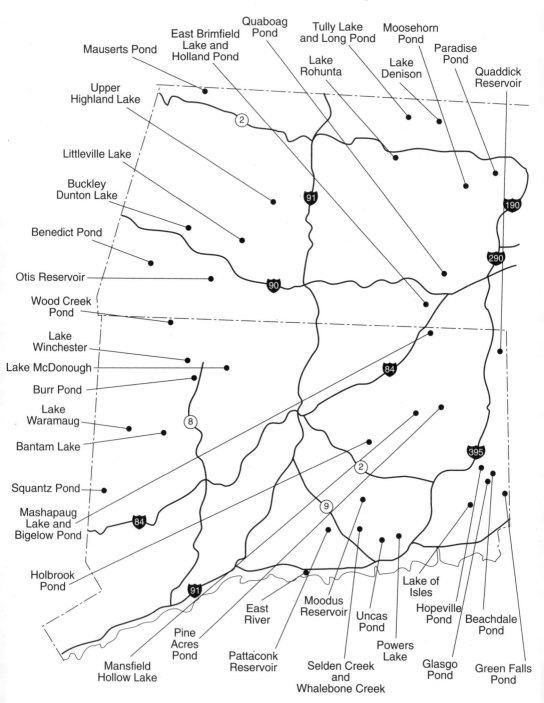

Mauserts Pond

Upper Highland Lake

East Brimfield Lake and Holland Pond

Quaboag Pond

Tully Lake and Long Pond

Moosehorn Pond

Paradise Pond

Lake Rohunta

Lake Denison

Quaddick Reservoir

Littleville Lake

Buckley Dunton Lake

Benedict Pond

Otis Reservoir

Wood Creek Pond

Lake Winchester

Lake McDonough

Burr Pond

Lake Waramaug

Bantam Lake

Squantz Pond

Mashapaug Lake and Bigelow Pond

Holbrook Pond

Mansfield Hollow Lake

Pine Acres Pond

East River

Pattaconk Reservoir

Moodus Reservoir

Selden Creek and Whalebone Creek

Uncas Pond

Powers Lake

Lake of Isles

Hopeville Pond

Glasgo Pond

Beachdale Pond

Green Falls Pond

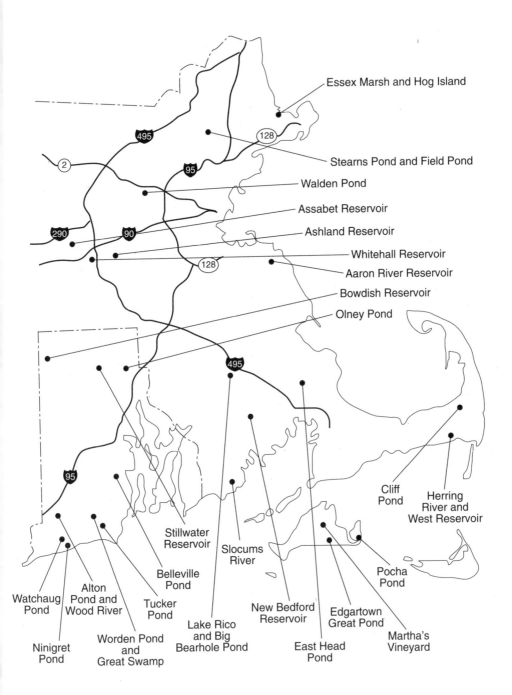

Essex Marsh and Hog Island

Stearns Pond and Field Pond

Walden Pond

Assabet Reservoir

Ashland Reservoir

Whitehall Reservoir

Aaron River Reservoir

Bowdish Reservoir

Olney Pond

Cliff Pond

Herring River and West Reservoir

Stillwater Reservoir

Slocums River

Pocha Pond

Belleville Pond

Watchaug Pond

Alton Pond and Wood River

Tucker Pond

New Bedford Reservoir

Edgartown Great Pond

Ninigret Pond

Worden Pond and Great Swamp

Lake Rico and Big Bearhole Pond

East Head Pond

Martha's Vineyard

Introduction

For some, the lure of paddling is the exhilarating sound of white water churning through narrow gorges and the adrenalin rush as you round the bend and approach the next set of rapids. Indeed I enjoy a bit of white-water canoeing now and then, but for the most part, I'm a different kind of paddler. What lures me to canoeing are the marshy coves and inlets of our out-of-the-way lakes and ponds where wood ducks hide amid the pickerel weed, and the lazy, meandering river or estuary channels where one can watch the playful antics of river otters, reflect on the meaning of life, or simply relax.

With quiet water canoeing, you can focus on being there instead of getting there. You don't need a lot of fancy equipment and high-tech gear—though a nice light canoe is great if you have to portage into the more out-of-the-way places. Other than my paddle and PFD (personal flotation device), my most important gear is a pair of binoculars and field guides to the fauna and flora I'm likely to encounter on my explorations. This is not to say that quiet water canoeing is without risks. You can get yourself into lots of trouble on the larger lakes in bad weather (more on that later), but for the most part the risks are low—low enough that my older daughter donned a PFD for her first canoe trip on her one-month birthday, and low enough that even with two children under seven, my wife and I feel comfortable enough to head out for three- and four-day family canoe camping expeditions.

Being an avid quiet water paddler, I have long made it a habit to explore New England's lakes and ponds. Not all my searches have been successful, though. Our canoe-topped car has logged many miles, some of them fruitless as the pond I sought turned out to be off limits to boating, or chock full of speedboats and water-skiers. My searches for great places to paddle were seldom helped by books. I always found great books on canoeing, but they were all on river canoeing. There was nothing on the types of places I could enjoy with my family and without complicated logistics. I had to do my own exploring. When an opportunity arose to assemble this type of guide for the Appalachian Mountain Club, my explorations spread out and became more systematic. This book is the result of that effort.

Like its companion volume—the AMC *Quiet Water Canoe Guide: New Hampshire/Vermont*—this book fills a void that has existed in the literature, providing information on where you can go for a quiet day or half-day of paddling in Massachusetts, Connecticut, or Rhode Island. From the many hundreds of lakes and ponds in these three states, sixty-one have been selected for inclusion—places with particularly nice features. The book describes how to get there, where you can park, camping opportunities in the area (in many cases), and most important, what's special about the body of water and what you might see there.

How These Lakes and Ponds Were Selected

This guide includes only a small percentage of the lakes and ponds in the three states. I started the selection process with some definite likes and dislikes when it comes to canoeing. Among the features I look for in a lake or pond are the following: pretty scenery; not too much development around the shoreline; not too many motorboats; a varied shoreline with lots of coves and inlets to explore; and interesting plants, animals, and geological features.

I wanted to include a variety of types of bodies of water in the book: some big lakes for when you want to cover a lot of distance, and some protected ponds that are just right for young paddlers, short excursions, or when it's windy. To make the book useful to more people, I tried to spread out the bodies of water geographically, making it possible to visit nice spots without spending half your time in the car.

I had a few favorite canoeing locations in these states when I took on this project, but I knew that I'd be exploring lakes and ponds I had never even heard of, let alone paddled on. Finding the nicest would take some work. I asked friends and friends-of-friends—anyone I could find who shared an interest in quiet water canoeing—for suggestions. They proved a big help, but I went further, spending days poring over United States Geological Survey (USGS) topographic maps for the three states, and studying literature provided by the states on public boat access, reviewing fishing guides and information from the U.S. Army Corps of Engineers. From the USGS maps, I could get a sense of how developed a lake or pond was (although, as I found out, some of these maps are quite out-of-date).

I compiled an initial list of over 200 lakes, ponds, and tidal estuaries in Connecticut, Massachusetts, and Rhode Island. Quite a few of these were eliminated by phone calls to municipalities—finding out that the body of water was off-limits to boating—but I still visited more than 150 lakes and ponds, and paddled on about 90 of them. Some two-thirds of these I found nice enough to include in this guide.

I have by no means found all the best places. As I proceeded with the project, I constantly discovered new lakes and ponds—through someone's tip or just a reexamination of the maps. I'm sure there are still dozens of other lakes and ponds around the three states that really *should* be in a guide like this. That's what future editions are for.

Do I Really Want to Tell People about the Best Places?

Throughout this project, many people have asked me how I could tell others about my favorite hidden lakes and ponds—the remote, pristine places still unspoiled by too many people. After all, increased visitation would make these places less idyllic. That has indeed been a difficult issue for me and one I've spent many an hour grappling with as I paddled along.

What I've come to is this: By getting more people like you and me—people who value wild remote areas for what they are—out enjoying these places, we will be able to build support for greater protection of these bodies of water. For many lakes and ponds, protection means the purchase of fragile areas by such groups as the Nature Conservancy to prevent further development. On other bodies of water, the best form of protection is restriction on motorboat use, which is generally handled by state government.

My hope is that you will become involved in helping protect some of our most treasured water resources. For many of the lakes, ponds, and estuaries in southern New England, the most vocal users right now are people who use motorboats to fish and water-ski. When surveys are done about the recreational use of these places, the loudest voice is from those people who are having the greatest impact on these delicate environments. The policymakers need to hear from the low-impact users as well. I hope that in a few years, I'll be able to report that many more of the lakes and ponds included here are better protected than they are today, and thus likely to remain enjoyable to quiet water paddlers for years and years to come.

Safety First

You might be attracted to quiet water because you paddle with small children and don't want to risk capsizing in a swift-flowing river. Or maybe you just don't like dangerous places, such as raging white water on rivers in the spring, or places where you have to concentrate too much on your paddling skills. So you turn to the lakes and ponds, envisioning tranquil paddling on mirror-smooth water reflecting the surrounding hills.

You will certainly find these conditions, especially in the early morning hours. But if you spend any time at all paddling in New England, you may also encounter quite dangerous and even life-threatening conditions. Strong winds can come up very quickly, especially in coastal areas, turning a tranquil lake into a not-so-quiet, whitecap-filled inland sea. On a big lake or estuary, strong winds can stir up two-foot waves in almost no time—waves that can quickly swamp a canoe. Unlike river paddling, on the larger lakes you are often far from shore, and capsizing in cold water can bring on hypothermia rapidly.

On some of the bodies of water included here, you also need to be careful about big boats with big wakes. On the section of the Connecticut River by Selden Neck, for example, large tug-drawn barges and cabin cruisers can throw out a three-foot wake—more than enough to roll or swamp your canoe. And there are horror stories on the big lakes like Candlewood of motorboat operators not even seeing canoes and colliding. A good motorboater will know to slow his or her boat when nearing paddlers, but you can't always count on that—believe me.

The bottom line is that you can encounter dangerous conditions on most lakes and ponds. Always use care, and be sure to have one PFD for each person in the canoe. The best practice is always to wear your PFD in the canoe. Certainly all children should wear them, and if there are children in the boat, you too should wear a PFD so that if the boat capsizes, you can be of more help to the children. If you don't normally wear your PFD while you paddle, at least put it on when wind comes up, when you're crossing a large lake, when there is substantial motorboat traffic, or when you have to deal with strong tidal currents. It may be an inconvenience, it may make you a little hotter in the summer, it may interfere a bit with your paddling. But it could save your life! So far, I've avoided any serious canoeing mishaps, but there have been numerous occasions—especially when my children were with me—when strong winds have come up unexpectedly, making me glad that we were well protected with high-quality PFDs.

Also, in the name of safety, be ready to change your plans. If you've just driven an hour or two to get to a sizable lake and it's too windy, be ready to find a smaller pond that's more protected, or go hiking instead. Even if the forecaster promises a beautiful sunny day with no wind, it could end up blowing a gale and raining. So, be flexible in your plans.

On some lakes, ponds, and estuaries described in this guide, you should also be aware that hunting season can bring a big influx of activity. I have tried to note those places where waterfowl hunting is popular—avoid these areas during hunting season. If you don't know when hunting season is, you can find out from state fish and wildlife offices. In Massachusetts, contact the Massachusetts Division of Fisheries and Wildlife, 100 Cambridge Street, Boston, MA 02202; 617-727-3151; in Connecticut, contact the Connecticut Department of Environmental Protection, Wildlife Division, Room 254, 165 Capitol Avenue, Hartford, CT 06106; 203-566-4683; in Rhode Island, contact the Rhode Island Division of Fish and Wildlife, Oliver Stedman Government Center, 4808 Tower Hill Road, Wakefield, RI 02879; 401-789-3094.

Special Considerations for Tidal Rivers and Estuaries

The numerous tidal estuaries, marshes, and rivers along the coast of Massachusetts, Connecticut, and Rhode Island provide some of the finest canoeing in New England. Eight such bodies of water are included in this book, from Essex Marsh and Hog Island north of Boston to East River in Connecticut, and Martha's Vineyard. Tidal paddling can be dangerous, though, and requires some special safety precautions. As the name implies, tidal wetlands are influenced by tides—the twice-daily cycling of high and low tides resulting from the gravitational attraction of the moon as it revolves around the earth. Except at a turning or ebb tide, the tide is always either coming in or going out, alternately filling or emptying the estuary.

For the paddler, this means that you will have to be paddling in flowing water. How fast the tidal current is depends on the height differential between high and low tide, which ranges from two to twelve feet along the southern New England coast, how large the area being drained and filled is, and the configuration of the tidal channel. A very narrow channel will have a faster tidal current than a broad one. Even a slow-moving tidal river can have a quite fast current where it narrows under a highway bridge or at a breachway into the ocean. While tidal currents can make paddling quite difficult, they can also work with you if you plan carefully. For example, on a tidal river like the Herring River on Cape Cod or East River in Connecticut, you can launch a boat near the mouth of the river as the tide is coming in, follow the tidal current upstream as high tide approaches, enjoy some exploring at high tide, then paddle back downstream with the current as the tide drops. In other words, you can enjoy a day of river canoeing, always paddling with the current, and end up where you began.

Predicting high and low tides on these estuaries can be difficult, though. High tide in some of these areas can lag an hour or two behind high tide at the ocean. If the channel connecting the ocean to the estuary is narrow, you can find yourself fighting against an incoming tidal current even after the high tide should have passed. This is because the channel does not let water through quickly enough to allow the estuary to keep pace with the rising and falling tide on the ocean. This happens at Ninigret Pond in Rhode Island, as you may discover if you launch your canoe along the narrow breachway connecting the pond to the ocean. The conditions change daily depending on the height of the tide.

When paddling in tidal areas, check the local tide chart, or pick up a current copy of the *Eldridge Tide and Pilot Book* (Marion Jewett White, Publisher, 34 Commercial Wharf, Boston, MA 02110), which includes tide information for the entire Northeast and has lots of other pertinent information relating to saltwater boating—including the speed of tidal currents in selected locations. In some areas, the tidal currents are just too fast to paddle safely unless you are a skilled white-water paddler, and with some the currents are simply too fast to paddle against. Wearing a PFD is especially important with tidal paddling.

Also keep in mind the fact that tidal bodies of water are often quite windy. A stiff offshore breeze can compound the difficulty of paddling against a tidal current, making paddling extremely difficult and tiring. If the day is windy, or if strong breezes are expected to come up, be ready to change your plans and find a quieter inland body of water where you can enjoy some relaxing easy paddling.

Other Concerns: Lyme Disease and Poison Ivy

Tick-borne Lyme disease has become a significant health threat in southern New England. Some coastal areas have very high concentrations of deer ticks, which carry the bacteria. Deer ticks are tiny, about the size of a pinhead. They are found in grassy and wooded areas, especially locations with high mammal populations. The greatest risk from deer ticks is from April through September, and risk is lowest in the dead of winter. Deer tick bites are not painful and they often go unnoticed. If you are bitten, you still might not contract Lyme disease. Not all ticks carry the disease, and even if the tick does, it might not pass the bacteria along to you. Removing ticks promptly will reduce your chances of getting sick. Use fine-point tweezers to remove the tiny ticks, and swab the area with antiseptic or soap and water. The most common early symptom of Lyme disease is a slowly expanding red rash that may swell slightly. Not all people develop this rash, though. If untreated, later symptoms of Lyme disease include joint aches (thus the earlier name of Lyme arthritis), heart problems, and nervous system complications. Sometimes these symptoms take many months to appear. If you experience unusual symptoms, contact your doctor right away. Rapid treatment is important to ensure complete recovery.

Poison ivy is far less of a concern than Lyme disease, but a bad case can be very debilitating. Some individuals have fairly severe allergic reactions. There is a lot of poison ivy in southern New England, especially in coastal areas. Learn to identify this plant so that you can avoid it. If you do come into contact with it, try to wash the area thoroughly with soap and water.

Starting Out Right: Equipment Selection

To get started with quiet water canoeing, you don't really need a whole lot of fancy, high-tech gear. Almost any canoe will do, as long as it isn't a high-performance racing model or a tippy boat designed for white water. If you're new to canoeing, try borrowing a canoe for your first few trips. Once you've had a little experience, you'll be in a much better position to select a canoe to buy.

If you're buying a canoe, look for one that is stable. Canoe manufacturers often refer to both the initial stability and the secondary stability of their boats. A canoe with good initial stability and poor secondary stability will be unlikely to begin tipping, but once it tips up a bit it may keep going (this is the case with some older aluminum canoes). Look for a model that does pretty well with both initial and secondary stability. The best canoe for lake and pond canoeing has a keel or shallow-V hull and flat keel-line to keep it tracking well across the water, even in a breeze. White-water canoes, on the other hand, have rounded bottoms and what's called *rocker,* a curve to the bottom from front to back. Rocker provides maneuverability in white water, but makes tracking difficult in open water.

If you like the out-of-the-way lakes and ponds, especially those that require portaging in, you should try to stretch your budget to afford a Kevlar® canoe. Kevlar is a very strong fiber similar to fiberglass, but much lighter. My full-size Kevlar canoe weighs just fifty-five pounds, and my solo canoe (also Kevlar), around forty. If you plan to do a lot of canoeing by yourself, you should consider a solo canoe, in which you sit or kneel close to the center of the boat. You will be amazed at how easily a well-designed solo canoe handles compared with a standard two-seater used for solo canoeing.

Look for a good canoe carrying rack. I prefer a simple two-bar system that clips onto the car's rain gutters. You can save money by purchasing just the mounting brackets and cutting sections of two-by-four for the racks. (With newer cars that do not have gutters, you may need to buy one of the more expensive rack systems.) I strap the canoe onto both racks and also secure it to both front and rear bumpers. The sales people in any good outdoor equipment store should be able to set you up with an easy-to-use system.

Though not essential, a portage yoke in place of the canoe's center thwart makes portaging a lot easier. (A thwart is a wood or metal support that spans the width of the canoe from gunwale to gunwale.) If you expect to do a lot of portaging, you might also want to choose a PFD with padded shoulders. Even with a portage yoke, this extra padding can make a long carry much more comfortable. Also, always attach a rope—called a *painter*—to the front of the canoe so that you can tie it up when you stop for lunch or, more important, so that you or someone else can grab onto the canoe if need be.

Paddles should be light and comfortable. My favorite paddle is relatively short (fifty-six inches) with a blade made of various laminated woods, including both softwoods and hardwoods. It also has a special synthetic tip to protect the blade from damage if you hit rocks or push off from shore. You can try out one of the new bent-shaft paddles, but I prefer a straight-shaft paddle.

As mentioned earlier, life preservers are a must—both by common sense and by law. The best type of life preserver is a Coast Guard–approved Type I, II, or III personal flotation device or PFD. A Type IV PFD (floating cushion) is acceptable by law for adults, but is far less effective than a life vest that you wear. A good PFD is relatively expensive, but it is designed to keep a person's face above water, even if he or she loses consciousness. There must be one PFD in the boat for each occupant, according to Connecticut, Massachusetts, and Rhode Island laws. (New federal regulations may soon specify that only Type I, II, and III PFDs are acceptable, not Type IV.) Massachusetts and Rhode Island go further with their boating safety regulations. In Massachusetts, a Type I, II, or III PFD must be worn by all canoe and kayak occupants at all times between September 15 and May

15, and a Type I, II, or III PFD must be worn at all times on all vessels by children under twelve years of age. In Rhode Island, all children under ten years of age must wear PFDs on boats under sixteen feet in length. With children, it is extremely important that the PFD be the right size so that it won't slip off. Adult PFDs for children are not acceptable. If adults in the canoe are not wearing their PFDs, they must be readily accessible. As explained previously, however, I recommend that you wear your PFD at all times, especially if you are paddling with children. You'll set a good example.

As for clothing, plan for the unexpected—especially on longer trips. Even with a bright sunny day forecast, I have frequently had a shower come along. So I make it a habit to always take a small stuff sack with my rain gear in the canoe. On longer trips I also carry a dry change of clothes. Along with rain coming up unexpectedly, temperatures can drop very quickly. Bring plenty of warm clothes if you will be out for a few hours with children. The kids are probably just sitting while you're doing the work. Even though you may be plenty warm from paddling, they can be getting cold. Watch for signs of discomfort.

Bringing the Kids Along

Quiet water canoeing is a great activity to do with kids, as long as the conditions are all right and as long as you've taken adequate safety precautions. Maintain flexibility in your plans in case of adverse weather, and always make it a rule to wear PFDs in the canoe. We have a simple rule in our family: If you don't wear the PFD, you don't get in the canoe. Period. To make wearing the life vest more acceptable to our three- and six-year-old daughters, my wife and I also wear ours.

When paddling with kids you should also set up some rules about suddenly changing position in the boat. When both kids and the dog (well, that's another issue...) suddenly shift from one side of the canoe to the other, it can rock the boat precariously, especially if there's a strong breeze or waves. Two children side by side in the center of the canoe often works fairly well. We've rigged up a rope fence to keep our dog approximately in the center of the boat. Fortunately, we have a particularly mellow golden retriever, who is very good in a canoe; I wouldn't want to paddle with a lot of dogs I know.

My final suggestion for canoeing with kids—and perhaps the most important—is to make it fun. If the parents are arguing about who should be paddling on which side of the boat, or yelling about rocks ahead, the kids will be affected. Try to keep calm. Your kids will do better, and you'll have a better time. On long trips, set up a cozy place where young children can sleep. We find that after the initial excitement of paddling fades, the gently rolling canoe often puts our kids to sleep, especially near the end of a long day. If you haven't taken your kids canoeing before, they might be anxious on the first trip or two, but after they are used to it, they will be much more relaxed.

Respect for the Outdoors

Lakes and ponds are among our most heavily used recreational areas. Keeping them in good shape requires special attention. Even such a low-impact pastime as canoeing can have a substantial effect on a fragile marsh habitat. Our wetlands are extremely important ecosystems for wildlife and home to many rare and endangered species. An unaware paddler can disturb rare turtles, nesting waterfowl, and fragile aquatic environments. Paddling through a shallow marsh can even injure the roots of ecologically important plants. So use care as you enjoy these waters.

You even can go further than the old adage, "Take only photographs, leave only footprints." On the most pristine of our lakes and ponds, I make it a habit to carry a bag with me and pick up the leavings of other less-thoughtful individuals. If each of us can do the same, not only will we end up with much more attractive places to paddle, but we will also be appreciated. While motorboaters tend to have a bad reputation when it comes to leaving trash, I want canoeists to have the opposite reputation—which could come in handy when we are seeking greater paddling access on some of the region's more remote lakes. To learn more about how to enjoy a wild area without damaging it, see the excellent book, *Soft Paths* by Hampton and Cole (Stackpole Books, 1988).

What You'll See

Wetland ecosystems are diverse and exciting—by far the richest ecosystems we have access to. In Connecticut, Massachusetts, and Rhode Island, you can visit everything from saltwater estuarian marshes to deep, crystal-clear mountain ponds and unique bog environments. You'll have the opportunity to observe hundreds of species of birds; dozens of species of mammals, turtles, snakes; and hundreds of plants. Some of these species are quite rare and exciting to discover—such as a delicate orchid or a family of otters. But even the ordinary plants and animals are a storehouse of information and discovery, providing hours of observation.

I've picked out a few of the more interesting plants and animals that you might encounter on the lakes and ponds of southern New England and written up some notes on them. You will find these write-ups—and accompanying pen-and-ink illustrations by Gordon Morrison—interspersed in the lake and pond descriptions. By learning a little more about these species, you'll find them all the more fun to watch.

Have a Great Time

The purpose of this guide is to help you enjoy and appreciate our outdoors. I hope you will enjoy using this book as much as I enjoyed researching and writing it. Let me know what you like or dislike about the places I've described, and tell me about any others that you think should be included. Send comments to Alex Wilson, c/o AMC Books, 5 Joy Street, Boston, MA 02108. Also pass along any inaccuracies found in this edition as well as suggestions for additional information that could be included in future editions.

Finally, don't consider this guide as a limit to the areas you can visit. There are other lakes and ponds—hundreds more in these three states—many of which offer excellent quiet water canoeing. Buy some topographic or other maps and explore. You'll find, as I did, that many of the ponds shown on maps are municipal water supplies and off-limits to canoes. Others are private. And others are too built up with summer homes. But there are many gems out there that are not written up in this guide—hidden beaver ponds, quiet meandering channels of slow-moving streams and rivers, old mill ponds with ruins of long-abandoned mills, bird-filled estuaries—places whose secrets you can either reveal to others or keep to yourself. And that's as it should be.

Alex Wilson
October 1992

# Massachusetts

Essex Marsh and Hog Island
Essex, MA

Within an hour's drive of Boston a more splendid canoeing spot simply does not exist. The Essex Marsh is a broad saltwater estuary north and east of Essex, comprising the Essex and Castle rivers and several thousand acres of tidal creek and salt-marsh environment between Route 133 to the south and west, Castle Neck to the north, and Essex Bay to the east. Castle Neck, with its sand dunes and beach plum/bayberry highlands, protects the marsh from the open ocean. In the middle of the marsh sits Hog Island (also known as Choate Island), a tall island that dominates the local topography. Hog Island is a rather dramatic glacial drumlin, rising steeply on the western side to 177 feet, then sloping more gradually to the east. Drumlins are glacial deposits formed by the receding glacier. They frequently look like the bowl of an inverted teaspoon—steeper on one side than the other. Hog Island and several smaller surrounding islands are owned by The Trustees of Reservations and maintained as the Crane Wildlife Refuge. In the right conditions, paddling here is wonderful—about the nicest salt-marsh canoeing you will find. But because all the water is tidal, with a tide differential of eight to ten feet and extensive areas that are entirely drained at low tide, you need to plan your trip carefully.

GETTING THERE: There is a good put-in point on the Essex River in the Town of Essex right on Route 133. If driving from Boston or points west on Route 128, get off at Exit 14, and drive west on Route 133 towards Essex. In 3.3 miles you will see the Essex River on the right and Woodman's Restaurant on the left. There is a small boat launch right across the road from Woodman's where you can unload your canoe and gear. Then park behind the restaurant at a small roadside park.

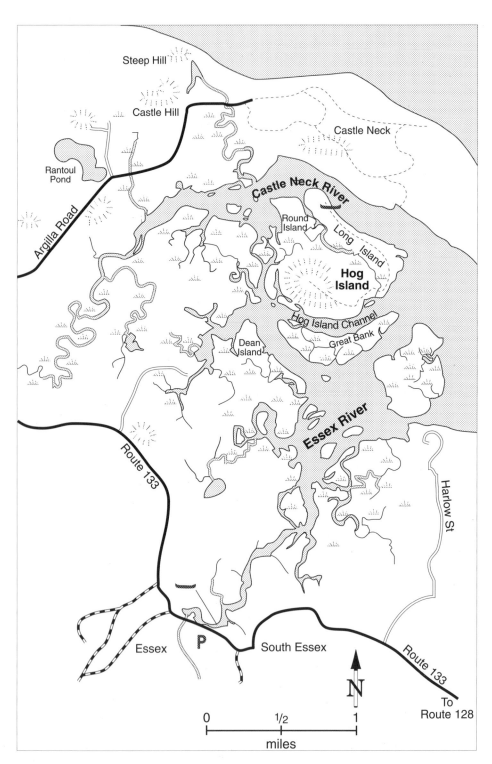

Steep Hill

Castle Hill

Castle Neck

Rantoul
Pond

Argilla Road

Castle Neck River

Round
Island

Long Island

Hog
Island

Hog Island Channel

Great Bank

Dean
Island

Essex River

Route 133

Harlow St

Essex

P

South Essex

Route 133

To
Route 128

N

0   1/2   1
miles

Approaching from the south, you will see Hog Island's distinct profile rising above the salt marsh.

As you launch your boat, paddle to the right (downstream if the tide is going out; upstream if the tide is coming in) and follow the widening channel toward Hog Island. (If you paddle the other way on the Essex River you will quickly come to a dock and marina, then the Route 133 bridge. The Essex River on the other side of the bridge is attractive and rich with wildlife, but be forewarned that the tidal current under the bridge, where the channel is constricted, is very fast. You may have trouble paddling against the current.) As you round successive curves heading generally north, Hog Island will come into view. Look back periodically as you paddle towards Hog Island and note landmarks that will guide your return. At different water levels, the area can look quite different, and it's possible to get disoriented. (Also, remember that at low tide you will be about eight feet lower than you are at high tide.)

To reach the boat landing on the north side of adjoining Long Island, initially aim for the steeper western end of Hog Island. As you get near, you will see a channel heading off to the right in front of the island. You can follow this Hog Island Channel to the right and then around the island, or—if the tide is high enough—continue around the west side of the island. The western route is a little more direct, but on either side of low tide it is blocked off by exposed tidal flats. To avoid problems with low water it is a good idea to plan a trip here so that you are arriving and leaving within three or four hours of high tide. You can land your boat at Long Island between 9 AM and 3:30 PM from Memorial Day weekend through Columbus Day weekend. Upon landing, register with a Trustees of Reservations staff member. Hiking here is free to members of The Trustees of Reservations; the fee for others in 1992 was $2 for adults, $1 for children aged six to twelve, and no fee for children under six. Also pick up a self-guided tour map and description of the Crane Wildlife Refuge.

Hog Island

A wonderful trail extends southeast from the dock on Long Island and then across to Hog Island. This trail, maintained by The Trustees of Reservations, takes you past a large barn on Long Island, a newer Cape-style cottage (part of which serves as a visitor center), and the original Choate House on the main island. The house was built by Thomas Choate between 1725 and 1749. It is a beautiful example of early eighteenth-century architecture. Restored in 1977, it is open to the public by appointment with the refuge staff. From the Choate House, you can walk uphill to the island's peak, passing the oddly out-of-place spruce forest that was planted in the 1930s by Richard Crane, the Chicago plumbing magnate, who purchased the entire island and a great deal of surrounding land in the early 1900s.

Until recently, the Crane Wildlife Refuge housed a quite large population of deer, typically numbering from fifty to seventy-five. Because hunting was not permitted at the refuge and there were no native predators, the deer became quite tame and visitors could watch them at close range. Since the mid-1980s, however, Lyme disease borne by deer ticks has become a major problem on isolated islands such as this. To reduce the deer population in an effort to control the ticks, limited hunting has been permitted in recent years, and the deer are fewer in number and much more wary of humans.

Getting back in your canoe, you can explore a little way into Lee's Creek between Hog Island and Round Island, but much of this area is protected as bird-nesting habitat. The water around Hog Island seemed exceptionally clear when I paddled here, with white sand visible even ten or fifteen feet down. You might also want to paddle across to Castle Neck and explore the sand dunes and Crane's Beach, also owned by The Trustees of Reservations. (If you pull your canoe up on Castle Neck be sure to account for rising tide and pull it up far enough. Also, be careful not to damage the fragile dune ecosystem.)

On your way back to the Essex River landing, you might also want to explore portions of the Castle Neck River and the inlet creeks and channels that reach into the salt marsh. For the birdwatcher or wildlife enthusiast, salt marshes provide an extremely interesting ecosystem, dominated by saltwater cordgrass (*Spartina alterniflora*) and salt-meadow grass (*S. patens*). At high tide, you can explore deeply into the little side creeks and inlets and look out over the thousands of acres of *Spartina*. At low tide you will see mussels clinging to the sod banks, green crabs, perhaps horseshoe crabs, and clumps of seaweed clinging to rocks. On the mud flats, keep an eye out for various sandpipers and gulls. You may also see osprey here, which wildlife experts have been hoping would return to northern Massachusetts since their decline several decades ago from DDT poisoning. Over 20 species of birds nest at the refuge and more than 180 migrating species have been sighted here.

If you want to take advantage of tidal currents as you paddle to and from Hog Island, you will have to plan to stay on the island at least three or four hours—through a low-tide cycle. Leave the Essex River landing within a few hours after high tide and paddle with the current out to the island as described above. Spend the day on the island and return two or three hours after low tide so that you can ride the tide back in. If you don't have this much time, you can paddle against the current on the Essex River. This is what I've done, and as long as you aren't fighting both the current and a strong wind, you shouldn't have too much trouble. Be sure to check a weather forecast before starting, especially if you plan to stay on the island through a low-tide cycle, since you are pretty well trapped there for a few hours when the tide is at its lowest. Also be aware that you need to paddle across a fairly broad expanse of water and low salt marsh; strong winds can generate sizable waves. Wear your PFD when paddling here.

For more information on the Crane Wildlife Refuge, Hog Island, Crane Neck, and the surrounding area, contact The Trustees of Reservations, Northeast Regional Office, P.O. Box 563, Ipswich, MA 01938; 508-356-4351. The refuge is maintained with support from TTOR members (individual membership costs $35 per year and family membership $50). There is also an excellent description of the area in the AMC book *More Country Walks Near Boston* by William Scheller.

Stearns Pond and Field Pond
North Andover and Andover, MA

A collection of small ponds in Harold Parker State Forest, a half-hour north of Boston, provides opportunity for very relaxing, quiet water paddling. Of the nine named ponds in the forest, I've paddled on the two largest: Stearns Pond and Field Pond. Gasoline-powered motorboats are prohibited on all ponds in the Forest. In fact, there aren't even any real boat ramps, so access is effectively limited to carry-in boats.

Both Stearns and Field ponds have highly varied shorelines—full of coves, inlets, and islands—so despite their small sizes, you can do a surprising amount of exploration. The shorelines are wooded with mixed conifer and deciduous trees. Along the shore, shrubs are fairly dense, but there are plenty of places to get out and enjoy a picnic or take a walk on the needle-carpeted forest floor. There is a small swimming beach on Stearns Pond. Some areas of these ponds are thick with both floating and submerged vegetation—great habitat for bass. There are also many mossy hillocks in the shallows—remains of trees killed years ago when the dams were built. Look for the small carnivorous sundew plants amid the sphagnum moss on these hillocks. Along the shallow sandy shores, you are likely to see lots of freshwater mussel shells left by the area's industrious raccoons, and you may well see a great blue heron or two and the oddly proportioned kingfisher as you paddle here.

The 3500-acre state forest provides plenty of opportunity for exploring with your canoe, especially if you don't mind a small portage. You can paddle on any of the ponds as long as you park off the pavement. If there seem to be too many canoes on the larger ponds described above, do a little exploring. You can put your canoe in across the road from Field Pond into Collins Pond, for example; paddle to the north end and then carry over to Brackett Pond, where you're unlikely to see other boats. Salem Pond is the most remote pond here and requires a considerable carry. To explore these areas, pick up a Harold Parker State Forest Trail Map, which shows the network of trails and unpaved roads through the forest—most of the unpaved roads are closed to vehicles.

GETTING THERE: Harold Parker State Forest can be reached from Interstate 93 by getting off at Exit 41 and driving north on Route 125 for 2.6 miles (passing the intersection with Route 28) to Gould Road and the state forest entrance. Turning off Route 125, take a shallow right

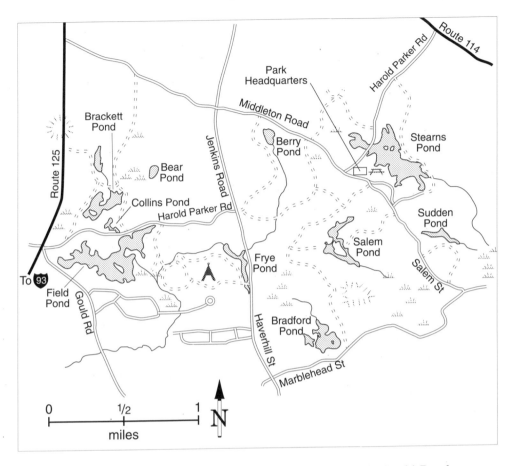

onto Harold Parker Road; a hard right would put you on Gould Road. You will reach Field Pond on the right after about 0.6 mile, with parking along the road (you must park off the pavement, but there is quite a bit of space along here). To get to Stearns Pond, continue on Harold Parker Road to the stop sign, turn left on Jenkins Road then right on Middleton Road and drive for 1.0 mile to the continuation of Harold Parker Road. Turn left here, and the canoe access onto Stearns Pond will be on the right after about 0.3 mile (again, there is not a real parking area; you have to pull onto the side of the road off the pavement).

Camping is available here. The camping entrance is on Jenkins Road just south of the intersection with the western extension of Harold Parker Road (see map). Camping rates in 1992 were $12 per night. For more information, contact Harold Parker State Forest, 1951 Turnpike Road, North Andover, MA 01845; 508-686-3391.

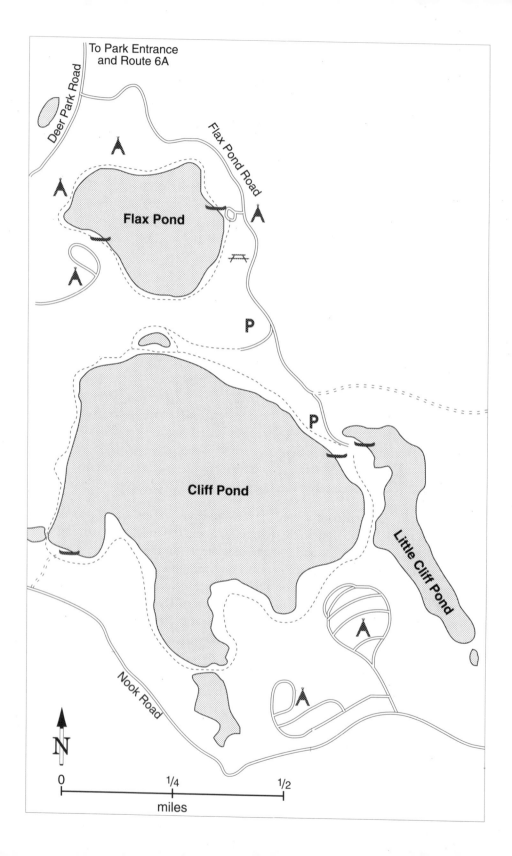

Cliff Pond, Little Cliff Pond, Flax Pond

Nickerson State Park, Brewster, MA

Nickerson State Park, with over 1700 acres and 420 campsites, is one of the largest state parks in Massachusetts and about the best spot for camping and freshwater canoeing on the Cape—especially if you can avoid the peak summer visiting season. The park has more than a dozen kettle ponds—shallow depressions that were formed ten thousand years ago as the receding glaciers left large chunks of ice buried in glacial debris. As the ice gradually melted, the shallow depressions filled with water. Because most kettle ponds are not fed by significant streams, their levels fluctuate considerably with the season and the amount of rainfall.

Three of these ponds—Cliff, Little Cliff, and Flax—provide excellent paddling. Cliff Pond is the largest pond in Nickerson State Park. You can launch a canoe either on the west side (the primary launch point), or on the east side, between Cliff and Little Cliff. The wide, shallow, sandy shorelines of these ponds are typical of kettle ponds. In fact, in some areas at some water levels you will have to drag your canoe out a few hundred feet until the water is deep enough to float the canoe with you in it. That was the case at the launch area between Cliff and Little Cliff Ponds when I visited. Some of the shallower sections of shoreline are quite thick with vegetation, but most of the shoreline is sandy and readily accessible to either paddler or swimmer. Little Cliff Pond is narrower than Cliff Pond, and Flax Pond is rounder, but otherwise these ponds are very similar.

Surrounding the ponds you will see large stands of pitch pine and black oak, along with white pine, hemlock, and spruce that were planted by the Civilian Conservation Corps in the 1930s. Except for the campgrounds and park features, there is no development around these ponds and in the park.

Nickerson State Park was created in 1934 when the Roland Nickerson estate—the largest private holding of forest land on the Cape—was given to the Commonwealth. Along with the ponds, numerous hiking and bicycle trails wind through the forested park, and the scenic Cape Cod Rail Trail passes through the north end of the park. On the Cape Cod Rail Trail you can bicycle approximately twenty miles. Going southwest from Nickerson State Park, the trail leads to Dennis in 11.6 miles; heading northeast, you reach the Salt Pond National Seashore Visitors Center in Eastham in 7.9 miles. Occupying the bed of an abandoned railway, this is almost an ideal bicycle trail, with generally flat terrain and minimal road crossings and interruptions. You can pick up a map of the trail and rent bicycles at Nickerson State Park.

The ponds at Nickerson State Park are popular for fishing. The major ponds are stocked yearly with trout and bass. It is also of note that a new world-record American eel was caught at Cliff Pond in 1992: an 8-pound, 4-ounce eel, measuring 46 inches in length with a girth of $10\frac{1}{2}$ inches. While not popular today, eel was so common in the diet of nineteenth-century New Englanders that it came to be known as "Derryfield beef." The eel is returning to favor, though, via Japanese sushi bars. Eels are a unique fish in that they breed at sea, then return inland until they reach adulthood. The eel caught at Cliff Pond was probably cut off from the sea many years ago, as they are reported to live thirty to fifty years.

GETTING THERE: To reach Nickerson State Park, take Route 6 east to Exit 12, then turn onto Route 6A west, following signs for Nickerson State Park. You will reach the park entrance in 1.6 miles. Pick up a map of the park at the headquarters and follow the map or signs to one of the boat launch locations. Tent camping is available from April through October (call for exact dates). You can camp with a self-contained vehicle year-round (self-contained vehicles have water and toilet facilities). Campsites were $12 per night in 1992. This is a great place, but be aware that camping occupancy is near 100 percent from late June—when kids get out of school—until Labor Day. All campsites are on a first-come, first-served basis; there are no reservations. Campsite occupancy is limited to two weeks from the last Sunday in June to the Sunday before Labor Day, and there are no hookups. Canoe rentals are available on Flax Pond. For more information, contact Nickerson State Park, Route 6A, Brewster, MA 02631; 508-896-3491.

Herring River and West Reservoir
Harwich, MA

Well away from the usual recreation destinations on Cape Cod, the Herring River provides superb quiet paddling through bird-filled salt-water and freshwater marsh. Even on a fairly windy day, the river is canoeable—especially if you can time your paddling to coincide with the tides. The best canoeing on the Herring River is from Route 28 in West Harwich up to West Reservoir. (You can also paddle on down to Nantucket Sound, but there are lots of houses south of Route 28.)

Put in by the Route 28 bridge over the Herring River. Paddling upriver from here (north), you will initially pass a few houses on the west shore, but these are quickly left behind as you enter the broad, wild salt marsh through which the gently flowing river winds. This is a tremendous spot for birding. You're likely to see gulls, snowy egrets, great blue herons, green herons, yellowlegs, Canada geese, cormorants, mallards, black ducks, mute swans, redwing blackbirds, and various hawks as you paddle along here. The marsh is thick with the common grasses and cattails of the salt-marsh environment that provide nesting habitat for some of the species of birds that one hears but rarely sees: marsh wrens, swamp sparrows, Virginia rails, and least bitterns. In the trees on both sides of the marsh are many woodland species, including the Northern Parula warbler, which use the beard moss that hangs from many trees here, in making its nest.

The Herring River is tidal all the way up to the dike containing West Reservoir, though the farther up you paddle, the less saline the water, as the river's flow dilutes the ocean water. Your paddling will be somewhat easier if you can paddle upriver as the tide is coming in, though the river's flow is gentle enough so that wind is usually a bigger factor than current, and wind is a common companion on the Cape! Near high tide, you can explore numerous little canals and inlets along the river. At the outlet from West Reservoir, you have to carry your canoe up over the dike to get onto the reservoir. Pull over on the left side as you paddle upstream, just beside the outlet from the fish ladder. During the spawning season for herring (alewife), you can watch the fish swimming from pool to pool in this fish ladder; in fact, this is a popular place for netting herring (regulations are posted).

West Reservoir is all fresh water and a great location for studying aquatic plants, birds, and other wildlife inhabiting the reservoir and sur-rounding woodland. I saw a dozen black-crowned night herons here as I paddled around the reservoir. But even more exciting was the turtle

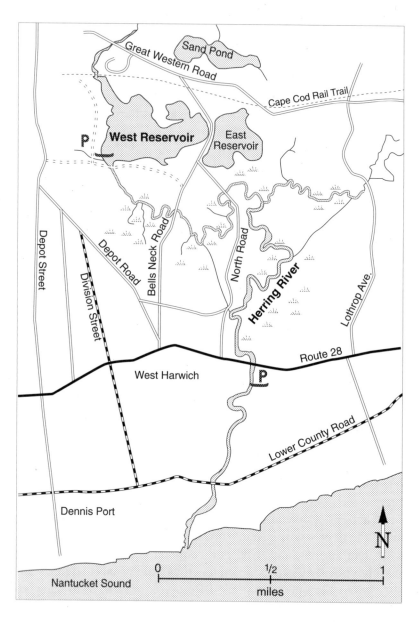

life. I saw literally hundreds of painted turtles, a good-sized snapper, and two far-less-common stinkpot turtles. This latter species is a curious one—with a steeply humped carapace that seems undersized, a pointed "beak," and a musky smell you will probably notice if you pick one up (a defensive musky secretion is released from glands on both sides of the body). It is from this smell that both the stinkpot and the broader musk turtle genus get their names. Generally, these turtles are seen underwater, but on occasion they will sun themselves on protruding logs or rocks, and unlike painted turtles, you can often paddle right up to them for close observation if you are quiet.

The reservoir is fairly deep and the water brackish. Most of the surrounding land is wooded with black oak, white oak, and pitch pine. By the water's edge you will see some black gum or tupelo, with foliage that turns a brilliant crimson in the fall. Much of the land surrounding the reservoir and Herring River is protected by the Town of Harwich and known as the Harwich Conservation Land.

Be aware that this area is used for duck hunting in the fall—notice the duck hunting blinds. You would do well to avoid this season when paddling here.

GETTING THERE: There are two primary canoe access points to this area: the boat launch by the Route 28 bridge over the Herring River, and via a dirt road into the reservoir. The Route 28 access is very easy to find. Traveling east on Route 28, go 2.2 miles past the intersection of Route 28 and 134. Just after crossing the bridge over the Herring River, turn right into the boat access. If driving west from farther out on the Cape, the access is on the left .9 mile from the intersection of Routes 28 and 39, just before the Herring River bridge. There is parking at the put-in point for about fifteen cars.

Finding the other access to the Herring River and West Reservoir is a lot tougher. From the Herring River bridge, drive .5 mile west on Route 28 to Depot Road. Turn right here (north), and drive another .8 mile until Depot Road bears to the right with Depot Street coming in from the left. Continue another .2 mile and turn right onto an unmarked dirt road. In about .1 mile you will see a sign indicating the Town of Harwich Conservation Land, and just a few hundred yards past that is the reservoir. There is parking space for eight or ten cars here. Along with the put-in spot for the West Reservoir and the Herring River below the dike, a pleasant trail and several dirt roads lead through the Harwich Conservation Lands from here. Also, the Cape Cod Rail Trail passes by the north end of West Reservoir, where the Herring River flows into the reservoir through several culverts. This wonderful bicycling and walking trail extends nearly twenty miles along an abandoned railway bed through the towns of Dennis, Harwich, Brewster, Orleans, and Eastham.

If you don't have a canoe, they are available from Cape Cod Waterways a few miles west from the Herring River on Route 28, right where the highway crosses the Swan River—another good paddling spot, though not as remote as the Herring River. For information, call 508-398-0080.

Martha's Vineyard

Martha's Vineyard, MA

Long known for sailing, beachcombing, bed-and-breakfast hopping, gift shopping, and general vacationing, Martha's Vineyard is also a great place for canoeing. There are at least a dozen spots worth paddling and several that are truly spectacular. Detailed write-ups on two of these locations are included in this guide: Edgartown Great Pond and Pocha Pond, which connects to Poge Bay on Chappaquiddick. Other places worth visiting by canoe, with a few comments on each, are listed below:

Tisbury Great Pond. There is a new canoe access on Tiah's Cove on land that has been purchased by the Martha's Vineyard Land Bank. While somewhat more developed than Edgartown Great Pond, Tisbury Great Pond offers some great canoeing.

Long Cove. Located just east of Tisbury Great Pond, Long Cove is totally undeveloped and protected by The Trustees of Reservations. Access is off of Deep Neck Road, via two-and-a-half miles of rough sand roads. Canoe access requires a considerable carry from the parking lot. For information, contact The Trustees of Reservations, Box 319X, Lambert's Cove Road, Vineyard Haven, MA 02568; 508-693-7662.

On a calm day, paddling on one of the many ponds on Martha's Vineyard can be wonderful. Quitsa Pond (an arm of Menemsha Pond) is shown here in the late afternoon.

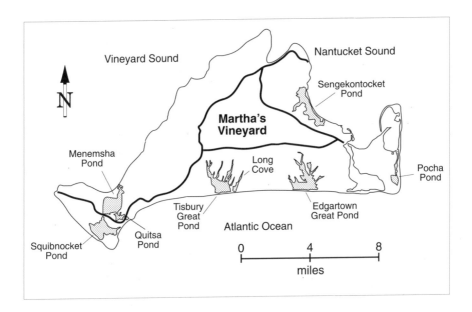

Menemsha Pond and Quitsa Pond. The classic New England fishing village of Menemsha can be seen from a canoe at the north end of Menemsha Pond. Some of the fishing boats that dock here are very large. Smaller fishing and sailing boats are moored along the perimeter of both Menemsha and Quitsa ponds. There is a large public beach area with boat access at the north end of Menemsha Pond at the end of Dutcher Dock, but tidal currents on Menemsha Creek leading into the pond can be very strong, so use caution here. Another small public access is located at the southeast tip of Quitsa Pond where South Road crosses the water. Really adventuresome canoeists can paddle from the southwest corner of Menemsha Pond—via a tiny connecting creek partially blocked by weirs and passing through a one hundred-foot-long concrete culvert—into Squibnocket Pond. Squibnocket is one of the most picturesque and remote bodies of water on Martha's Vineyard, but the shores are private, and some areas are heavily patrolled for security.

Sengekontocket Pond. Located between Oak Bluffs and Edgartown, this large pond has a fair amount of development on it, but offers nice canoeing nonetheless. On Felix Neck near the midpoint of the pond (reachable from Vineyard Haven Road) is Felix Neck Wildlife Sanctuary of the Massachusetts Audubon Society. Canoe access is off Beach Road. Fortunately, you don't have to be able to pronounce its Indian name to paddle on the pond.

GETTING THERE: Most people reach Martha's Vineyard via the ferry out of Woods Hole. Be prepared for the high cost of getting over with a car and canoe; in 1992, rates were $72 round-trip for a car, plus $9 per passenger. You can bring a canoe over on your car, but if the canoe makes the overall height of your car over 6 1/2 feet, you may have to pay a surcharge. Reservations are highly recommended, but they require prepayment (Mastercard or Visa can be used), and there is a substantial penalty for cancelling or changing a reservation. For ferry information or reservations, contact the Woods Hole, Martha's Vineyard and Nantucket Steamship Authority, P.O. Box 284, Woods Hole, MA 02543; 508-540-2022 or 508-548-3788.

Canoe Safety on Martha's Vineyard

If you are considering paddling on Martha's Vineyard ponds, keep in mind that the island is often very windy (that's why it is so popular with windsurfers), and sudden weather changes are common. Keep your paddling plans flexible, and don't take any chances. Be sure to wear life vests (PFDs) if the conditions are at all threatening, if children are with you, or if you are not a skilled swimmer; simply having the PFDs in the boat with you is not enough. (One PFD for each person in the boat is required by law in Massachusetts.)

Also be aware that ponds that are open to the sea can have extremely strong tidal currents—in some places the tidal current will be much faster than you can paddle. When combined with a strong breeze, this can make for very hazardous open-boat paddling conditions. Use caution and good sense when canoeing here, so that you can fully enjoy what the Vineyard has to offer. If the conditions aren't right for paddling, go for a hike or enjoy some other safe activity.

When to Visit

Along with concern about the weather, there is one more warning that is necessary for anyone thinking about canoeing on Martha's Vineyard: tourists. The Vineyard population increases from about twelve thousand in the winter to more than sixty thousand during the summer months. If you can even get over to Martha's Vineyard on the ferry, there may not be camping space or room in the island's inns or bed-and-breakfast establishments. Most of the visitors seem to scoot around on mopeds when they aren't shopping. Traffic can be a real problem—

in fact, I suspect the risk of traffic accidents exceeds that of canoeing manyfold. The solution to this problem is to try to schedule your visit after Labor Day or before school's out in the spring. You might not get the warm sun during off-season visits, but at least the competition to enjoy that sun will be less.

Camping and Other Lodging on Martha's Vineyard

Camping is available at two private campgrounds on Martha's Vineyard, both of which are located close to Vineyard Haven on the northern side of the island. Martha's Vineyard Family Campground (P.O. Box 1557, Vineyard Haven, MA 02568; 508-693-3772) has 180 sites and is open from mid-May until mid-October. Webb's Camping Area (RFD 2, Box 100, Vineyard Haven, MA 02568; 508-693-0233) has 150 sites and is open from mid-May until mid-September. The Manuel F. Correllus State Forest, in the center of the island, does not permit camping.

For those who want more luxurious accommodations (and are willing to pay for them), there are dozens of inns and bed-and-breakfast establishments on Martha's Vineyard. For a packet of information on these facilities, contact the Martha's Vineyard Chamber of Commerce, P.O. Box 1698, Vineyard Haven, MA 02568; 508-693-0085. More affordable dorm-style lodging is available from an American Youth Hostel located between Edgartown and West Tisbury. The hostel operates from April until mid-November; 1992 rates are $10 per person per night for members and $13 for nonmembers. For information, write to American Youth Hostel, P.O. Box 158, West Tisbury, MA 02575; 508-693-2665.

An excellent map of the island is available from the Martha's Vineyard Land Bank, which has been purchasing and protecting wild land on the island since 1986. For a copy of the map, contact the Martha's Vineyard Land Bank Commission, P.O. Box 2057, Edgartown, MA 02539; 508-627-7141.

Double-Crested Cormorant
The Ancient Angler

Two of our most common water birds in southern New England—the wood duck and the double-crested cormorant—couldn't be more different. One is the essence of beauty, shimmering red and blue and chestnut brown. The other is a drab greenish black with a long, lanky, reptilian neck and hooked beak—frankly, it's pretty ugly. Cormorants have been described as looking like a cross between a crow and an eel. The beautiful wood duck gets all the attention, but few birds found on lakes, ponds, and estuaries of southern New England are as fascinating as the much-maligned cormorant.

The double-crested cormorant (*Phalacrocorax auritus*) ranges widely throughout North Ameri-

ca, both along the coasts and on inland lakes and ponds. In southern New England, cormorants can be found on almost any body of water. On coastal ponds and estuaries it is not unusual to see hundreds. Once severely threatened by fishermen, who shot cormorants as standard practice whenever they got the chance, and by DDT, which weakened their egg shells, cormorants began a dramatic rebound several decades ago.

Perhaps more than any other species, the cormorant reminds us of avian evolution from reptiles. Cormorants, of which there are thirty species worldwide and six in North America, have changed little in 40 million years, and close relatives are found in the fossil record of 100 million years ago—not long after reptilian scales evolved into feathers and the first birds took flight. The bird looks primitive, whether you see one swimming along low in the water—somewhat like images we've seen of the supposed Loch Ness Monster—or perched atop a pier with wings outspread drying. Their habit of perching with wings outstretched has long been assumed to be for drying the poorly oiled feathers, but you might see them doing this even in the rain, leading some ornithologists to speculate that it may also have to do with balance—helping compensate for legs that are positioned far back on their bodies.

Cormorants are in the same sub-order as pelicans, another ancient and odd-looking bird. The double-crested cormorant is the only species seen regularly in New England, though an occasional great cormorant strays into this region from its usual range in northeastern Canada. Our species gets its name from double crests that appear briefly on most adults during breeding season. Adults have an yellow or orange chin pouch that is obvious if you get close enough for a good look. Sexes are identical in appearance.

When flying, cormorants are quite distinctive. They fly low, almost dipping their wing tips into the water with each flap, with necks outstretched. They are heavy birds that have difficulty taking off from the water, but once they get going they can fly at speeds approaching fifty miles per hour. When you watch one take off from a rock perch or pier, it almost invariably drops down to the water's surface. During migration, cormorants fly in large flocks. They look like geese from a distance as they fly in a V formation, but they are totally silent. It was quite an odd sensation when I first saw a large flock fly over; I thought they were geese, but heard no honking.

Like loons, cormorants can control how high they float in the water by storing or expelling air from special internal sacs. Their bones are heavier than those of most birds, and there is some evidence that they sometimes swallow stones to improve their diving ability. They are excellent swimmers, using primarily their large webbed feet for propulsion, but also gaining quick bursts of speed with their wings—literally "flying" underwater. The twelve tail feathers are very stiff and used as a rudder. They are known to dive as deep as eighty feet, catching fish underwater, then bringing them to the surface for swallowing. An adult cormorant needs about a pound of fish per day if it is not also feeding young, but there have been some remarkable examples of their prodigious appetites in the literature. The crop and gullet of one individual was found to contain seventy-six four-inch-long anchovies; another swallowed a fish sixteen inches long (the bird only stands thirty-six inches tall!). They fish primarily by sight, but rely on hearing as well, as has been evidenced by the discovery of healthy cormorants that were totally blind and observations of them fishing successfully in murky water with zero visibility.

The cormorant's superb fishing skills did not go unnoticed by humans. As long ago as 1000 B.C. trained cormorants were used in fishing. In China, Japan, and India, fishermen tied collars around their necks to prevent them from swallowing fish. In China, where cormorant fishing attained a true art form, the birds were specially bred and trained to catch and retrieve fish using whistle signals, even without tethering. In Japan, they were always tethered with long leather leashes. Groups of cormorants, both those fishing for their human masters and wild groups, have been known to herd fish to one end of a pond, then swim in, a few at a time, to catch the concentrated fish.

This same fishing skill brought unrelenting persecution from American fishermen, who thought the birds were taking too many of their fish. Indeed, cormorants were hunted almost to extinction in the early 1900s. Today, catfish farmers in the Southeast suffer annual losses to the bird in the millions of dollars. It is likely that catfish ponds will have to be redesigned to more effectively exclude this voracious eater.

Cormorants generally nest on rocky islands, laying two to four eggs in rather simple-looking nests of twigs, sticks, grasses, and feathers. They nest widely off the New England coast. Interestingly, while most birds incubate eggs with skin contact by plucking some feathers from their breasts, cormorants keep their eggs warm using their feet (warm blood circulates through their highly vascular webbed feet). Both parents partake equally in incubating eggs, guarding the young, and feeding. On a hearty diet of fish, young cormorants grow quickly. By three or four weeks of age, they begin leaving their nest to wander about their islands in roving bands of juveniles (a sort of *West Side Story* of the Isles of Shoals), returning only at feeding time. They can dive at five or six weeks of age, and they are fully independent by ten weeks. Primary enemies during nesting are black-backed gulls and herring gulls, which will rob unguarded nests of eggs or young.

Having survived for 40 million years and now rebounded from hunting persecution and DDT poisoning, the cormorant appears to have a bright future. You are sure to see this bird often as you paddle the lakes, ponds, and estuaries of southern New England.

Edgartown Great Pond

Edgartown, MA (Martha's Vineyard)

Edgartown Great Pond is one of the Vineyard's real gems, and indeed one of my favorite paddling spots in all of Massachusetts. The pond has very little development, lots of wildlife, a ten-horsepower limit for outboard motors, and more than fifteen miles of shoreline to explore. The south edge of the pond backs up against the barrier beach that separates it from the Atlantic Ocean, and as you paddle here you can hear the crashing waves just across the low dunes. Most of the time the pond is totally isolated from the ocean and thus free of rising and falling tides and tidal currents. Three or four times a year, however, a channel is dug between the ocean and the pond to allow a mixing of the water.

Edgartown Great Pond and Tisbury Great Pond are among the best remaining examples anywhere of great salt ponds, a geological feature of coastal outwash plains produced from melting glaciers at the end of the last ice age. As glaciers receded to the north, meltwater flowed south off the glacier. These streams and rivers carried silt and sand, which they deposited to form the outwash plains found here and on Nantucket Island, Cape Cod, and Long Island. The rippling topography on Martha's Vineyard is a result of these glacial streams depositing this till as they flowed away from the glacier. Depressions formed where remnant blocks of glacial ice forced these streams to flow around them. The common kettle ponds on the Cape were formed when blocks of ice became totally isolated; on Martha's Vineyard, the glacial till produced mainly ridges. Moving coastal sands then sealed off the south end of these ponds with barrier beaches.

The varying salinity in great salt ponds results in considerable diversity of vegetation and animal life. (Even before channels were opened up several times a year, mixing of ocean and pond water occurred periodically with storms. Hurricane Bob in 1991 swept ocean water over the barrier beach, thoroughly mixing Edgartown Great Pond's water with sea water in the course of a few hours.) At the tips of some coves on Edgartown Great Pond are found freshwater ecosystems with plants that are intolerant of high salinity, such as cranberry, woolgrass, and grass pinks (a type of orchid). Along the main pond are salt-tolerant species such as salt-marsh grasses (*Spartina spp.*), glasswort, and marsh orach. Piping plovers and least terns, both of which are threatened species, frequently nest on the dunes here. Ospreys nest on several platforms around the pond, and numerous warblers and other

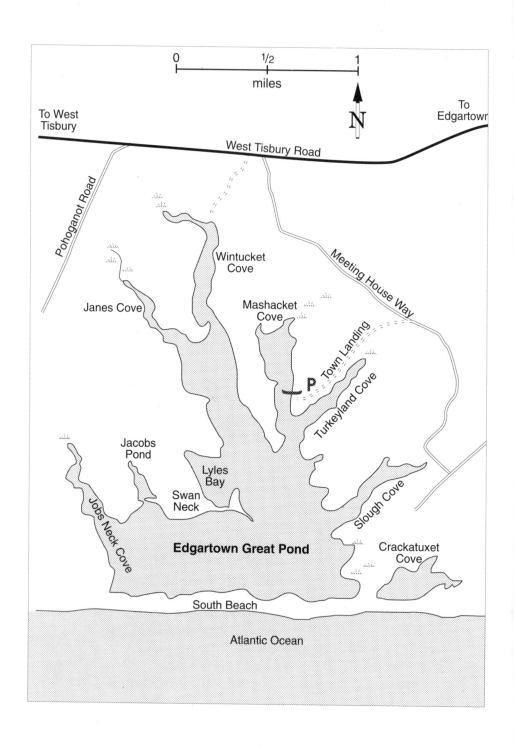

songbirds nest in the surrounding area. Paddling here in September I saw lots of great blue herons, snowy and great egrets, black-crowned night herons, black-backed and herring gulls, and various sandpipers and plovers. I was also lucky enough to see a family of five otters. To come across otters you usually have to paddle early in the morning or late in the day toward dusk.

Of the various coves on Edgartown Great Pond, Janes Cove seems to be the most remote. It was here I saw the otters and a pair of large snapping turtles. As you paddle up here, note the thick moss hanging from some of the old red maples and beetlebung trees (a local name for black gum). Jobs Neck Cove is another very pretty cove, with just one house on it. As you paddle along the shores of Edgartown Great Pond, watch for blue crabs scurrying away. Specimens up to eight inches across are commonly found here (note the bright blue on the claws on some individuals).

While I tend to focus on the natural history of a body of water, Edgartown Great Pond has a lot of social history to it as well. The pond was commercially fished by settlers of European descent as long ago as 1660. Alewife was the primary fish caught here for about 250 years, and you are likely to see schools of this fish in the pond (if the water is fairly calm, a school of alewives feeding looks like a mass of bubbles breaking the surface). They come into the pond in the spring to spawn, entering through the opening in South Beach, and they leave in the fall, when the barrier beach is again breached. Also caught here are yellow and white perch, eels, and occasional oceanic fish such as striped bass, flounder, and bluefish that enter the pond through the opening in South Beach and get trapped. Today the primary commercial fishing in Edgartown Great Pond is for shellfish: oysters and steamer clams. It is primarily for the benefit of the shellfishing industry that the pond is opened to the ocean several times each year. (Without the periodic mixing with sea water, the water would not remain saline enough for shellfish.)

Paddling the full perimeter of Edgartown Great Pond could easily take a full day, especially if you spend time studying its varied wildlife or fishing. Remember to respect the property owners. Except for the public landing on Mashacket Neck, the entire shoreline is privately owned: camping is not permitted anywhere here. This is not a place to get out and enjoy a stroll along South Beach. Remember, also, to keep the access area clean. Take a few minutes to pick up litter you find here to help make sure that paddlers will remain welcome on Edgartown Great Pond.

GETTING THERE: To reach the public access to Edgartown Great Pond take the Edgartown–West Tisbury Road to Meeting House Way. If driving west from Edgartown, the road is on the left, 1.8 miles from the turnoff from the intersection with Main Street in Edgartown. If driving east from West Tisbury, Meeting House Way is on the right, 6.3 miles from the intersection of State Road and South Road in West Tisbury, or 2.9 miles from the airport. After turning onto Meeting House Way, drive 1.4 miles on a fairly rough, sandy road, then take a sharp right turn on a less-traveled, unmarked sand road. You will reach the boat access in 0.8 mile. There is room for fifteen or twenty cars along the road, which loops around at the end. Be careful not to block one of the access points to the water with your car, however; these are used by commercial shellfish harvesters for loading baskets of oysters or clams into their cars.

Pocha Pond

Edgartown, MA (Chappaquiddick Island, Martha's Vineyard)

Pocha Pond and the connecting channel into Poge Bay provide some wonderful paddling, with public access across the Cape Poge sand dunes to several miles of beautiful, remote ocean beach. From the canoe access at the now-closed Dyke Bridge, you can paddle south into Pocha Pond. Except for a couple of houses near the end of Dyke Road and a few at the south end of Pocha Pond, there is no development along here, just acres and acres of salt marsh to explore.

Paddling on a late-summer morning I saw dozens of great blue herons, great egrets and snowy egrets, sea gulls, and cormorants, plus a few black scoters and kingfishers. Pocha Pond is open to the sea via the Cape Poge Gut, so only plants that can withstand regular saltwater flooding survive here. Among them are sea lavender (*Limonium nashii*), glasswort (*Salicornia virginica*), and several species of salt-marsh grass (*Spartina patens* and *S. alternaflora*). On the exposed peat at low tide, beneath the salt-marsh grass, you will see various seaweeds and mussels. In the water are more seaweeds, sponge colonies, various crabs, and mollusks (I found some very large whelk shells here). Past the open marsh you will see pitch pine, scrub oak, swamp white oak, and black gum, known locally as beetlebung.

Just south of the Dyke Bridge and to the west is a narrow inlet creek that you can paddle up. Watch out for mollusk-encrusted rocks and shell conglomerations here, particularly near low tide. Near the end of this little creek is a phragmites marsh and dense grove of beetlebung, whose leaves turn a brilliant crimson in the early fall. Be careful during the hunting season; I saw at least one old hunting blind and expect the area is used fairly heavily for waterfowl hunting.

North of the Dyke Bridge the channel is quite narrow along Toms Neck (an area called the Lagoon) but it opens up in Poge Bay. In a strong breeze, the water on Poge Bay can get quite rough, so be careful. If the wind is coming from the south, you can probably make it without too much difficulty around to Pease Pond and explore that (close to low tide, it may be hard to get around some exposed sandbanks). You can also beach your canoe on the Atlantic side of the Lagoon or Poge Bay and hike along the beach. Be forewarned that there are jeep trails along here, so it may not be much of a wilderness experience, though jeeps are prohibited from the beach itself south of Arruda's Point. Also watch

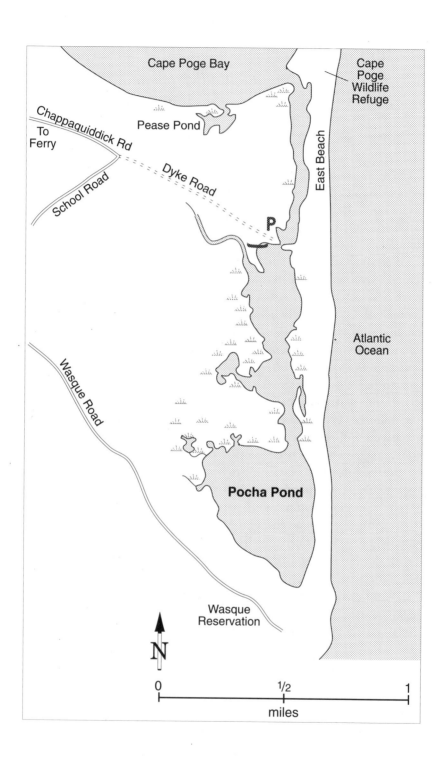

Cape Poge Bay

Cape Poge Wildlife Refuge

Pease Pond

Chappaquiddick Rd

To Ferry

School Road

Dyke Road

East Beach

P

Atlantic Ocean

Wasque Road

Pocha Pond

Wasque Reservation

N

0   ½   1

miles

out for poison ivy amid the sand dunes. It grows in profusion here. This section of beach is quite wild and beautiful, with waves crashing on the sandy shore. Surf fishing here is considered to be among the best on the Atlantic Coast—for stripers and blues—and you may find some interesting things washed up on the beach. When I visited in 1992 I came across the remains of a whale.

GETTING THERE: To reach Dyke Bridge where you can launch a canoe, take the ferry across to Chappaquiddick Island from Edgartown (the ferry holds three to four cars and runs back and forth fairly steadily during periods when you are likely to be canoeing). After getting off the ferry, drive east on Chappaquiddick Road (the only way you can go). Stay on the paved road for 2.4 miles and then continue straight on a dirt road (Dyke Road) where the paved road curves sharply to the right and turns into School Road. You will reach a dead end and the remains of the old bridge in another 0.8 mile. There is parking for about fifteen cars here (there is more room on the left side of the road than the right), and you can carry your canoe to the water on either side of the road.

The Cape Poge Wildlife Refuge on the barrier beach north of Dyke Bridge and the Wasque Reservation at the south end of Pocha Pond are owned and managed by The Trustees of Reservations. TTOR also owns the unique Mytoi Japanese-style garden that you pass on Dyke Road. Restrooms can be found there. For more information and an excellent map of the area, contact TTOR Islands Regional Office, Box 319X, Vineyard Haven, MA 02568; 508-693-7662.

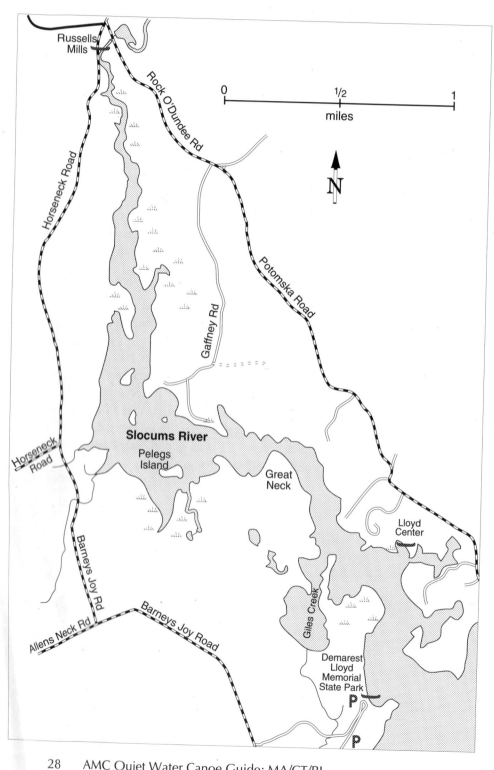

Slocums River
Dartmouth, MA

Slocums River is a real treat, one of the best tidal rivers in New England for quiet paddling, birds, and salt-marsh plants. One could easily spend a day or two exploring the river, getting to know its different personalities at high and low tide. There are a few houses along the river, but not enough to detract from the peace and quiet. This isolated corner of Dartmouth township was originally settled by members of the Slocum family, distantly related to Joshua Slocum, who, in the early 1900s, sailed a small ketch out of nearby Fairhaven and around the world in the first solo circumnavigation of the earth in a small craft. This feat perhaps epitomizes the rigor and determination of the early Slocums: Anthony, who first cleared the land, and Giles, who, in 1638, founded the Society of Friends Apponeagonsett Meeting, still active not far from Russells Mills.

The best place to launch your canoe is the Demarest-Lloyd Memorial State Park at the south end of the river. There is a $5 entrance fee. Even parking at the northernmost parking lot, though, you will have a fair carry across sand flats to the water—quite far at low tide (apparently, there used to be a real boat ramp here, but shifting sand has covered it). That helps keep motorboats out, so I don't mind. Near the put-in, watch for interesting gulls and terns. Out on the bay from here (a cove of Buzzards Bay), there will be some swells, but the water is fairly calm because it is so well protected.

Head upstream (north) on Slocums River. Giles Creek can be reached by paddling around to the left. It is a wonderful cove with egrets, herons, and gulls feeding amid the salt-marsh grass (*Spartina*). Depending on the timing of your visit relative to the tide, you may only be able to see the egrets' heads extending above the grasses as you paddle along. Back out on the main river there are a few houses along the east shore, but not many, and they seem to fit in well with the curves of the river.

After a rather narrow section along Great Neck, the river opens up by Pelegs Island. Near this island, an unnamed creek offers a superb spot to learn about the salt-marsh ecosystem—especially at low tide. I paddled up this creek early in September at just about low tide and saw thousands of fiddler crabs along the banks (the fiddler crab has one claw that is much larger than the other, making it look as if it's holding a fiddle). I had seen fiddler crabs many times before, but never in such

Slocums River is one of New England's most beautiful tidal rivers— and a great spot for wildlife observation.

numbers as I saw on this little inlet creek. The exposed mud flats seemed to move as I paddled close and the startled crabs scurried to safety, with the clickety-clack of thousands of tiny legs on the pebbles and mud. They were also thick on some of the undercut sod banks, along with mussels.

Following the wide section of river, a narrow channel continues north, first in a wide flood plain, then along a bank on the right, with a few houses looking out over the water. Eventually, you reach a town boat access at the village of Russells Mills. Even though this access point is limited to town residents, it is a fine place to get out for a stretch if you've paddled up from Demarest-Lloyd State Park, and I'm told it is all right to use as a drop-off point for a one-way paddle downstream. If you want a snack or need to make a call, walk up Horseneck Road to the right (north) several hundred yards to the general store.

The distance from the park to this northern access is about four miles, but if you like to explore the shoreline and any coves and inlets you come across, as I do, a round trip will easily take three to five hours—longer if you have a leisurely picnic lunch along the way. While you are here, you might well want to visit the Lloyd Center for Environmental Studies, which is across the mouth of the river from Demarest-Lloyd State Park. This highly regarded nature center, on fifty-five acres of land, offers a wide range of educational programs, nature walks, lecture programs, and canoe trips. You can paddle over, beach your canoe, and walk up; or you can drive around (see directions below). You cannot launch a canoe from the Lloyd Center because the path to the water is too steep, but you can leave your boat at the water and walk up to view the center's exhibits and enjoy their trails.

GETTING THERE: To reach Demarest-Lloyd State Park, get off Interstate 195 just east of Fall River onto Route 88 South. Drive 8.0 miles and turn left onto Hix Bridge Road toward Handy Four Corners and South Westport. Stay on Hix Bridge Road for 1.5 miles, then turn right on Horseneck Road in South Westport. (Horseneck Road makes a large loop—south, east, and then north, with some maps showing an extension by the same name to the south.) Drive south on Horseneck Road for 3.4 miles and turn left, staying on Horseneck Road. Follow this section of Horseneck Road for 1.0 mile, then turn right onto Allens Neck Road. Allens Neck Road makes a sharp left turn, then Barneys Joy Road comes in from the left. Continue straight (on Barneys Joy Road) and drive another mile to the entrance to Demarest-Lloyd State Park on the left. Drive past the main parking lot to a smaller lot farther north, and carry your canoe to the water from there. There is no camping in the park, and its season is limited. The park is open from Memorial Day until Labor Day; hours are 10 AM to 6:30 PM. For more information, contact Demarest-Lloyd State Park, Barneys Joy Road, South Dartmouth, MA 02748; 508-636-8816.

To reach the Lloyd Center by car, drive up around Slocums River on Barneys Joy Road, Horeseneck Road (the eastern arm), Rock O'Dundee Road, and Potomska Road. After turning onto Potomska Road, the Lloyd Center is 1.7 miles farther south on the right, marked by a blue sign. For more on the Lloyd Center, including information on organized canoe trips they offer on Slocums River, the Westport River, and other area bodies of water, contact the Lloyd Center, 430 Potomska Road, P.O. Box 87037, South Dartmouth, MA 02748; 508-990-0505.

Osprey
Fish Hawk Back from the Brink

Ospreys, or fish hawks, are seen regularly on many lakes, ponds, and estuaries in southern New England. On the inland lakes and ponds you are most likely to see them during migration, when they are passing through and stop over to feed along the Westport River and a number of other tidal locations. You may see dozens and you'll have an excellent opportunity to observe them nesting.

The osprey, *Pandion haliaetus,* is a large raptor with a wingspan up to six feet. It is the sole species in the family Pandionidae, and is among the world's most widely distributed birds—occurring on all continents except Antarctica. The bird is dark brown to almost black above and white below, with a characteristic bend to the wings that gives it an **M**-shape as it soars. From close range, the face markings are easily recognizable. Ospreys have proportionally smaller heads and longer tails than gulls, with which they are sometimes confused.

Ospreys feed exclusively on fish. They soar or hover at a height of about 150 feet, using their keen eyesight to locate fish near the surface of the water. Then they dive, crashing into the water feet-first, thrashing around in the water briefly and, quite often, emerging with fish tightly grasped in their talons. Osprey feet are specially adapted with sharp spiny projections that enable them to hold on tightly to their slippery prey.

Osprey generally mate for life and return to the same nesting site year after year. Males are first to arrive in the spring from their wintering grounds in the Gulf states or northern South America, followed a week later by the females. When they first return, you may see males engaged in a fascinating sky dance, in which they repeatedly fly steeply up, hover with tail fanned and talons extended, then dive down. This may be a courtship behavior, or one designed to delineate territory, or both.

Traditionally, ospreys have nested in tall dead trees, but more recently they have taken to artificial nesting platforms erected for the birds. Hundreds of these platforms have been put up since the early 1970s in southern New England. The actual nest is typically about five feet in diameter and two to seven feet in height, depending on how many years it has been used. Nests are made of sticks and are somewhat sloppy. To collect sticks, the male uses a very sensible technique: alighting near the end of a dead branch to break it off, then carrying the stick off to the nest. The female collects most of the nest lining material (moss, bark, twigs, grass, seaweed).

Two or three eggs—whitish with reddish-brown blotches—are laid over a period of several days. After a thirty-four- to forty-day incubation period during which the female does most of the sitting, the chicks hatch. Because the young hatch over several days, they vary in size. In a year of food shortage, the larger chick will outcompete its smaller sibling(s) and may be the sole survivor. The male osprey does virtually all the fishing during the incubation and nestling stage. Young ospreys first take to flight after seven or eight weeks, but they do not become fully independent for another month or two. After migrating south, the young spend two winters and the summer between in the wintering ground. They return to the general area where they were raised the following year, when they may pair up and begin building a nest, but they do not actually breed until their third year.

Ospreys are remarkably content to nest in close proximity to humans and have been known to nest on chimneys and light poles in parking lots. Their primary natural enemy is the bald eagle, which is far less adept at fishing and often tries to steal their fish. A far more significant enemy, however, has been our chemical warfare against insect pests.

The insecticide DDT was introduced in 1947 and widely used in controlling mosquitoes on our coastal salt marshes. DDT is an extremely long-lasting chlorinated hydrocarbon. Over the years it accumulated in fatty tissue of animals, gradually moving up the food chain. Small fish would eat insects that had been sprayed, larger fish would eat the small fish, and so on up the food chain to such predators as ospreys. At each step along the way, DDT was ingested but stored in fatty tissue rather than being excreted. By the time the top of the food chain was reached, DDT concentrations were very high, especially in a bird like the osprey with a long life span. High DDT levels resulted in a thinning of their eggshells and an extremely high failure rate. Osprey populations plummeted. Along the Connecticut River delta in Connecticut, for example, the population of ospreys dropped from two hundred nesting pairs in 1938 to twelve by 1965. By the end of the 1960s the bird was almost gone from the eastern United States. The realization that DDT was causing this decline (along with other environmental and human health problems) led to a ban of the pesticide in the early 1970s. Since that time, osprey populations have gradually recovered, at least through the 1980s.

Most recently, however, there has been a disturbing decline in nesting success. Along the Westport River, for example, 133 osprey were fledged in 1991, compared with only 84 in 1992. Hopefully, this is simply an aberration resulting from colder-than-normal weather, but various other possible causes are being investigated, including the ingestion of pesticides at the southern wintering quarters where environmentally dangerous chemicals including DDT have not been banned, increased competition with sea gulls since area landfills have been closed, and elevated water pollution. Efforts are underway to eliminate use of such chemicals worldwide, or at least to prevent U.S. chemical manufacturers from selling them abroad. With such efforts and better controls on water pollution here, we will be able to enjoy watching ospreys hover over our waterways for many years to come.

East Head Pond
Plymouth and Carver, MA

East Head Pond is a small, undeveloped pond in Myles Standish State Forest, one of the largest publicly owned tracts of land in Massachusetts. The pond itself is actually owned by the A.D. Makepeace Company, a member of the Ocean Spray Corporation (the largest cranberry grower in Massachusetts), but state forest land extends right up to the shoreline, and canoeing is permitted. The shallow, sandy pond is typical of kettle-hole ponds, which were formed as the last glacier receded ten or twelve thousand years ago and left large chunks of glacial ice behind, usually buried in debris. As these ice blocks melted they left depressions in the surrounding sand that filled to form ponds. Because kettle-hole ponds generally have very little inflow and outflow, their water levels often fluctuate considerably, depending on rain and drought conditions.

East Head Pond is surrounded by quite different species than are found in most of New England. Dominant species include pitch pine and scrub oak in what is known as a pine barrens ecosystem. Myles Standish State Forest has one of the largest pitch pine/scrub oak communities north of Long Island. This forest community develops on sandy soil and is well adapted to frequent fires: in 1957 an area of fifteen thousand acres here, including some state forest land, burned in a forest fire. Along with pitch pine and scrub oak, you will see such other trees as red maple, gray birch, white pine, black gum, scarlet oak, and big-tooth aspen as you paddle around East Head Pond. There is also a rich diversity of shrubs along the shoreline: two species of blueberry (highbush and black highbush), sweet pepperbush, leatherleaf, sweet gale, laurel, wild raisin (*Viburnam cassinoides*), and inkberry (*Ilex glabra*). Even in mid-September I found some of the blueberry bushes just laden with berries—you could pick them by the handful!

The water here is brackish and rich in iron. In fact, during the eighteenth century this area was mined for bog iron, which is deposited in thin layers here. After that industry petered out, cranberry production took over; many commercial cranberry bogs are in this area. There is considerable pond vegetation both on and in East Head Pond, including water shield, fragrant water lily, and bladderwort. Living on the sandy bottom are freshwater mussels. The pond also contains largemouth bass, pickerel, and yellow perch. You may be lucky enough to see an osprey join the human anglers fishing here.

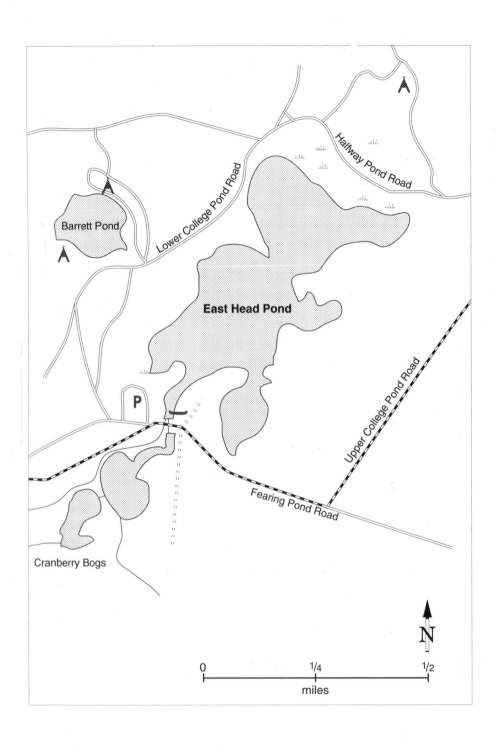

Barrett Pond

Lower College Pond Road

Halfway Pond Road

East Head Pond

Upper College Pond Road

P

Fearing Pond Road

Cranberry Bogs

N

| 0 | 1/4 | 1/2 |

miles

East Head Pond is a great spot for a morning of relaxed paddling or fishing. Gasoline-powered motors are prohibited from the pond, so it stays pretty quiet. If you and your family want a change of pace, a nice trail extends around the pond—one of many trails in Myles Standish State Forest. In all the state forest has twenty-three miles of hiking and horse trails, fifteen miles of bicycle trails, and thirty-five miles of off-road-vehicle trails that crisscross the pine barrens. Some of these trails are not so quiet, but if you ask at the ranger station you can be directed to the trails most likely to be free of motorcycles and all-terrain vehicles.

GETTING THERE: Directions to Myles Standish State Forest are confusing, but fortunately the route is well marked—follow the signs for Myles Standish State Forest and you shouldn't have any trouble getting there. Get off Interstate 495 (Route 25) at Exit 2 and drive north on Route 58 for 2.3 miles. In South Carver, continue straight on Tremont Street where Route 58 bears to the left. Continue on this street for 0.8 mile, and then turn right onto Cranberry Road. Stay on the paved road and the Myles Standish State Forest Headquarters will be on the left in 2.8 miles. The boat launch for East Head Pond is just past the headquarters. Park on the right side of the road and put your canoe in on the left. If there isn't enough parking room here, you can park at the Forest Service office after unloading your boat.

There are 475 campsites in Myles Standish State Forest. That's a lot, but camping here doesn't seem so bad because the campsites are divided into a number of widely separated areas. Many of the campsites, in fact, are located on smaller ponds that you can paddle on. There are campgrounds on Barrett Pond, New Long Pond, Charge Pond, Fearing Pond, and Gurley Pond. Camping rates are modest ($10 per night in 1992), and camping areas have flush toilets and washrooms. Some areas also have hot showers. The campground is open from mid-April to mid-October. The day-use areas at College Pond and Fearings Pond are generally staffed from Memorial Day through Labor Day. For more information, contact Myles Standish State Forest, Cranberry Road, South Carver, MA 02366; 508-866-2526.

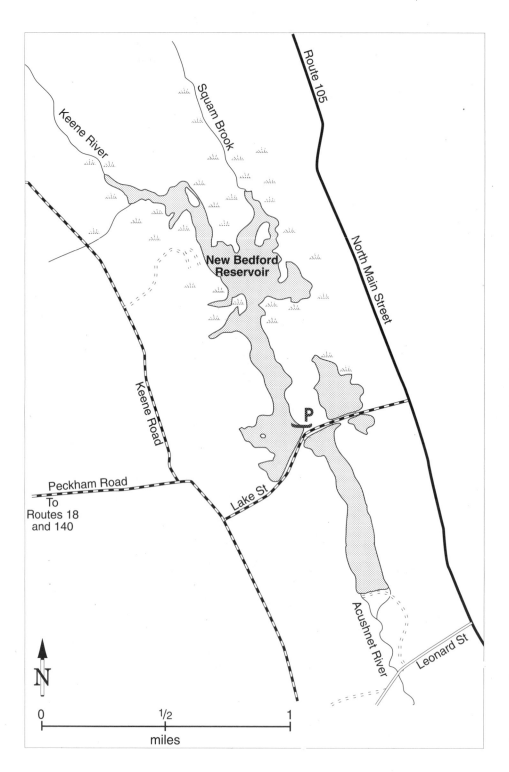

Keene River

Squam Brook

Route 105

New Bedford
Reservoir

North Main Street

P

Keene Road

Peckham Road

To
Routes 18
and 140

Lake St

Acushnet River

Leonard St

N

0   1/2   1
miles

New Bedford Reservoir
Acushnet, MA

The New Bedford Reservoir is just the sort of spot I like. Its highly varied shoreline and marshy coves provide a haven for all sorts of waterfowl and wetland plants. Don't expect easy paddling, though. Much of the reservoir is so choked with vegetation that paddling is quite restricted. (My partner and I joked that if we didn't pay attention we might find ourselves poling through an upland meadow, not having noticed the gradual transition from open water.) By late summer, algae blooms on this eutrophic body of water may give the place a somewhat strong aroma.

The reservoir is fed by the Keene River and Squam Brook, the latter flowing out of the heavily developed Long Pond to the north. Below New Bedford Reservoir, the Acushnet River flows to New Bedford and Buzzards Bay. By the time the water reaches the reservoir it is fairly laden with pollutants. In fact, notices were posted in 1992 at the town park along Lake Street that swimming was prohibited because of water pollution. Despite the pollution, you will see lots of birds here (in fact, a number of people fishing here blamed the pollution *on* the birds, which I found quite ironic). I saw perhaps two dozen wood ducks in mid-September, along with blue-wing teal, black ducks, Canada geese, and great blue herons. In the spring I'm sure the surrounding area is filled with nesting songbirds. You can also expect to see painted turtles sunning on logs or floating vegetation, and you might see a snapping turtle. This large reclusive turtle is present in considerable numbers in marshy bodies of water, and pollution doesn't seem to bother it. Most of the time, all you see of this shy reptile is the triangular tip of its nose reaching above water for air, though in late spring or early summer you may sometimes see one on land when it is off to find new habitat or lay eggs. I have also seen this turtle underwater on occasion as I've paddled on a lake or pond—though that is not likely here because of the dense underwater vegetation.

In some parts of the reservoir are heavy infestations of the introduced Eurasian milfoil, a plant that has choked many lakes and ponds in the Northeast (there is some evidence of success in controlling the plant with an insect that feeds on the species: Very rapid reductions in Eurasian milfoil populations have been observed on several Vermont lakes where the larva was first discovered). Other plant species in and on the water include water meal, duckweed, water shield, fragrant water lily, bullhead lily, bladderwort, fanwort, and coontail. Closer to shore are pickerel weed, cattail, and various grasses, sedges, and reeds.

Because of the extensive vegetation, it is a little difficult to sort out where the reservoir is and where it isn't. Some areas that show on topographic maps as open water are truly impassable by early summer, so to be able to paddle as much as possible here you would need to visit in early spring before the various floating and underwater plants send out the new year's growth. By midsummer you may have difficulty figuring out just where you are relative to the map, but you can't really get lost. Midway up on the western shore is a small cluster of houses, and paddling north you eventually reach a few houses and cranberry operations at the upper end of the western branch (by the Keene River inlet), but otherwise most of the development is at the south end, closer to Lake Street.

If you look carefully, near the northern end of the reservoir on the western arm, there are a few canals that connect with and run parallel to the main (weed-choked) reservoir. These canals are shaded and much less weedy, thus easier to paddle most of the season. I believe these were dug to get water to the cranberry bogs, where it is needed for periodic flooding. Paddling up these little canals has a very different, almost eerie, feel to it, with a dark canopy of maples and grapevines overhanging from both sides.

GETTING THERE: Take Route 140 to Exit 7 and drive east for about 0.4 mile following signs for Route 18. Then turn left (north) onto Acushnet Avenue (Route 18). Take the second right (after 0.3 mile) onto Peckham Road. Stay on Peckham for 1.7 miles, curving sharply to the right at one point, then turn left onto Lake Street. You will pass along the reservoir, then reach a parking area with carry-in boat access on the left in 0.5 mile.

Lake Rico and Big Bearhole Pond
Taunton, MA

Lake Rico and the collection of other small ponds in Massasoit State Park provide superb quiet water canoeing—some of the best in this part of the state. Some maps show as many as six bodies of water (Lake Rico, Kings Pond, Furnace Pond, Middle Pond, Little Bearhole Pond, and Big Bearhole Pond), but Lake Rico, Kings Pond, and Furnace Pond are connected. (They were separate ponds when used by cranberry growers, but the water level was raised when the state purchased the land.) From the boat access on Middleboro Avenue, you can do a lot of paddling, extending quite far east on Kings Pond and quite far south on Furnace Pond—an area of about 250 acres.

There is some development on the western side of Furnace Pond and Lake Rico, and on the eastern end of Big Bearhole Pond, but the rest of these ponds are fully within the fifteen-hundred-acre Massasoit State Park, so the only development is related to recreation. You can launch a canoe onto Lake Rico without entering the park, but the primary access onto Big Bearhole Pond is through the park and requires paying a day-use fee (you can also access Big Bearhole Pond off Turner Street). All of these ponds are limited to non-gasoline-powered boats, and all require a hand-carry.

In the early morning light, Lake Rico can be almost magical. Gasoline-powered boats are off-limits here, as they are on the several other ponds in Massasoit State Park.

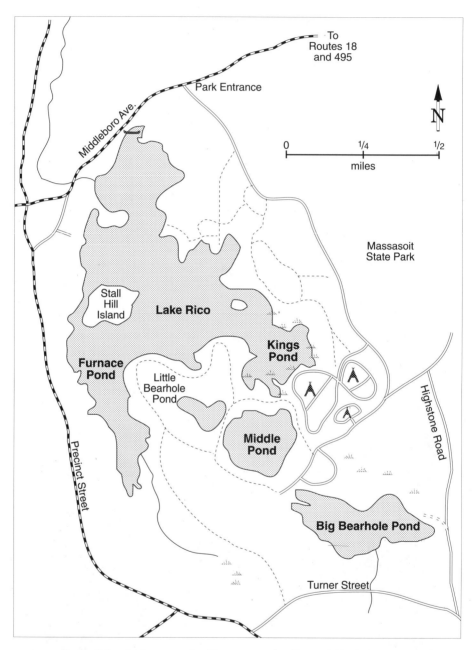

Lake Rico is large and offers several miles of shoreline paddling. Along here you will pass some quite large stands of pine with open forest floor—easily accessible if you want to get out for a picnic lunch or a short walk. The evidence of shoreline erosion on Lake Rico makes me wonder if the area used to be open to powerboats. If so, the boating restriction is a definite improvement. From the boat access point on Middleboro Avenue, all you can really see of Lake Rico is the northern cove. Paddling out of here to the south, you leave road noise behind and get into some very nice country. Kings Pond is very marshy. In fact, as I approached I didn't think I'd be able to paddle into this section of Lake Rico at all because of the vegetation, but you can pick your way through, paddling carefully around the bulrushes, pickerel weed, stands of cattail, and floating water lilies. Near the tip of this cove you can hear the small waterfall inlet from Middle Pond. Watch for great blue herons, green herons, wood ducks, teal, and pied-billed grebes in here; the bird habitat is superb.

Big Bearhole Pond is a lot smaller than Lake Rico, but still very nice for a morning or afternoon of paddling, and it offers the best large-mouth bass fishing. White pine dominates the shoreline vegetation, mixed with red maple, black gum, scarlet oak, gray birch, sweet pepper-bush, blueberry, winterberry, and alder. Patches of swamp loosestrife grow along here and some shallow coves have bullhead lily and fragrant water lily. There is quite a bit of underwater vegetation in the pond, including fanwort and bladderwort. Large bass are taken from here regularly, including some over eight pounds. Other species caught in Big Bearhole Pond and Lake Rico include yellow perch and chain pickerel.

I carried a canoe into Middle Pond and paddled around it as well, but the carry is not very convenient and the pond quite small. You will do better to stick with Big Bearhole Pond and Lake Rico, unless you are camping close to Middle Pond, in which case the carry down may not be that far (the camping area closest to Middle Pond was closed when I visited).

GETTING THERE: Take I-495 to Exit 5 and drive south on Route 18. Drive a little less than 1 mile (the exact distance depends on whether you were driving north or south on 495) and turn right onto Middleboro Avenue, following signs to Massasoit State Park. You will pass the entrance to the park in 2.1 miles (drive in here to get onto Big Bearhole Pond), and the boat access for Lake Rico in 2.4 miles. To launch your canoe on Lake Rico, park in the small lot on the left and carry your boat down to the water. If the parking area is full, there is additional space along Middleboro Avenue by the dam.

Massasoit State Park offers 126 wooded campsites, a swimming beach on Middle Pond, and lots of trails for hiking, mountain bikes, or horseback riding. For information contact Massasoit State Park, Middleboro Avenue, East Taunton, MA 02718; 508-822-7405.

Aaron River Reservoir
Cohasset, MA

The Aaron River Reservoir in Wompatuck State Park near the town of Hingham is one of those places that few people know about. Even if they've hiked or bicycled at Wompatuck, many are unaware that canoeing is permitted on the reservoir. And it's not too surprising, as you may discover when you try to get onto the reservoir. Even after I finally got into the park, after circumnavigating it for what seemed like a half-hour, I almost gave up on boat access seeing the many locked gates leading towards the reservoir. I assumed it was a public water supply and that the tip I had been given about canoeing here was somehow incorrect. But I asked at the campground registration office and found out that you can pick up a key to the gate leading into the reservoir, drive in, and hand-launch your boat.

Something seemed odd about the Aaron River Reservoir as soon as I launched my canoe here; it took me a while to figure out why. There are paved roads everywhere, most of them barred off and long unused by all except bicyclists, joggers, and walkers. A six-foot barbed-wire-topped chain-link fence separates the reservoir from private property outside the park along the eastern shore. The security seemed strange since this didn't seem to be a public water supply, but what made it even stranger were gates through the fencing at every house. Finally, at the end of an arm of the reservoir extending to the west there was an old concrete structure maybe twenty feet high and eighty feet long with huge old rusted steel doors, built into the side of what looked like an artificial earthen mound. That's when I began to put two and two together: The structure is an old ammunition bunker, and the park is an old military facility.

Until 1966 this was the Hingham Naval Ammunition Depot, and it served as a principal supply facility for military operations during World War II. After it closed in 1966, there were efforts to resurrect it, but finally in 1970 the commonwealth took it over for use as a state park.

Having figured out the origin of Wompatuck State Park, I was able to enjoy envisioning what must have been a dramatic transition from a military compound fifty years ago to deep woods, rolling bicycle trails, and a fairly wild reservoir today. One still sees the mark of the land's previous use, but nature is reclaiming the property, providing great recreation in the process. There are some unsettling aspects: I detected

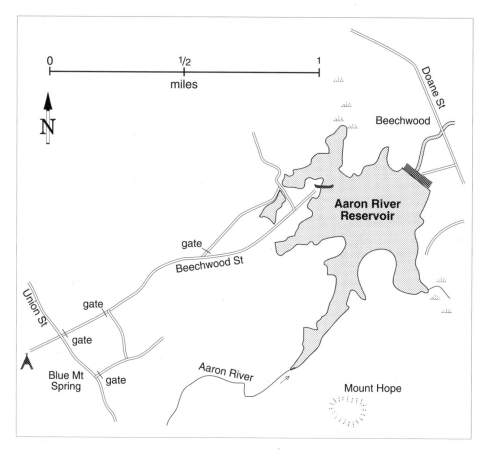

some smell of pollution and noticed quite a few dead or dying trees around the perimeter, so I wonder if there still remains some legacy of its years as a military base.

The shoreline of Aaron River Reservoir is generally rocky. There are lots of protruding (sharp) rocks along the reservoir as well as some hidden stumps. Surprisingly little vegetation is visible in the reservoir—pickerel weed along the shallower shores, a few floating water lilies, and some underwater vegetation—but really very little. The surrounding woodlands are predominantly white pine, hemlock, red oak, beech, black birch, and red maple. During a September visit, I saw an osprey, a few cormorants, lots of seagulls, and quite a few painted turtles. With huge rock slabs extending out into the water in places, you will find lots of nice spots for picnics here.

GETTING THERE: To reach Wompatuck State Park, take Route 3 to Exit 14 and drive north on Route 228 toward Hingham. Stay on 228, which becomes Main Street, for about 4.0 miles (a little less if you got off Route 3 driving south), and turn right onto Free Street. Drive 0.9 mile on Free Street, and turn right onto Union Street, following signs to Wompatuck State Park. In 0.2 mile you pass the gate house (there is a day-use fee during the summer months) and the visitor center. You might be able to pick up a key to the gate for canoeing access at the visitor center; if not, you will have to drive another 1.5 miles on the main road through the park (the continuation of Union Street) to the campground registration office, on the right. When you register for boating, you will be directed to drive another 0.3 mile down the road, passing Blue Mountain Spring (where you are likely to see long lines of people filling containers with fresh spring water) to the first gate on the left past the spring entrance. After passing through the gate (closing it behind you), follow the arrows on the pavement to get to the boat access. You will make first a left turn, then a right turn, in all driving about another 1 mile to the hand-carry boat access. On a busy summer weekend you may need to park some distance from the water and carry your boat in.

Wompatuck State Park comprises almost three thousand acres and has more than twelve miles of bicycle trails and numerous hiking trails. Motorized vehicles are excluded from the roads and trails, except for access to the boat launch area. Boating is limited to non-gasoline-powered boats. The park has four hundred campsites and is open for camping from early May until mid-October—though the dates of operation are affected by state budgets, so may not be predictable. The park is open for day-use year-round. For more information, contact Wompatuck State Park, Union Street, Hingham, MA 02043; 617-749-7160.

Walden Pond
Concord, MA

To be honest, Walden Pond is not a great canoeing spot. It is crowded, the shoreline is badly eroded and fenced off, and the pond is very small with relatively little shoreline variation. However, it is rich in historical significance. It's worth a visit simply to paddle the same water that Thoreau and Emerson—two of the grandfathers of the environmental movement—knew so well. Henry David Thoreau lived at Walden Pond, on land owned by Ralph Waldo Emerson, from March 1845 until September 1847, and he later reflected on the experience in his book *Walden,* published in 1854.

At the time Thoreau lived here, the woods surrounding Walden Pond were among the last remaining woodlands in the Concord area, most of the land having been cleared for farming. He built a small one-room cabin near the northern tip of the pond, and spent his days studying the area's natural history, gardening, reading, and writing. It was here, in fact, that he began his career as a writer, drafting his first book, *A Week on the Concord and Merrimack Rivers.* At Walden Pond, which he had known as a boy growing up in Concord, Thoreau was deeply affected by society's destruction of the forests: "When I first paddled a boat on Walden it was completely surrounded by thick and lofty pine and oak woods...but since I left those shores, the woodcutters have still further laid them waste." While living here, Thoreau planted some four hundred white pine trees. Most of the trees were knocked down by the great hurricane of 1938, but a few stumps can still be found above the house site.

When Thoreau lived here, Walden Pond was still visited occasionally by loons, but they disappeared shortly thereafter, pushed away by encroaching civilization and a lack of fish. (Today, loons nest on only four bodies of water in Massachusetts, all of which are public water supplies off-limits to canoeing.) In the twentieth century, Walden Pond became far more crowded than Thoreau could have imagined. In part from the fame he had given to the pond, Walden became a favorite recreation site. Even before the boat houses were built in 1917, crowds as large as 2000 per day visited the pond. By the summer of 1935, after an eighty-acre parcel of land around the pond had been granted to the Commonwealth of Massachusetts as a public park, as many as 485,000 people visited the pond each summer, with up to 25,000 visitors on a single Sunday!

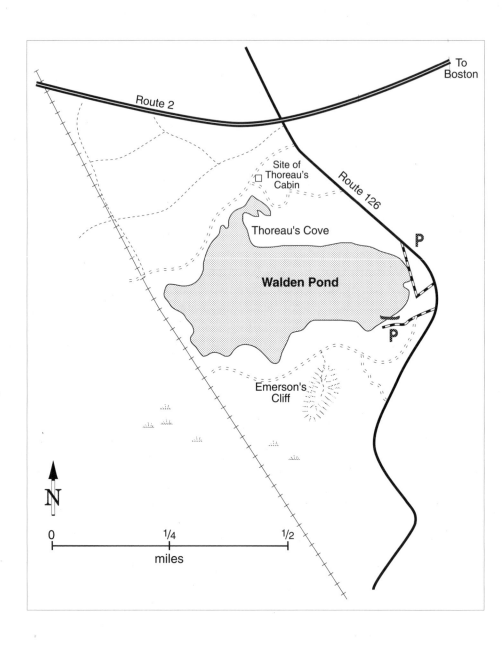

To
Boston

Route 2

Route 126

Site of
Thoreau's
Cabin

Thoreau's Cove

P

Walden Pond

P

Emerson's
Cliff

N

0   1/4   1/2
miles

Since 1975, Walden Pond has been managed by the Massachusetts Department of Environmental Management (DEM). DEM is working to restore the pond's eroded banks—thus the fencing—and they limit the number of people using the park to one thousand at any given time. That is still a lot of people for a small pond and surrounding woodland. If you want to visit here and your schedule permits, come midweek after Labor Day or before Memorial Day. Or perhaps on a drizzly day that will make you more reflective of the pond's historic past as you paddle the deserted shores.

Geologically, Walden Pond is a kettle hole, formed ten to twelve thousand years ago when receding glaciers left behind a large chunk of ice buried in glacial till. As this ice melted, it left a deep sandy-bottomed pond with a maximum depth of about 100 feet. There are many other kettle-hole ponds in southeastern Massachusetts, including Cape Cod (see section on Cliff Pond). The sandy bottom provides superb swimming, but the absence of any major inlet streams keeps Walden Pond and most other kettle ponds relatively sterile. (With other types of ponds, inlet streams carry in a great deal of organic matter, providing nutrients for aquatic life.) If it were not stocked, Walden Pond would provide little in the way of fishing.

GETTING THERE: To reach Walden Pond from the west, take Route 2 East for 3.5 miles past the rotary in Concord, then turn right onto Route 126 South. The main entrance to Walden Pond State Reservation is on the left 0.3 mile from Route 2, and the boat access is on the right another 0.3 mile farther down Route 126. If you are coming from the east on Route 2, turn left onto Route 126 a little over four miles from Route 128 (I-95).

The boat access is open to boaters only. Though this policy could change, in 1992 a chain was kept up across the boat access road, but boaters were permitted to lower the chain to drive in while the park was open (5 AM until one-half hour after sunset). The pond is open to non-gasoline-powered boats only. There are numerous trails through the park; pick up a trail map at the park headquarters. For more information, contact Walden Pond State Reservation, 915 Walden Street (Route 126), Concord, MA 01742; 617-369-3254.

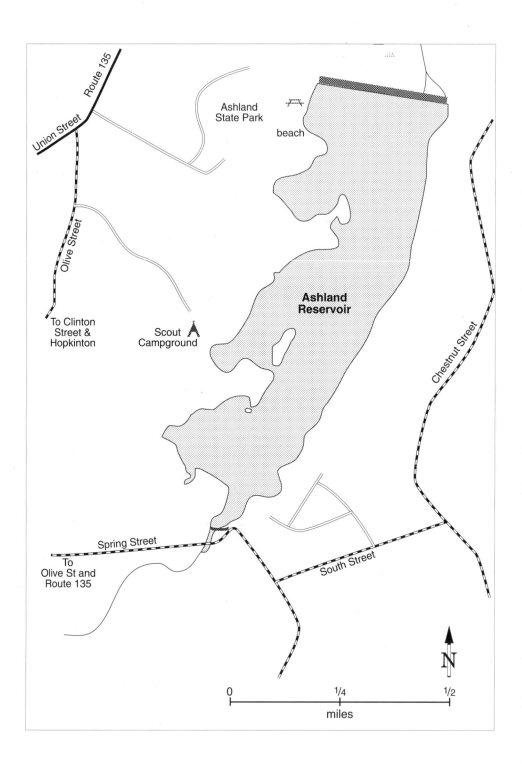

Route 135

Union Street

Ashland
State Park

beach

Olive Street

To Clinton
Street &
Hopkinton

Scout
Campground

**Ashland
Reservoir**

Chestnut Street

Spring Street

To
Olive St and
Route 135

South Street

N

0   1/4   1/2

miles

Ashland Reservoir

Ashland, MA

Ashland Reservoir is a great spot for a quiet morning or afternoon paddle. With a largely undeveloped shoreline, a 12 MPH limit for motorboats, a sandy bottom, and attractive deep woods surrounding the reservoir, Ashland offers some of the best paddling within the 495 loop. The reservoir is a little over a mile long and about a quarter-mile wide in most places. The reservoir seems quite deep, with little floating or underwater vegetation. Ashland State Park, with picnic and swimming areas, is located at the north end.

The boat access for Ashland Reservoir is at the south end by the inlet. As you paddle north the reservoir quickly opens up, with some deep coves on the western shore. You will probably find the western shore more interesting to paddle along than the eastern shore, since there is more variation here and no development (there are a few houses on the eastern side). The shoreline of the whole reservoir is heavily wooded, with red oak and white pine the dominant species. You will also see red maple, American chestnut, scarlet oak, white oak, gray birch, black birch, sassafras, black gum, and pitch pine. Right along the shore, the shrubs are fairly dense: sweet pepperbush, alder, blueberry, and winterberry. During a mid-September paddle here I found some delicious grapes overhanging the water along the eastern shore.

The bottom is generally sandy or rocky, and the water somewhat brackish—due, most likely, to natural tannins in the water. In places you will see numerous shallow depressions a foot or two in diameter in the sand that are free of debris and organic matter. These are spawning locations for sunfish. During the summer you can watch adult males valiantly guarding these depressions and fanning the eggs to provide good aeration. Along with lots of sunfish, Ashland Reservoir has healthy populations of bullhead catfish, largemouth bass, yellow perch, and stocked rainbow trout.

GETTING THERE: To reach Ashland Reservoir, take Interstate 495 to Exit 21, then get onto West Main Street heading toward Hopkinton and Ashland. West Main Street merges into Route 135, becoming East Main Street in Hopkinton. After crossing Route 85 in Hopkinton, continue on Route 135 for another 1.7 miles, then turn right onto Clinton Street. Stay on Clinton Street for 0.6 mile and turn left onto Olive

Street. After 0.2 mile, turn right off of Olive Street onto Spring Street; you will reach the boat access and parking area on the left after 0.7 mile. If you are coming west on Route 135 from the Framingham area, drive 2.2 miles past the intersection with Main Street in Ashland, turn left onto Clinton Street, then follow directions as above.

To reach the main entrance of Ashland State Park, drive back from the boat access to Route 135 and turn right. The entrance to the park will be on the right and is clearly marked when the park is open. Ashland State Park has walking trails, picnic areas, and a good swimming beach. The park has a limited season of operation, though, and the boat access on Spring Street is where you should launch a canoe. For more information on paddling and other recreational opportunities at Ashland Reservoir, contact Ashland State Park c/o Hopkinton State Park, 71 Cedar Street, Hopkinton, MA 01748; 508-435-4303.

Whitehall Reservoir

Hopkinton, MA

Whitehall Reservoir is great. Of the canoeable lakes and ponds within an hour's drive from the Boston area, it just can't be beat—most of the time, that is. The large (575-acre) reservoir at one time served as a water supply for the suburban areas west of Boston, but when the Quabbin Reservoir was created in 1939, drinking water from Whitehall was no longer needed and eventually the area was turned into a state park. Its years of restricted access mean great boating today.

I stumbled on the Whitehall Reservoir pretty much by surprise. I had seen it on a map and assumed it would be off-limits to boating, as so many of the less developed lakes are. But it isn't, though some boating restrictions are sorely needed—see below. The entire shoreline of the reservoir is owned and protected by the state. Homeowners are permitted to have small docks on the reservoir, but the size of these docks is regulated, and mooring of larger boats is not permitted. From the water, the reservoir feels very undeveloped and wild.

The shoreline is highly varied, with numerous deep coves and dozens of wonderful islands to explore. You will find some marshy areas, but most of the shoreline is heavily wooded, with the woods open and inviting. The difficulty in picnicking here is deciding which great spot to choose! Along much of the shoreline, the trees are typical of this part of Massachusetts—mixed deciduous trees and conifers, with laurel and highbush blueberry along the shoreline. Near the center of the reservoir, however, close to the west side, is a fantastic grouping of islands with far different vegetation on them. Here you'll see Atlantic white cedar, larch, and spruce—trees one would expect to see much farther north. The area is almost magical. On a quiet weekday morning you can feel lost weaving in and out of these islands and the channels that cut through them. Whether you're fishing, birdwatching, or simply enjoying a few hours of paddling, be sure to paddle over to this part of the reservoir.

While the islands near the center of the reservoir are quite wet and not suitable for exploration on foot, some other islands in the reservoir are. The islands farther north are higher and perfect for a picnic or blueberry-picking excursion. Also north, by the dam at the northeastern tip, are some gorgeous open woodlands—tall white pine with a thick carpet of pine needles underfoot.

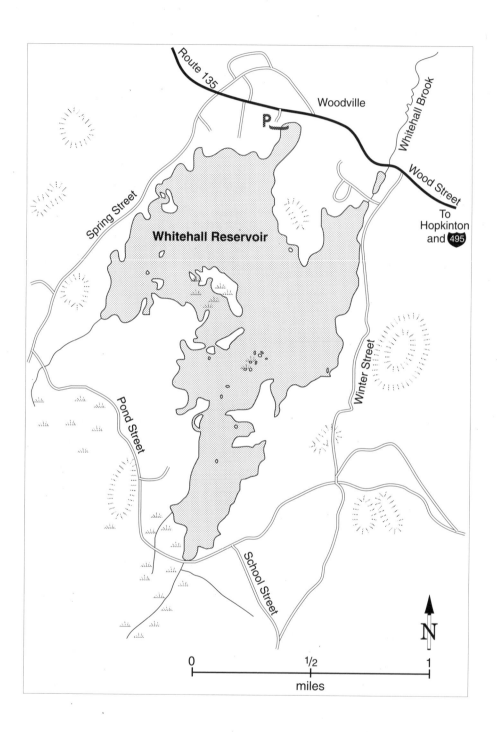

Route 135

Woodville

Whitehall Brook

Spring Street

Wood Street

Whitehall Reservoir

To
Hopkinton
and **495**

Winter Street

Pond Street

School Street

N

0	1/2	1

miles

While Whitehall Reservoir offers some great canoeing, it has its drawbacks. On a sunny summer weekend motorboat use can be excessive. There is supposed to be a boating speed limit of 12 MPH, but that rule is not widely respected. As I was paddling out from between two small islands, a large power boat came churning by at a good 35 MPH within 15 or 20 feet, its occupants oblivious to the wake being created, the disturbance, and the potential danger. I was told by someone who paddles on Whitehall regularly that he's pretty much given up even coming here on weekends because of some very close encounters he's had with motorboats. And the concern is not only one of safety and enjoyment for paddlers; the wakes from large motorboats are causing significant erosion in some parts of the reservoir.

Whitehall Reservoir is the perfect example of a lake that could be preserved in almost pristine condition for the enjoyment of low-impact paddlers and the protection of the shoreline—if only the state could be convinced to restrict access. Carry-in-only access at the boat launch off Route 135 at the north end would make all the difference in the world. Perhaps once enough of us have experienced how wonderful paddling here can be, we can collectively convince the powers that be at the Massachusetts Department of Environmental Management, Division of Forests and Parks (100 Cambridge Street, Boston, MA 02202), and the Massachusetts Public Access Board (100 Nashua Street, Room 915, Boston, MA 02114) that this one should be left to us.

GETTING THERE: Take Route 495 to Exit 21 (the first exit south of the Mass Pike), and drive northeast on West Main Street toward Hopkinton. Just as you get into Hopkinton, turn left on Wood Street (Route 135). (This turn is about a mile from the end of the exit ramp—a little more if you were driving south on Route 495, a little less if you were driving north.) After turning onto Route 135, drive 2.7 miles, heading generally northwest. You will first pass under Route 495 and through the small village of Woodville; then the boat launch will be on the left, marked with a sign indicating Whitehall State Park. There is no camping here. For more information, contact nearby Hopkinton State Park, 71 Cedar Street, Hopkinton, MA 01748; 508-435-4303.

Assabet Reservoir
Westborough, MA

The Assabet Reservoir, just a few miles from busy Route 9 in Westborough, is a fascinating place, well worth a visit by canoe—and canoes are definitely the craft of choice for this body of water. There are thousands of closely spaced dead trees and stumps left over from the creation of this flood-control reservoir in 1969. For some reason the trees were not cut before the area was dammed, making boating here a challenge, but providing great nesting habitat for birds.

The eastern end of the 310-acre reservoir is fairly open and easy to paddle, but once you round the point of land extending down from the north side, the Assabet Reservoir is a forest of standing dead trees and stumps. In places, you will literally have to weave your canoe around these trees to get through, watching carefully for more stumps hiding just beneath the surface. Tree swallows nest in the dead trees in abundance and help keep the population of mosquitoes in check.

Near the western edge of the reservoir there is a great blue heron rookery, where approximately twenty pairs of this large wading bird hatch and raise their young. If you get a chance to visit here in the spring, be sure to take a look at the rookery. Don't get too close, though. Not only will you risk scaring the herons, you could be in for

Perched precariously atop the standing dead trees in Assabet Reservoir are about two dozen great blue heron nests.

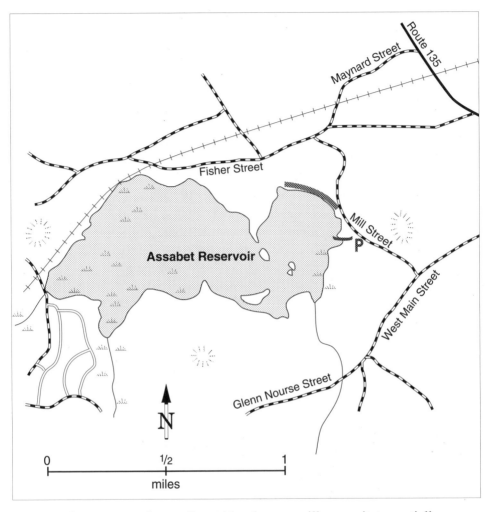

an unpleasant experience. Great blue herons will regurgitate partially digested food—mostly fish—on intruders as a defense. Yuck! (For more information on this remarkable bird, take a look at the companion volume to this book: *AMC Quiet Water Canoe Guide: New Hampshire/Vermont.*)

Most of Assabet Reservoir is quite shallow. The deepest point is only fifteen feet. As such, it is an excellent spot for largemouth bass fishing, with plenty of cover provided by the underwater vegetation. Someone caught a six-pounder while I was there. Most of the shoreline is quite marshy, with cattails and bulrush growing around the perimeter, and water shield floating on the open water. Somewhat surprisingly, the bottom is quite sandy—looking at the reservoir one would guess that the bottom would be thick muck. Freshwater mussels can be found here with piles of their shells as evidence of many a meal raccoons have enjoyed. Surrounding the reservoir are willows, alder, red maple, red oak, and aspen. A number of islands are scattered around the reservoir, but these offer little in the way of access for rest or a picnic. Along with swallows and great blue herons, keep an eye out for green herons, cedar waxwings, ospreys, wood ducks, and lots of painted turtles.

GETTING THERE: To reach the Assabet Reservoir, take Route 9 west from Interstate-495 (Exit 23B) toward Westborough. Drive about 3.3 miles to Route 135 and turn right at the stop sign (south) toward Westborough. Drive 0.7 mile on Route 135, and turn right onto Maynard Street. After crossing the railroad tracks, bear right onto Fisher Street, then take an almost immediate left onto Mill Street. Pull-over parking space and a boat ramp are on the right after 0.4 mile. There is room for ten to fifteen cars along both sides of the road, plus another three or four off the road by the boat ramp. If you are coming from a different direction, or get lost, don't expect a lot of help when you ask about the Assabet Reservoir. It is known most commonly as the A-1 Site, George Nichols Dam, or Stump Pond.

The Assabet River begins its journey to the confluence with the Concord River here. If you are interested in paddling down the Assabet and Concord rivers, refer to the *AMC River Guide: Massachusetts/ Connecticut/Rhode Island* or the more detailed *Concord, Sudbury, and Assabet Rivers: A Guide to Canoeing, Wildlife, and History* by Ron McAdow (Bliss Publishing Company, 1990). Both the reservoir and the Assabet River that flows out of it vary in water level. After a drought, the reservoir may be a little smaller than shown on the accompanying map.

Paradise Pond
Princeton, MA

Bordering Leominster State Forest, undeveloped, and free of gasoline-powered motorboats, Paradise Pond is a great spot for a morning or afternoon of paddling—almost a little paradise in the center of Massachusetts. The only problem is a highway running along most of the west shore of the pond. Though Route 31 is not heavily traveled, the road interrupts the peace and quiet.

The pond is small, at just thirty-eight acres, but the shoreline is quite varied, with a number of coves and several islands to explore. The vegetation here includes a number of species that you rarely see this far north: swamp honeysuckle (a fairly late-blooming azalea with honeysuckle-like sticky white flowers), sweet pepperbush (a late-blooming shrub with clusters of small, fragrant white flowers that you can still find in bloom at the end of August), and sassafras. Also found along the shoreline here are buttonbush, mountain laurel, highbush blueberry, alder, shadbush, sweet gale, leatherleaf, black gum, white pine, oak, and birch.

The islands on Paradise Pond are very much worth visiting. Instead of white pine and the various deciduous trees that comprise most of the woods around Paradise Pond, the dominant tree on the islands is pitch pine, a three-needled pine with large plates of bark on the older trees. Away from the water's edge, the islands are open and carpeted with a thick bed of needles—ideal locations for a picnic lunch.

The water in Paradise Pond appears quite clean. In some sections, the surface is covered with water shield, which you can easily distinguish from other water lilies because the stem extends down from the center of the oval leaves; there is no cut in the leaf. Feel the slippery underside of these leaves. In the water you will see lots of bladderwort. This unusual plant has feathery leaves with small bulbs or "bladders" that serve a fascinating role. Bladderwort (*Utricularia spp.*) is actually a carnivorous plant that obtains some of its nourishment from animal matter. The bladders are really traps, about 1 millimeter in diameter, that are sealed closed by a small layer of tissue, surrounded by tiny hairs. The fluid in this bladder is gradually absorbed by the surrounding tissue and a negative pressure develops inside the bladder. When a small aquatic animal brushes against one of these trigger hairs, the "door" suddenly springs open, pulling water and the prey into the bladder. The tiny animal is digested by enzymes over a period of a few days. Most of the prey consists of protozoa, minute water insects, tiny crustaceans, and the like, but some bladderworts can ingest mosquito

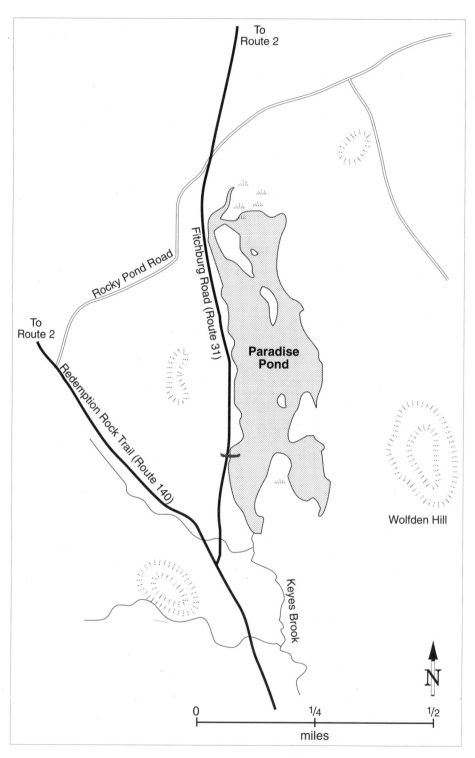

larvae as well—which is nice to know. Mosquito larvae and other large prey can be captured in stages, the bladder closing around just a portion of the larva initially, then resetting and pulling a second section in after ingesting the first. It is really quite a remarkable process that long mystified botanists. These carnivorous bladderworts are among the most common of our underwater plants. Look for feathery underwater plants with tiny bulbous bladders as you paddle around this and other New England ponds. In the summer, bladderworts have yellow or purple flowers above the water's surface.

If you look carefully as you paddle around Paradise Pond, you will also see sundew on floating logs and sphagnum hummocks in some parts of the pond. Sundew is another carnivorous plant that captures insects with a sticky substance on hairs that protrude from the leaf and stem. You may also see painted turtles here, though they do not seem as abundant as I expected. I saw a water snake here as well—entwined on a branch over the water. The pond is fished for largemouth bass, pickerel, and yellow perch.

At the southern tip of the pond you will see ruins of an old mill building. An 1870 map shows an E.B. Walker Saw Mill here. Earlier maps show other saw mills on this Keyes Brook branch of the Stillwater. Another tidbit of local history: Princeton was chosen by early colonial negotiators as the site for a prisoner redemption. Redemption Rock is about two miles north of Paradise Pond, near the Westminster town line and lying deep in woods. It was here in 1675 that Mary Rowlandson, who had been captured during the midwinter massacre at Lancaster and held in Quebec for eight weeks, was freed for twenty pounds sterling and some whiskey. Route 140, which passes just south of Paradise Pond, is known as Redemption Rock Trail.

On the east side of Paradise Pond, Leominster State Forest provides some great hiking on old logging roads and trails that wind through pine-needle-carpeted open woodland. You'll see lots of wildflowers here in the spring. However, camping is not permitted, so you'll have to content yourself with hiking and perhaps a picnic lunch or dinner. Trails here are also used for off-road vehicles.

GETTING THERE: Take Route 2 to Exit 28, and turn onto Route 31 South. In about 3 miles you should see Paradise Pond on the left; in another half-mile there is a sizable pull-off area on the left side of the road where you can park. There are several places along here, the largest of which has room for ten to fifteen cars. It is just a short carry from here to the water. For more information, call Leominster State Forest, P.O. Box 142, Westminster, MA 01473; 508-874-2303 or 508-368-0126.

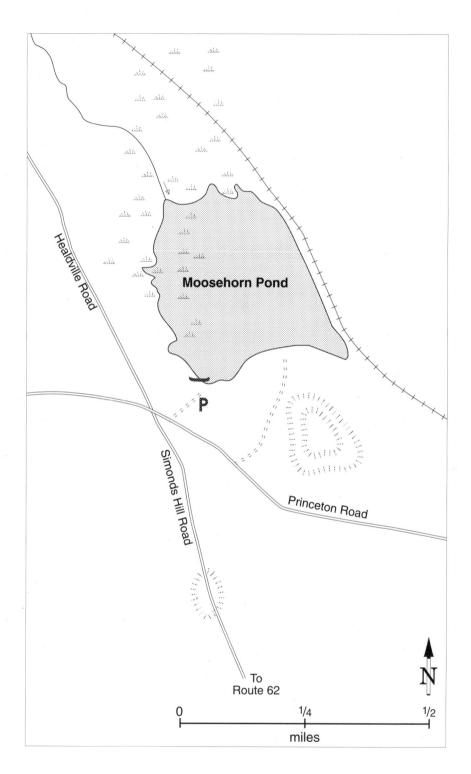

Moosehorn Pond

Healdville Road

Simonds Hill Road

Princeton Road

P

To
Route 62

N

| 0 | | 1/4 | | 1/2 |

miles

Moosehorn Pond
Hubbardston, MA

Moosehorn Pond is small but interesting—definitely worth a visit if you're in the area. The pond is undeveloped, some distance away from major roads, and access is limited to canoes and other carry-in boats. These features keep it very quiet and relatively pristine. Looking out over Moosehorn from the boat access, it has a very "northern" feel to it. Much of the pond is marshy, with spongy mats of sphagnum moss and dense stands of leatherleaf punctuated by the occasional tall spires of tamarack. Hidden amid the sphagnum moss are sundew, marsh fern, and, I suspect, an occasional pitcher plant (I was surprised to find only a single—deceased—pitcher plant during a visit in early September and suspect the plant could be found if one looked hard enough).

Along with tamaracks, you will see red maple, white birch, gray birch, white pine, red oak, American chestnut, sassafras, witchhazel, blueberry, winterberry (a member of the holly genus), and sweet pepperbush. On the water are a number of floating-leaf plants: fragrant water lily, bullhead lily, water shield, and pondweed. If you are quiet as you paddle through the marshy islands, you're likely to see wood ducks, which nest here, as well as great blue herons. Fish species caught at Moosehorn include largemouth bass, pickerel, and yellow perch.

During most seasons you can paddle considerably farther north than the border of the pond shown on the map—though it's not exactly smooth sailing with the floating sphagnum mats, half-submerged logs, and hillocks of grass. Indeed, in the northern section of the pond, poling might prove more effective than paddling if you're adequately equipped. Old but still-used railroad tracks run along the eastern side of the pond.

While there is no camping at Moosehorn Pond, you can camp a couple of miles away on the East Branch of the Ware River at the Pout & Trout Campground. The campground is a far cry from a wilderness experience but is not as bad as some private campgrounds, and it is located on a beautiful stretch of river. I camped here midweek in September and it was very quiet and relaxing. From the campground, a gently flowing canoeable stretch of the Ware River extends both north and south. The shores of the river are thick with pickerel weed, and you can expect to see turtles, wood ducks, mallards, and great blue herons. The open river is quite narrow, but a wide marsh and grassland extend a few hundred yards on each side of the river. You can put in at the campground if you are staying there, or at a public boat access on the west

Spindly tamarack trees are part of the bog ecosystem at Moosehorn Pond.

side of the river along Intervale Road, just north of a small, relatively modern, covered bridge. Downriver from the bridge are some rapids.

GETTING THERE: To reach Moosehorn Pond from the north, take Route 68 South from Route 2 (Exit 22) for approximately 7 miles, then turn left onto Route 62 East. Drive 1.0 mile and bear left onto Clark Road. After 0.3 mile, bear left onto Simonds Hill Road, staying on the paved road (a dirt road continues straight). Drive 0.9 mile on Simonds Hill Road and then turn right onto Princeton Road. The public boat access is on the left after about 100 yards. There is parking space for eight to ten cars, and you have to carry your boat to the water.

If you are driving up from the south, take Route 190 to Route 140 North (Exit 5). After 2.3 miles, turn left onto Route 62 West. Continue on Route 62 for 9.3 miles, through the town of Princeton, to Clark Road. Take a sharp right onto Clark Road, and follow directions as above.

To reach the Pout & Trout Campground, drive back down Simonds Hill Road and Clark Road to Route 62. Turn right on Route 62 (west) and then take an almost immediate left onto Intervale Road. The campground is on the left 0.6 mile from Route 62. In 1992, tent camping rates started at $14 per night without water and electricity. To reach the public boat access (carry-in only—no ramp), continue past the campground entrance for 0.3 mile. Access is on the left. For more information on camping, contact the Pout & Trout Campground, River Road, Rutland, MA 01543; 508-886-6677.

Quaboag Pond
East Brookfield, MA

Quaboag Pond is large, quite developed on the north and east sides, and popular with water-skiers—less than ideal from a canoeist's standpoint. But the inlet and outlet rivers are a different story and highly worth exploring. The East Brookfield River flows into Quaboag Pond at the northeastern tip. Traveling upstream from the Quaboag Shore Road bridge where it enters Quaboag Pond, the slow-flowing East Brookfield River hugs the road for a few hundred yards, then turns generally north and east. Initially, the channel is fairly wide as it winds through Allen Marsh. The sides are thick with pickerel weed, grasses, sedges, and buttonbush. In the water are the floating leaves of fragrant water lily, bullhead lily, and pondweed. Bladderwort and other submerged plant species are flowing in the current beneath the river's surface. Though rarely visible, the bottom is generally sandy with freshwater mussels thriving in it. I've seen lots of painted turtles along here, a stinkpot turtle—which had climbed up on a protruding branch well above the water's surface, as these turtles will—great blue herons, wood ducks, and muskrats.

The East Brookfield River, which flows into Quaboag Pond, is a wide, slow-flowing river that meanders through a broad marsh. This is an excellent place to see wildlife.

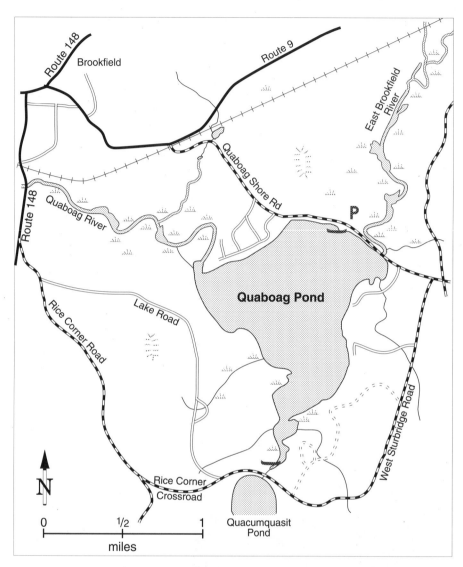

As you paddle farther north on the East Brookfield River, the channel gets narrower and more defined; there are fewer wide backwater (oxbow) ponds to explore. Eventually, about two miles up the river, you reach a fork. From here on, your path may be restricted by fallen trees or brush, though if you persevere you might make it to Lake Lashaway (left fork), or to East Brookfield, where the right channel flows generally along Route 9 toward Spencer (I have not been up this far).

At the northwestern tip of the generally triangular Quaboag Pond, the Quaboag River flows out of the pond, beginning its journey westward to the confluence with the Ware and Swift rivers to form the

Chicopee River. The first several miles of this river are quiet meandering flatwater; white water is not encountered until you get to Warren, about eight miles from Quaboag Pond, so you can get in a full day of quiet water paddling through some gorgeous country by making a round-trip of it. Initially, the Quaboag River winds it way through the marshy Quacumquasit Wildlife Management Area. There is considerable vegetation on and along the river here. Like the East Brookfield River, underwater vegetation grows in profusion in the channel. Close to the banks are floating-leaf plants, with grasses and shrubs lining the banks. Along much of this stretch of river, the tree line is quite far from the river—several hundred yards across the marsh. In general, the Quaboag River is quite a bit wider than the East Brookfield River. Both the East Brookfield and Quaboag rivers are used for duck hunting in the fall, so try to schedule your paddling to avoid those times.

In years long past, the Quaboag River served as a major thoroughfare for the region's Native Americans. The route of connecting waterways from west and south met at Quaboag Pond. A short portage connected the pond to the nearby Quinaboag River, which ran south through Nipmuk and Eastern Niantic country to meet other tributaries of the Pawcatuck River system, which meanders from southern Rhode Island through Narraganset country. In this way, nations of this south coastal region could communicate, trade, and journey north to Quaboag Pond, then turn west and down the Chicopee River to the Connecticut country.

In the native uprising known as King Philip's War, indigenous nations along this route ravaged the more isolated settlements of colonial New England. Old Brookfield, a frontier village a few miles to the northwest of Quaboag Pond on Foster Hill, became an easy target. On August 2, 1675, Quaboag warriors ambushed an armed team of English negotiators from Boston, there to extract a pledge of neutrality amidst growing Indian warfare in southeastern New England. The retreating English took hasty refuge with Brookfield's families in their largest structure, Ayres' Tavern. Ephraim Curtis, a scout of that party, finally crept through a determined siege in which all other structures were burned, to bring about eventual rescue from Marlborough. Fifty women and children and thirty-two men held the tavern, while two sets of twin babies were born within. The town was soon abandoned for safer and more central Hadley, in today's Pioneer Valley near Amherst. (For more on King Philip's War, see the section on Worden Pond, pages 199–206).

Back on Quaboag Pond, the nicest area for the paddler to explore is along the west shore from the Quaboag River outlet down to the connection with Quacumquasit Pond at the southern tip. The southern half of this shoreline is part of the Quacumquasit Wildlife Management Area. You'll see white and red oak, red maple, willow, alder, white pine, and sugar maple along the shore here—plus some blueberry bushes, which can make for considerable delays in late July and early August! At the southern end, there is a barrier gate under the Lake Road bridge. When the gate is closed, boat traffic between the two ponds is blocked—there are public boat access ramps on both bodies of water here.

GETTING THERE: To reach Quaboag Pond from the Mass. Pike (I-90), get off at Exit 9 and start south on I-84 toward Sturbridge. Get off at the first exit and follow Route 20 east for a little over a mile, then turn onto Route 49 North (follow signs carefully). Route 49 passes over the Mass. Pike almost immediately and continues north. From the intersection with Route 20, drive 4.0 miles and turn left (west) onto Flagg Street. After just 0.1 mile, Flagg Street ends at Podunk Road. Turn right (north) on Podunk and drive 1.5 miles to a fork where Podunk bears off to the right and Quaboag Shore Road bears to the left. Bear left here (heading generally west) and stay on Quaboag Shore Road, passing West Sturbridge Road to the left almost immediately. You will soon see Quaboag Pond on your left and the state boat access and parking lot between the road and the water shortly thereafter. The boat access is 0.7 mile from the fork of Podunk Road and Quaboag Shore Road.

As mentioned, there is another boat launch at the southern tip of Quaboag Pond, which you can reach by driving south on West Sturbridge Road and around the bottom of the pond on Rice Corner Crossroad. The boat launch and parking area are on the right just past the bridge on the west side of the channel connecting Quaboag and Quacumquasit Ponds. You can also hand-launch a canoe on the Quaboag River where the Fiskdale Road (Route 148) crosses it. There is room for only a few cars here and the access off the road is very poor. This access is 0.6 mile south on Route 148 from the intersection with Route 9 in Brookfield. For information on other access points on the Quaboag and East Brookfield rivers, which will be especially useful if you are planning a one-way trip with drop-off or pick-up, consult the *AMC River Guide: Massachusetts/Connecticut/Rhode Island.*

East Brimfield Lake and Holland Pond
Sturbridge, Massachusetts

Near historic Sturbridge, Massachusetts, you will find plenty of water for a full day of paddling on the various bodies of water that collectively comprise what is known as East Brimfield Lake. Long Pond to the north and Holland Pond to the south are connected, in normal conditions, by the slow-flowing Quinebaug River. Because of periodic flooding, the U.S. Army Corps of Engineers constructed the Brimfield dam, which enables this entire basin to be filled. This shouldn't get in the way of your paddling, however. Most of the time these bodies of water are quite manageable—a great spot for a few hours or a full day of canoeing.

From the boat launch on the north side of Route 20, Long Pond extends about 1.5 miles north, almost to Interstate 90. Most of the shoreline here is heavily wooded, with white pine, red oak, white oak, sugar maple, and red maple the dominant species. Unfortunately, there are also a lot of Eurasian milfoil and some development along the east shore. Two-thirds of the way up, you have to paddle under a very low bridge where Champeaux Road crosses (the bridge is so low that you have to lie back in your canoe and pull yourself through). The bridge

The gently flowing, marshy, Quinebaug River flows into East Brimfield Lake from Holland Pond.

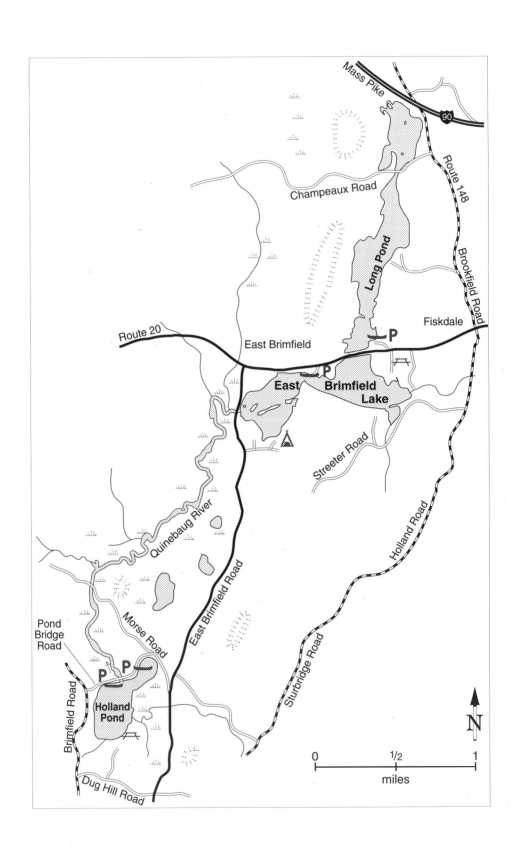

keeps out the larger motorboats, and the shoreline north of this bridge seems more interesting, with marshy coves, floating pond vegetation, ferns along the banks, and lots of birds. A grove of red oak and white pine jutting out into the water makes a great picnic area on the western side of this northernmost section of Long Pond. The only problem with the north end of Long Pond is that you have to put up with vehicle noise from I-90—the highway is just a few hundred feet from the northern end of the pond, though it is shielded pretty well by trees.

The section of East Brimfield Lake south of Route 20 is also nice, though between the looming dam at the east end, a public beach and picnic area, a large and well-used boat ramp, a private campground (replete with an armada of paddleboats and hundreds of screaming children on a nice summer weekend), and the highway running along much of it, one doesn't feel very alone here. You can paddle through a tunnel under Route 20 to get into this part of Long Pond, or put in on the south side of the highway. Paddlers wanting more solitude should canoe right on through this section of water, crossing under East Brimfield Road, and paddle up the slow-flowing Quinebaug River that flows into the west end of the lake.

From the west end of East Brimfield Lake to Holland Pond is about a three-mile paddle. If you paddle fairly steadily, you can make it in about an hour, but you'll enjoy it more if you take the time for observing wildlife, fishing, or a picnic. The river passes some farmland near the north end, but mostly it winds through thick marsh filled with birdlife. Sections of bank are lush with ferns, and in the few places where the woods rise steeply from the water, you'll see laurel beneath the red oak and white oak woodland. The water level drops just one meter in the three miles, so there is scarcely a ripple. There is quite a bit of underwater vegetation in the shallow water.

You pass under two more bridges on the way to Holland Pond, one of which is right at the pond's outlet. Be careful paddling under this bridge, as there is a wall of boulders beneath it. I was able to make it through unscathed in late May, but by midsummer you may well have to carry around to get into Holland Pond. The pond itself is very attractive, with just a few houses on the west side, well away from and above the water. There is a small sandy beach near the outlet and another larger one across the pond at the Holland Pond Recreation Area. This recreation area has not been operated for the past few years (see Getting There below), but I would imagine that swimming is permitted here even if the recreation area itself is not open.

GETTING THERE: There are good boat access points on both the north and south sides of Route 20 in East Brimfield. To paddle on the northern part of the lake, the best place to launch your boat is on the north side of the highway, just east of Long Pond. If driving west on Route 20, the boat launch is on the right 0.7 mile past the junction of Routes 20 and 148. The entrance to the boat launch is directly across the highway from an entrance marked Streeter Road Beach. If driving east on Route 20, look for a sharp left turn just after passing the pond on both sides of the road.

If you are more interested in exploring the southern section of Long Pond and then paddling up the Quinebaug River towards Holland Pond, you can put in at a boat launch area 0.4 mile farther west on the south side of Route 20. There is lots of room for parking at both of these locations, though East Brimfield Lake can see some pretty heavy usage on a summer weekend. These boat launches are part of the Streeter Point Recreation Area, which is managed by the Massachusetts Department of Environmental Management, Division of Forests and Parks.

Finally, you can drive up to Holland Pond via East Brimfield Road, Dug Hill Road, Brimfield Road, and Pond Bridge Road, as shown on the map. and put your boat in there. The boat access area is a little more difficult to find, but you'll be farther away from the larger, higher-horsepower motorboats found on Long Pond. From the bridge at the outlet of Holland Pond, you can launch either into the pond or the river below the bridge (be careful paddling under the bridge, as mentioned above). Additional space for parking and an unimproved boat ramp can be reached a few hundred yards east of the outlet.

If you're interested in camping here, the Quinebaug Cove Campsite offers year-round camping with 125 sites. Though this campground caters primarily to trailers and RVs, its location is good and if you avoid the busy seasons it could be quite pleasant. For information, contact Quinebaug Cove Campsite, RFD 2, Box 56, East Brimfield, MA 01010 (413-245-9525). While you're in the area you might want to visit historic Sturbridge Village, which portrays life in an 1830s New England town.

For more information on the Streeter Point Recreation Area, including the boat launches and the large picnic area and public beach on Long Pond, write to the Streeter Point Recreation Area, c/o Wells State Park, Walker Mountain Road, Sturbridge, MA 01566; 508-347-9257.

Water Lilies
Fascinating Flowers of New England's Waters

Three different water lilies are found on nearly all of our shallow freshwater ponds, lakes, and quiet rivers: fragrant water lily, bullhead lily, and water shield. Like other members of the water lily family (*Nymphaeaceae*), these have underwater stems called rhizomes in the mud at the bottom of the pond and leaves that extend up to the surface. These floating-leaved plants are uniquely adapted to life in the water, and can grow in water as shallow as six inches or as deep as fifteen feet—as long as the water is clear enough for sunlight to penetrate to the bottom, where it is needed for photosynthesis until newly germinated plants are old enough for their leaves to reach all the way to the surface.

Fragrant water lily (*Nymphaea odorata*) is the most common

species. It has attractive white (or, rarely, pink) flowers and round leaves that are reddish underneath with a slit on one side. Like other water lilies, this one has stomata (small openings on the leaf for gas exchange) on the top of the leaf; most other plants have the stomata on the leaf bottom. It will grow almost anywhere, including in the most polluted, stagnant ponds, where its delicate fragrance has to compete against the strong aroma of fouled water. The beauty of a pond whose surface is covered with white blossoms from the fragrant water lily can thus belie the pond's true condition.

I had observed this plant for years as I paddled our quiet waters before I noticed a remarkable aspect of its physiology. After blooming, during which the flowers open up each morning and close in the afternoon over three or four successive days, the flower head is literally pulled back underwater by a coiling action of the stem. Underwater, the seeds develop in the fertilized flowerhead, taking three to four weeks to mature. The seeds are enclosed in a sort of capsule, called an aril, that eventually breaks off and floats to the surface. After a few days, the aril decomposes, releasing the seeds to whatever section of the pond the aril had floated to. The small seeds then sink, and some of them take root in the bottom mud.

Bullhead lily (*Nuphar variegatum*) has large oblong leaves and a yellow flower that may extend slightly above the surface of the water. The waxy cuplike flower is fascinating if you get a chance to study it closely. What look like yellow petals are actually sepals, and what look like small yellow stamens are actually petals. A disklike stigma is in the center. Carry a hand lens to get a really good look at this flower, which looks almost artificial. Bullhead lily rhizomes can be very large. Huge mats of them sometimes float to the surface, where they can be significant obstacles to your paddling.

Water shield (*Brassenia schreberi*), has smaller leaves than the other two water lilies described, and small obscure reddish flowers. It is readily distinguished from fragrant water lily and bullhead lily by its oval leaves that are not slit on one side. The petiole (leaf stem) joins the leaf in the center and the reddish underside is usually extremely slimy.

Numerous insects, snails, amphibians, and fish are closely associated with water lilies. One often finds speckled, sausage-shaped, jellied egg masses of pond snails on the underside of the leaves. Frogs and even young painted turtles may be seen sunning on the larger leaves of water lilies, and bass and pickerel often lurk in the shade just beneath the leaves.

The long stems of water lilies serve an interesting role in transporting gases to and from the underwater rhizomes. The stems have hollow tubes through which air is somehow pulled downward for respiration, and carbon dioxide is pushed upward. This process and the mechanisms driving it are poorly understood. A biologist friend of mine suggested that the "popping" or "snapping" sound frequently heard when paddling around shallow ponds on a sunny day might somehow be attributed to this air flow—a fascinating idea that I haven't been able to confirm or refute in the literature. (I had previously assumed this sound to be made by fish, though I never seemed to see the fish or their ripples.) Wondering about such mysteries makes one realize how much is left to discover about the natural world around us—including some of our most common wetland plants.

Lake Denison

Winchendon, MA

In north-central Massachusetts Lake Denison provides a fine spot for family lakeside camping and canoeing, particularly for beginning paddlers. The shallow, relatively round, eighty-two-acre lake has clear water and a sandy bottom—a combination that makes for great swimming. Gasoline-powered motorboats are prohibited from the lake, so you don't have to worry about a lot of noise or being run over by big boats. While undeveloped, the lake is heavily dominated by its recreational uses: 150 campsites, picnic areas, and a swimming beach. The entire eastern and northern sides of the lake are lined with campsites, with a boat ramp on the west side and the beach and picnic areas closer to the south end.

The Lake Denison Recreational Area is managed by the State Department of Environmental Management, Division of Forests and Park, but it is part of the nine-thousand-acre Birch Hill Flood Control Project of the U.S. Army Corps of Engineers. At times of severe flooding, the area can be cleared out and the Birch Hill Dam, a couple of miles to the south and west, can impound water, helping to reduce flooding of the Millers River downstream. If you camp here, you will be able to recognize it as an Army Corps of Engineers project, because all the red pine trees are planted in rows (perhaps tree planting is one of the only opportunities for regimentation for the Corps, so they need to take advantage of it). Camping beneath neatly manicured trees in absolutely straight rows feels a little like a Fellini flick—or perhaps gives you an idea of what a woodchuck must feel visiting a cornfield. Most of these plantings were carried out by the Civilian Conservation Corps (CCC) in the early 1930s. Back then Lake Denison had become the focus of an earlier experiment: an amusement park for city folk, complete with dance hall, sizable dock, and lake steamer, which plied the lake's shorelines. Excursion trolleys running through the country brought weekend and summer vacationers here from Gardner and other points south and east.

Interestingly, while Lake Denison is part of a large water catchment system, the lake itself is natural. It is a kettle-hole lake, formed by receding glaciers when a large chunk of glacial ice was left submerged in glacial till. As the chunk of ice gradually melted, it left this shallow lake with sandy shores and bottom—you will see many such

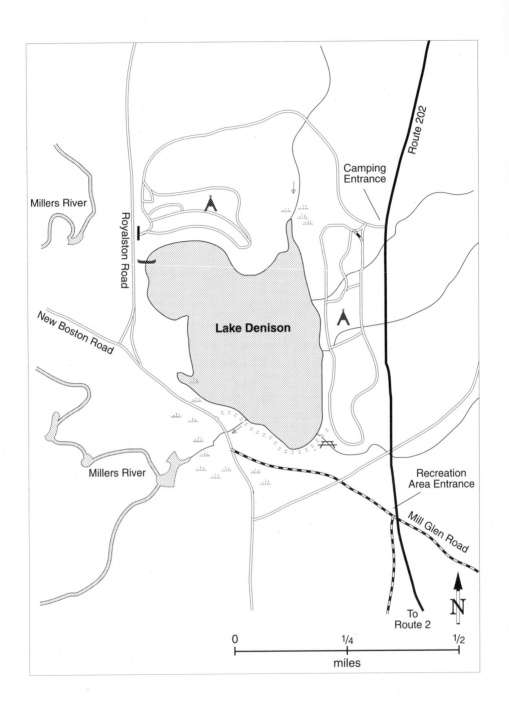

Millers River

Route 202

Camping
Entrance

Royalston Road

New Boston Road

Lake Denison

Millers River

Recreation
Area Entrance

Mill Glen Road

To
Route 2

N

0   1/4   1/2

miles

lakes and ponds farther east, especially on Cape Cod. The maximum depth of Lake Denison is only fifteen feet.

Lake Denison has a few shallow coves and inlets that offer some (limited) opportunity for exploration. Most interesting is the inlet at the northeastern tip. This area is dominated by swamp loosestrife and royal fern on mossy hummocks. Swamp loosestrife, over a few decades, can gain a foothold in shallow water and reduce a pond's perimeter. Here you will see characteristic spongy loosestrife islands and banks that effectively block canoe passage far into the inlet. Keep an eye out for painted turtles here. In a few other coves and shallow shoreline areas of Lake Denison you will see pickerel weed and both fragrant and bull-head lily. Farther from shore, white pine dominates the vegetation, with some red maple and gray birch at the water's edge. The red pine is planted farther from the lake.

GETTING THERE: Lake Denison is located off Route 202 west of Fitchburg. If you are coming from the east, take Route 2 to Exit 20 and drive 2.5 miles north, past the Narragansett Regional High School, to Route 202 in Baldwinville. Turn right on Route 202 and drive 2.4 miles to the entrance to the Lake Denison Recreational Area on the left. (The access for camping is another 0.6 mile up Route 202.) If you are coming from the west, get off Route 2 at Exit 19 and follow Route 202 directly to the Lake Denison Recreational Area entrance (a little over 6 miles). Follow signs to the boat ramp, which is about halfway around the lake. There is no fee to park and use the boat ramp, though there is a day-use fee for using the picnic and swimming areas. You can canoe here any time of year when the water is open, except on those rare occasions when the whole area is cleared out for flood-control reasons—the last such occurrence was in the spring of 1987 when ten inches of rain fell in one week and water was impounded behind the Birch Hill Dam. (The Lake Denison Recreational Area was closed for a month.)

For camping at Lake Denison, you have to drive 0.6 mile north on Route 202 from the primary Lake Denison Recreational Area entrance. Stop at the contact station to register just after turning off Route 202. The camping season runs from early spring (any time from the end of April until mid-May) until Columbus Day weekend. Camping fees in 1992 were $12 per night. The Lake Denison Recreational Area and Otter River State Forest (just to the south) are jointly managed. For more information, contact Otter River State Forest, New Winchendon Road, Baldwinville, MA 01436; 508-939-8962.

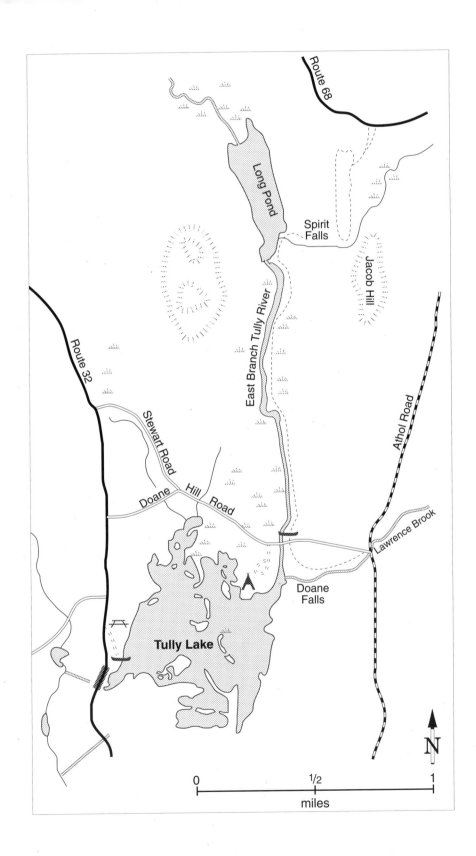

Tully Lake and Long Pond
Royalston, MA

Located in north-central Massachusetts, not far from the New Hampshire border, Tully Lake is a real gem. I am surprised so few people seem to know of its existence. The shoreline of the two-hundred-acre lake is highly varied with dozens of islands and deep winding coves to explore—my idea of a perfect paddling lake—and with no development around it. As an added bonus, there is a very nice primitive camping area at the north end. Though motorboats are permitted on the lake, there is a ten-horsepower limit, which keeps out water-skiers and jet-skis.

Tully Lake was created when the U.S. Army Corps of Engineers completed the 62-foot-high, 1570-foot-long dam in 1949. This is a flood-control dam, built in response to devastating flooding that occurred in the Connecticut River basin in 1937. At times of flooding, the water behind Tully Dam can be impounded, creating a single lake that encompasses Tully Lake, Long Pond, and an extensive marshy area north of Long Pond. In the spring of 1987, when the floodgates were closed because of heavy rainfall from two storms on top of snowmelt, the dam is estimated to have saved $3 million in damages downstream.

Around the shore, white pine predominates, mixed with red maple, hemlock, red oak, white oak, some quaking aspen, and white birch. By the water is a fairly dense border of shrubs, including buttonbush, various heaths, alder, blueberry, and—in places—cranberry with tiny oval leaves that are dwarfed by the large cranberries in the late summer and fall. But farther from shore, the woods open up, providing great picnicking and hiking. On the large island near the south end of the lake, I found a few highbush blueberry bushes covered with berries during a visit in early August. Along with the more common white pine, I saw scrub oak near the south end of the lake—a species that is more common on dry, sandy hills than around lakes.

Unfortunately, like many bodies of water in this area, Tully Lake suffers from high acidity (low pH), which has reduced fish populations. The water is classified as Class B (Class A is the cleanest; Class C the most polluted). Class B waters are suitable for fishing and swimming, though the U.S. Army Corps of Engineers does not permit swimming here. The lake bottom is generally sandy.

At the northeastern extension of Tully Lake, past the Lawrence Brook inlet from Doane Falls, you can paddle under the Doane Hill Road bridge and up the East Branch of the Tully River to Long Pond. (There is plenty of clearance under the bridge, but watch out for rocks

Tully Lake is undeveloped and full of islands and deep coves to explore.

in the water that might scratch your canoe.) This is a wonderful quiet paddle of about a mile-and-a-half. The gently flowing river has very little current; you can see the underwater vegetation swaying, but otherwise you would hardly know which way the current is flowing. The banks of the river are thick with pickerel weed, grasses, royal fern, buttonbush, and other marshy shrubs. Floating in the water along the edges are fragrant water lily, bullhead lily, pondweed, and water shield, but there seems to be plenty of open water for unrestricted paddling. I was quite excited to find along here a northern pitcher plant—an unusual plant, more common in northern bogs, that captures insects in the large cuplike leaves. You are also likely to see painted turtles, great blue herons, kingfishers, muskrats, and—toward evening—beavers.

As you round the last bend paddling north, the river opens up into Long Pond, a serene body of water surrounded by thick woodland on both sides. Most of Long Pond is open water—indicating it is reasonably deep—though at the north end the pond merges into marsh. I explored this north end for a while, but didn't find the main channel of the river—I'll leave that for my next visit. In early spring, before the floating vegetation restricts paddling, explorations of the north end will be much easier.

You might want to get out of your canoe near the south end of Long Pond on the east side and enjoy some hiking. Spirit Falls is reachable by hiking up a trail along Spirit Brook. Though most spectacular in early spring and after rains, Spirit Falls is worth the short hike anytime. There is a hiking trail along the east side of the Tully River between Spirit Falls and Doanes Falls on the Lawrence Brook. The trail crosses Doane Hill Road near the northern boat access by the bridge over the river.

The Tully Lake Camping Area has twenty-four primitive walk-in campsites. You park your car at the campground parking lot just off Doane Hill Road and carry your camping equipment in about 100 yards to the campsites, some of which are right on the water. This seems an ideal way to keep a camping area pleasant—by keeping out vehicles. To camp here you have to really like camping, even without an RV-powered television. I'd like to see more of the state campgrounds operated on a walk-in basis. Unfortunately, the future of the Tully Lake Camping Area is in question. Prior to 1992, the campground was managed by the Massachusetts Department of Environmental Management. In 1992, however, the state dropped the facility for budgetary reasons, and the U.S. Army Corps of Engineers took over management. According to one of the rangers in 1992, the Corps has not yet decided whether they will be able to keep the camping facility open. The token $5-per-night camping fee (1992 rates) just doesn't cover much of the cost of maintaining the facility, apparently. If you camp here and you like what you find, you might want to put in a word of support to the Corps. Camping is also available about ten miles east at Lake Denison State Park—see section on Lake Denison.

GETTING THERE: The main boat access for Tully Lake is located right off Route 32 approximately 4 miles north of Athol. From either the east or west, get off Route 2 at Exit 17 and drive north on Route 32 through Athol. Watch the highway signs carefully; it's easy to lose Route 32 as it meanders through the town. From the point at which Route 32 North splits off to the right from Route 2A West shortly after crossing the Millers River, drive approximately 3.7 miles north on 32 to the Tully Lake Recreation Area and boat launch on the right (the turn is about 0.4 mile past the gauging station and parking area overlook). To reach the Tully Lake Camping Area, continue on Route 32 for 0.4 mile past the boat access, and turn right on Doane Hill Road. Continue on Doane Hill Road where Stewart Road comes in from the left, and you will reach the campground entrance on the right 0.8 mile from Route 32 (the facility is well marked with signs). There is another boat launch site (with much less room for parking) a few hundred yards past the campground entrance just after crossing the Tully River—take a sharp left back toward the river. At the picnic area are restrooms and a boat launch at the southwestern tip of the lake and at the campground near the Doane Hill Road bridge over Tully River.

For more information on canoeing, picnicking, or camping here, contact the Park Ranger, Tully Lake, RFD #2, Athol, MA 01331; 508-249-9150.

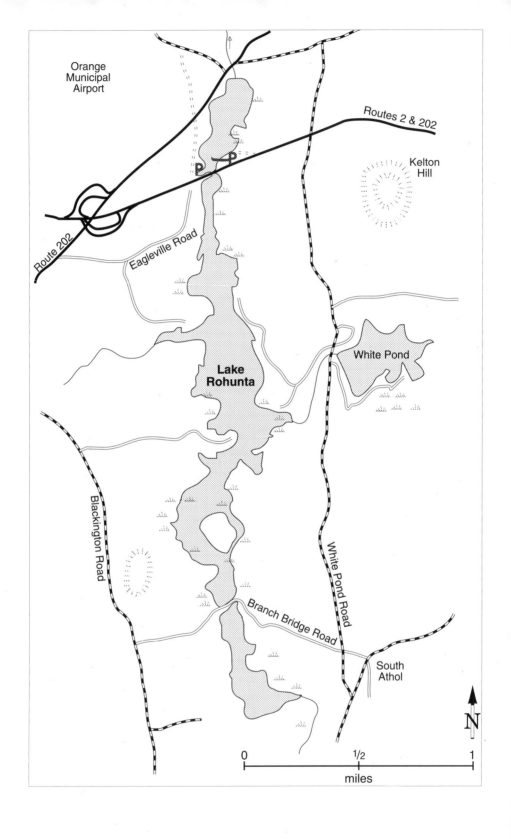

Orange Municipal Airport

Routes 2 & 202

Route 202

Kelton Hill

Eagleville Road

Lake Rohunta

White Pond

Blackington Road

White Pond Road

Branch Bridge Road

South Athol

N

0   1/2   1

miles

Lake Rohunta

Orange, MA

I had probably driven by Lake Rohunta fifty times—slowing down and wistfully glancing both north and south of Route 2—before I finally stopped and put a canoe in. From the highway it looks as if the main body of water is on the north side, but as a highway map will tell you, far more water is actually to the south. When I paddled here I fully expected to find development and power boats in the south where the lake widens. I couldn't have been more wrong. While there are some houses along the lake at its widest sections, the shallow weedy lake is really only appropriate for canoeing. For someone who far prefers weeds to power boats, this was a very pleasant surprise.

We spent a wonderful half-day here paddling the north end of the lake then down as far as Branch Bridge Road (where a small culvert blocks passage to the southernmost section of the lake), exploring the diverse aquatic vegetation, watching painted turtles basking in the sun, and gorging ourselves on blueberries, which were plentiful in the waning days of July. Among the flora we saw here were fragrant water lily, bullhead lily, water shield, pickerel weed, pondweed, both purple and swollen bladderwort, and buttonbush along the shores. In the most protected coves were the remains of trees killed when the lake was created. On the mossy tussocks built around these stumps you can find two species of the fascinating sundew plant: both round-leaved and spatulate-leaved. This carnivorous plant has sticky hairs on the upper side of its leaves that catch small insects. Enzymes in the leaf digest the insects to help nourish the plant. The surrounding woods are very enticing, just asking you to spread out a picnic lunch, particularly on the east side of the lake north of Route 2. These pine and hemlock woods are quite open with a dense carpet of needles underfoot and acid-loving laurels and blueberry bushes along the shore.

The farther south you paddle on the lake, the shallower and weedier it gets. In fact, by the midpoint, paddling is quite restricted by the floating vegetation, which covers more than 90 percent of the water's surface. Near the south end is a large, heavily wooded island. The easiest way around this is on the right (as you are paddling south), though we were able to work our way around to the left, and it was here we found the thickest stands of blueberry! Even on the main section of the lake, your paddling will be impeded by vegetation; at the end of July there was a narrow open channel of water the entire length of the lake, winding in a sinewy path up the lake. I'm not sure what keeps this channel open, but the serpentine shape leads me to believe that motorboats are not the cause. In the early spring, paddling here would be altogether different, with open water and easy navigation between the stumps as you paddle around the island.

You may see some exciting wildlife if you're attentive. We saw black ducks, Canada geese, a pair of broad-winged hawks (which I believe were nesting on the island), and a few wood ducks flying to safety as we paddled near (wood ducks are extremely wary and difficult to approach by canoe). Early in the morning I wouldn't be at all surprised to see a mink or even a river otter here. Be aware that the area is used for duck hunting in the fall, so try to time your paddling to avoid the waterfowl season. Fish caught here include chain pickerel, pike, and bullhead catfish.

Local historians believe that the name Rohunta is a derivative of the name Rodney Hunt. Hunt operated a hydro power facility at the south end of this waterway in the late 1800s. The area also has a bit of post-colonial history: in 1787 Daniel Shays led a straggling band of rebellious farmers along this way in retreat from Springfield. It was the desperate last hurrah of "Shays Rebellion," when farmers in western Massachusetts, suffering in the post-Revolution economic depression, protested the seizing of debtors by occupying the Springfield courthouse—an action that alarmed even President Washington. The uprising was quickly quelled and Shays, a reluctant leader, escaped to Vermont, where he was eventually pardoned.

GETTING THERE: Lake Rohunta is easy to find, with access right off Route 2 less than a mile east of Exit 16 (Route 202 South). There is a large pull-over area on the north side of Route 2, just east of the bridge across the narrowed lake, with room for at least fifteen cars (you shouldn't have to deal with boat-trailer parking since there is no ramp). This area north of Route 2 on the east side, I am told, is owned by the state. If there is no room to park here, you can also park across the bridge on the west side of the lake (also on the north side of the highway) where Eagleville Road used to cross Route 2. The carry to the water is not as easy here and the access to Route 2 is not as good.

Lake Rohunta is a wonderful spot for wildlife observation, marred only by the noise from Route 2 and a nearby municipal airport just west of the lake at the northern end. While this is not the wilderness experience that the nearby Quabbin Reservoir would offer (it's open to canoeing), Rohunta still offers a fine half-day of explorations.

Upper Highland Lake
Goshen, MA

Located within the Daughters of the American Revolution (D.A.R.) State Forest, Upper Highland Lake offers a great getaway spot for a relaxed weekend of family camping and canoeing. There are fifty-eight campsites here, including two that are wheelchair-accessible, a pleasant beach area, and plenty of hiking trails. The lake itself is small (about fifty acres), but there is no development on it other than recreational facilities and a private camp near its northwest corner. The camp is a Springfield Catholic Diocese Fresh Air Camp for urban children. Their use of the lake is limited to swimming. Because gasoline-powered motorboats are prohibited here, you should be able to enjoy some *quiet* paddling. Just to the south and also largely within D.A.R. State Forest is the somewhat larger Lower Highland Lake. Gasoline-powered motorboats are prohibited here as well, but there is considerable development on the southern half of the lake.

A ranger from the D.A.R. State Forest recalled finding a World War II photograph showing this boot-shaped lake from the fire tower atop Moore Hill (east side of lake and accessible from it by road or two trails). The tower, like others throughout southern New England in this uneasy time, was used as a warplane spotting lookout. The photo shows a nearly bare summit with young growth of hemlock and pines, reminders that much of this area had once been cleared as hilly farmland for sheep raising. The size of both lakes was increased by the Civilian Conservation Corps (CCC) through enlargement of the dams at their southern ends. The larger dams turned these small reservoirs, used for powering silk mills at Goshen, into the lovely paddling lakes we find today.

The vegetation around Upper Highland Lake is comprised primarily of deciduous trees—birch, maple, beech, and some oak—with a few hemlock and white pine mixed in. Along the shores are highbush blueberry, mountain laurel, and other shrubs. The water looks clean, and the banks are natural; the erosion resulting from motorboat wakes that you see on so many lakes is not found here. At the north end is an inlet to explore, though the inlet creek is not canoeable, and another cove extending to the northwest. Between these two is a beaver lodge, which you might want to visit around dusk or dawn to watch beavers either working on their lodge or feeding. Anglers will find yellow perch and sunfish.

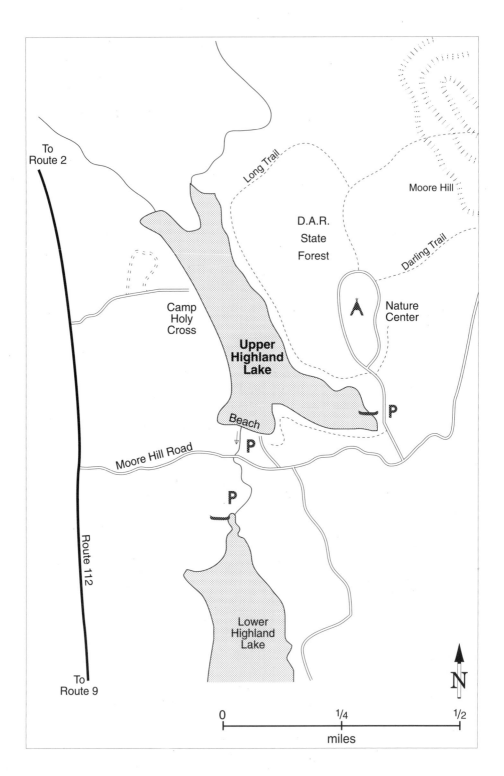

This is a popular spot for camping during the summer. The campsites generally fill up on Thursday, or even Wednesday, as the weekend approaches, and then open up by Sunday night. The sites are wooded and fairly typical of campsites you will find in state parks and forests— far better than what most private campgrounds have to offer. Campsites here are not right on the water. The camping fee in 1992 was $12 per night, and the season extends from about May 1 through Columbus Day weekend. The state forest is open year-round for day use, with a day-use fee charged from Memorial Day through Labor Day ($5 per vehicle in 1992).

GETTING THERE: If driving from the south up Interstate 91, get off at the exit for Route 9 West in Northampton. Continue on Route 9 past Williamsburg and Goshen, then turn right onto Route 112 North. The entrance to D.A.R. State Forest will be on the right in 0.7 mile (well marked with a sign). From the north or northwest, take Route 112 South from either Route 2 or Route 116. The state forest entrance will be on the left 12.8 miles south of Route 2, and 3.8 miles from the intersection with Route 116. Pick up a map of the park at the entrance booth. If there are no forest personnel, continue straight past the entrance booth (if you turn right you will get to the boat launch for Lower Highland Lake). After 0.4 mile turn left, following signs to the boat launch. You can unload your boat and gear at the water, but then drive to the parking area on the other side of the road. For further information, contact D.A.R. State Forest, East Street, Williamsburg, MA 01096; 413-268-7098.

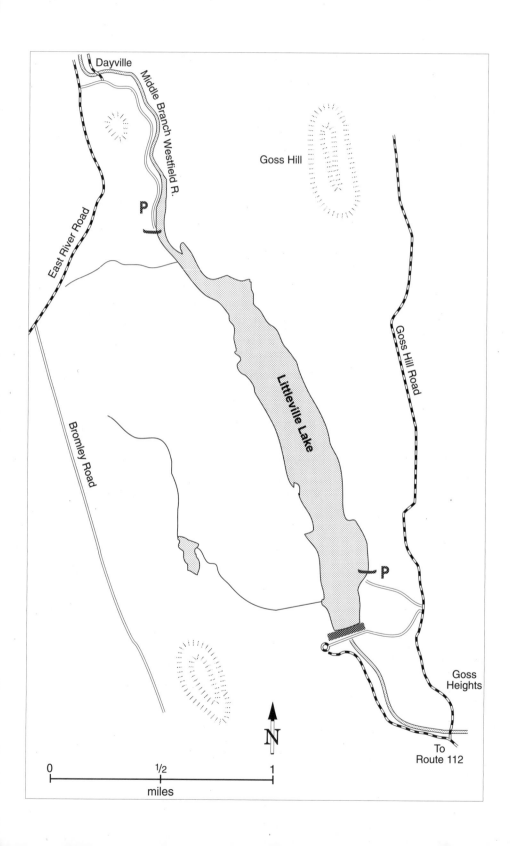

Dayville

Middle Branch Westfield R.

Goss Hill

East River Road

P

Littleville Lake

Goss Hill Road

Bromley Road

P

Goss Heights

To Route 112

N

0   1/2   1

miles

Littleville Lake
Chester, MA

Created when the U.S. Army Corps of Engineers built a flood-control dam on the Middle Branch of the Westfield River, Littleville Lake now offers superb canoeing, fishing, and picnicking. The 510-acre lake is long and narrow, with boat access points at both the north and south ends. As is true with many flood-control impoundments, Littleville Lake is totally free of development because at times of heavy rainfall and flooding the water level rises, putting the usual shoreline under water. While the lake is undeveloped, it must be noted that there is a fairly imposing dam looking down on most of the lake, precluding any illusions of wilderness.

Littleville Lake doubles as a backup water supply for Springfield, about thirty miles downstream, but has yet to be drawn upon since its completion in 1965. The dam was built in response to serious flooding that had occurred downstream as long ago as the 1600s. When the dam was built, a local fairground had to be relocated from the narrow valley; today's Dayville Fair continues to be a local attraction in mid-September.

The shoreline is generally rocky with fairly steep wooded banks. You will find typical woodland tree species here, including sugar maple, red maple, white ash, red oak, black birch, gray birch, quaking aspen, white pine, ironwood, and sycamore. At the north end are a few marshy areas, along with the inlet. About two-thirds of the way up the lake are signs of an abandoned farm: old apple trees, stone walls, and pastures grown into woodland. There is a beaver lodge here and generally more wildlife than elsewhere on the lake. You can paddle up the inlet river a short distance, but it becomes shallow fairly quickly with a lot of exposed rocks.

A ten-horsepower limit for motorboats on Littleville Lake and a prohibition on water-skiing help keep the lake relatively quiet, though you are likely to see quite a few smaller motorboats on a nice weekend day. Fishing is excellent for largemouth bass, yellow perch, and rainbow trout. Paddling around early one evening with the light just right, I saw about a dozen foot-long bass lurking beneath the surface along the west shore.

Despite the general lack of inlets and coves to explore, Littleville Lake offers a pleasant morning or afternoon of canoeing, with plenty of places to stop for a picnic. There is no camping here, and because the lake serves as a secondary water supply, recreational uses are carefully regulated. Swimming and wading, for example, are prohibited, and boat launching is permitted only at the designated areas at the south and north ends of the lake. You can pick up information on Littleville Lake, including complete rules and regulations, at the dam. The area is closed from 9 PM until 5 AM.

GETTING THERE: From Northampton, take Route 66 west to Route 112 South. Drive 2.1 miles south on Route 112, crossing the Westfield River. After crossing the river, take a fairly immediate right, following signs for the Littleton Dam. In 0.7 mile turn right onto Goss Hill Road, crossing a long and quite narrow bridge across the Middle Branch of the Westfield River, again following a sign for the Littleville Dam. In another 0.7 mile you will reach the entrance to the dam and, just past it, the road down to the boat launch at the south end of the lake. If driving from the south or west, take Route 20 to Route 112 North in Huntington. Drive north on 112 for 1.3 miles and turn left just before 112 crosses the Westfield River. Follow directions as described above.

To reach the northern boat access, continue on Route 20 West past Huntington, and turn right onto Chester Hill Road. Follow this until East River Road branches off to the right, and follow signs to the Dayville Access Area. There is plenty of room for parking at both access points.

Otis Reservoir

Otis, MA

One has to stretch the imagination a little to call Otis Reservoir "quiet," particularly on a nice summer weekend, but Tolland State Forest offers some pleasant lakeside camping, and the south end provides at least some opportunity to get away from most of the larger boats. For the most relaxing paddling, plan your visit midweek before school is out, or after Labor Day. At other times, motorboat traffic, water-skiing, jet-skis, and general rowdiness at the Tolland State Forest camping area can seriously detract from your enjoyment of the area.

The south end of the 1065-acre reservoir is by far the nicest from the paddler's perspective, particularly the far southern tip where fingers of the reservoir merge into a swampy area called Dismal Bay. You have to weave your way carefully through old rotted stumps here, as well as some large rocks, but these serve to keep out motorboats of all but the most dedicated bass anglers. On an early morning, with the mist rising over the water and no sign of anyone else except a lone great blue heron or deer browsing by the water's edge, you can almost feel as if you were in Canada .

The southern tip of Southwest Bay on Otis Reservoir is full of old stumps left over from the creation of the reservoir. This is an excellent place to see beavers in the early evening.

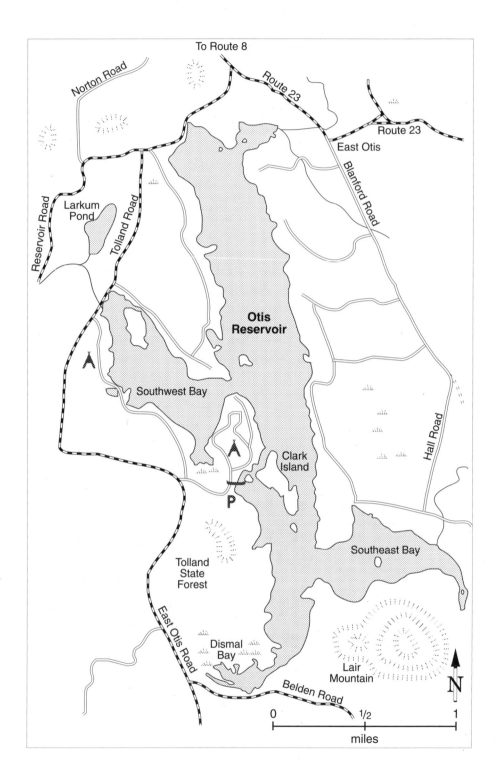

To Route 8

Norton Road

Route 23

Route 23

East Otis

Blanford Road

Reservoir Road

Larkum Pond

Tolland Road

Otis Reservoir

Southwest Bay

Clark Island

Hall Road

P

Tolland State Forest

Southeast Bay

East Otis Road

Dismal Bay

Lair Mountain

Belden Road

N

0   1/2   1

miles

The shores along the southern portion of Otis Reservoir are heavily vegetated with laurel, hemlock—its branches sweeping right down to the water's surface—hobblebush viburnum, highbush blueberry, ferns, and mosses. While most of the shoreline vegetation is fairly thick, there are places where you can pull up a boat and get out for a picnic lunch or break from paddling. The woodland is actually quite open, with a dense carpet of hemlock needles and mosses. Away from the immediate shore you'll see beech, white birch, yellow birch, and other hardwood species.

The extension to the east, called Southeast Bay, is also quite nice, especially once you get past the houses along the north shore. Near the tip of this inlet, where submerged rocks will discourage most motorboaters, there's a small island and an old beaver lodge. Watch for hawks perched in the tall trees in here.

Another place worth visiting is the cove around the campground peninsula from the public boat launch—the southern corner of Southwest Bay. There's an active beaver lodge in this marshy area, and numerous scattered rocks that require careful maneuvering around. The cattails, grasses, and sedges here provide protection for ducks, herons, and many songbirds. If you're staying in the campground, this makes a great late-evening or early-morning paddle when you're likely to see beaver and perhaps even a mink or otter.

North of the Tolland State Forest campground, Otis Reservoir is quite built up, with hundreds of summer homes—most with docks and many with big inboard motorboats tied up. A private campground, Camp Overflow, is located at the western end of Southwest Bay (P.O. Box 645, Otis, MA 01253; 413-269-4036), but if you're tent camping, Tolland State Forest, with ninety sites, will probably be a lot more enjoyable. In general, public campgrounds are more spread out, while private campgrounds tend to pack the sites closely together and cater to seasonal rentals. This is not to say, however, that public campgrounds are always idyllic. During a two-day stay during mid-June at Tolland I was surrounded by campers more interested in beer, loud music, and partying than in enjoying the peaceful surroundings. As mentioned above, it helps to plan your vacations carefully and choose, if at all possible, midweeks outside of the main vacation season. Camping is available from mid-May until Columbus Day weekend. Sites were $12 per night in 1992. Canoe rentals are available at Camp Overflow.

Fishing is very popular in Otis Reservoir. Largemouth bass, rainbow and brown trout, pickerel, perch, and pumpkinseed are among the fish caught here. In addition, the eight-thousand-acre Tolland State Forest offers superb hiking. For a great view, hike up to the fire lookout at Lair Mountain (1700 feet) near the south end of Otis Reservoir.

GETTING THERE: From the Mass Pike (I-90), get off at Exit 2 in Lee, drive east on Route 20, then turn south on Route 8 in West Becket. When you get to Otis, turn left (east) onto Route 23, and continue for approximately 3 miles. Then turn right onto Reservoir Road, following signs for Tolland State Forest. After 0.7 mile, turn left onto Tolland Road, and continue on this road past the gauging station on Southwest Bay (0.8 mile from Reservoir Road) until you get to a left turn 2.5 miles from Reservoir Road. Bear right almost immediately, following signs to the state forest, and you will reach the ranger station in another 0.4 mile. If you are driving up Route 8 from the south, turn right onto Reservoir Road 5.1 miles north of the intersection of Routes 57 and 8. Coming from this direction, turn right onto Tolland Road after 1.6 miles, and follow directions as above. The drive into the camping area and public boat launch is a bit circuitous, but the turns are well marked, and you shouldn't have any trouble finding your way.

For more information and maps of the state forest, contact Tolland State Forest, P.O. Box 342, East Otis, MA 01029; 413-269-6002.

Benedict Pond

Monterey, MA

Benedict Pond is tiny as lakes and ponds in this book go—just thirty-five acres—but it's hard to beat for a nice weekend of family camping and quiet paddling. The pond is located totally within Beartown State Forest, a relatively little known state forest, but actually the second-largest tract of public land in the state. There is no development around Benedict Pond except for park facilities, and gasoline-powered motorboats are prohibited. Camping is available year-round at Beartown, though there are only twelve campsites. Three of the campsites are right on the water, the others located nearby.

Benedict Pond is very picturesque, with huge fern-draped granite boulders along the shore, thick stands of mountain laurel, brilliant azaleas (blooming in late May), and a heavily wooded shoreline of mixed deciduous and conifer trees. The hemlocks, whose feathery branches reach down to the water's surface, are particularly attractive. Along with the laurel and azaleas in the understory, you'll see hobblebush viburnum (with large heart-shaped leaves in distinct pairs) and blueberries along the shore. There are several beaver lodges around the pond, and a small cattail marsh at the north end. Warm-water fish are caught

There are several beaver lodges along the shore of Benedict Pond. Paddle in the early morning or evening to see this fascinating mammal.

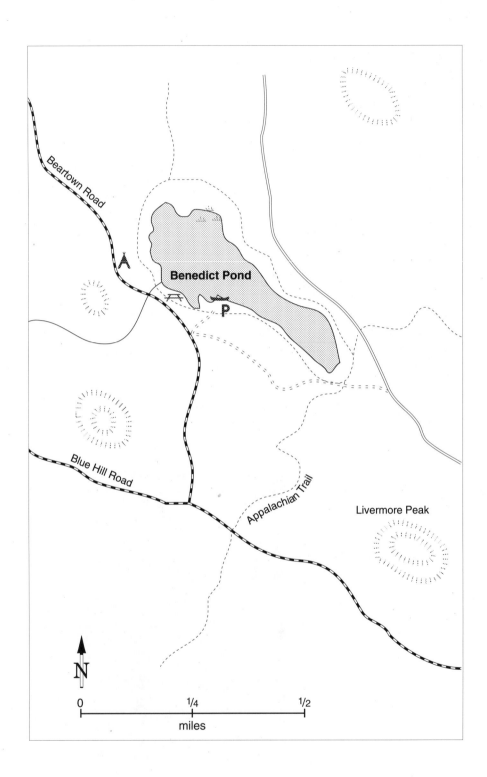

Beartown Road

Benedict Pond

A

P

Blue Hill Road

Appalachian Trail

Livermore Peak

N

0   1/4   1/2

miles

here, including bass, yellow perch, and pickerel. There is considerable underwater vegetation.

The Appalachian Trail runs past the southeastern tip of Benedict Pond, making this a great spot for a combination trip. Drop off the more adventurous of the family—say, Mom and the oldest nieces—for a couple of days of backpacking, planned so that they will end up at Benedict Pond where Dad and the younger kids are camping, fishing, and swimming at a wonderful little sandy beach—just right for young children. In addition to the Appalachian Trail, there are numerous other trails in Beartown State Forest, including a loop trail around the pond. There is a picnic area just west of the boat launch.

GETTING THERE: If you're driving from the east on the Mass Pike (I-90), get off at Exit 2 in Lee, and drive west on Route 102 until you get to Route 7. Take Route 7 south to Route 23 East, just before getting into Great Barrington. (If you're coming up from the south on Route 7, look for 23 East just after passing through Great Barrington.) Turn onto 23 East, and drive for 5.4 miles to Blue Hill Road (stay on Route 23 at the fork where Route 57 bears off to the right). Drive uphill on Blue Hill Road for 2.2 miles, then turn right into Beartown State Forest. You will reach the boat access and parking area in another 0.4 mile.

For further information and a trail map, contact Beartown State Forest, P.O. Box 97, Monterey, MA 01245; 413-528-0904. Canoes can be rented from Gaffer's Canoe Service (203-379-0948). The company will drop off and pick up canoes right at Benedict Pond.

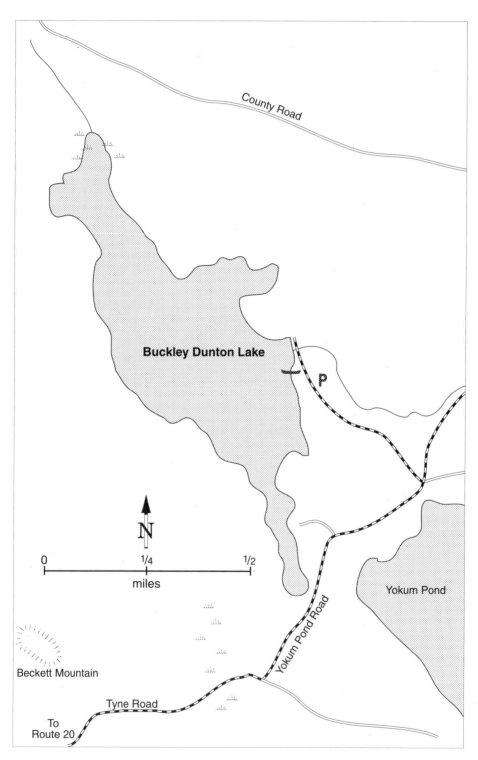

County Road

Buckley Dunton Lake

P

N

0   1/4   1/2

miles

Yokum Pond Road

Yokum Pond

Beckett Mountain

Tyne Road

To
Route 20

Buckley Dunton Lake
Becket, MA

Buckley Dunton is a very attractive 195-acre lake in the Berkshire Hills of western Massachusetts. There are just a few houses along the lake—at the extreme southern extension—the rest of the surrounding land being within October Mountain State Forest and thus protected from development. Even the houses on the south end do not seem too imposing. October Mountain is the largest tract of publicly owned land in Massachusetts, and it is somewhat off the beaten path and not too crowded. On nice weekends, though, you may see and hear heavy use of trails by off-road vehicles and a fair number of people out fishing on the lake. A nine-mile segment of the Appalachian Trail also passes through the forest.

Buckley Dunton Lake was created by damming up Yokum Brook in the 1800s to provide power for mills downstream. Another reservoir in the state forest that shows up on maps and looks very enticing, Washington Mountain Lake, apparently no longer holds water as the dam failed and was not repaired.

The shoreline of Buckley Dunton Lake, like most of October Mountain State Forest, is heavily wooded with trees and shrubs typical of the moderately high Berkshire Hills: hemlock, white pine, spruce, red maple, sugar maple, black cherry, ash, gray birch, yellow birch, and alder—to mention a few. Laurel is common along the shore, and you will see some blueberry bushes, which should provide for some flavorful rest stops if you visit in late July or August. There are a few very attractive picnic spots along the shore—where large boulders jut out into the water—but most of the shoreline is quite impenetrable due to the thick vegetation.

The north end of the lake is very shallow and marshy, with rotting logs and tree stumps forcing you to meander carefully in your canoe. Often you can't see the submerged mossy stumps as you paddle through this area, but you can feel them as your canoe glances off them. The inlet at the north end is not canoeable. You'll see bullhead lily, fragrant water lily, pondweed, blue flag iris, and cattail along here, plus—if you look carefully—the diminutive carnivorous sundew plant on mossy hillocks. Listen for bullfrogs as you paddle the north end. Early in the morning or in the evening you are also likely to see the lake's resident beavers.

Buckley Dunton State Forest is located in the heavily wooded Berkshire Hills of October Mountain State Forest. The dam is seen in the distance.

Fishing is popular at Buckley Dunton Lake for warm-water species, including bass, yellow perch, pickerel, and bullhead. Because of the stumps and rocks, the lake is not used by water-skiers, and most of the boats on the lake are small.

GETTING THERE: To reach Buckley Dunton Lake, take the Mass Pike (Interstate 90) to Exit 2 in Lee and turn onto Route 20 East. Stay on Route 20 for 4.0 miles, then turn left onto Becket Road. Drive 2.5 miles on Becket Road, which becomes Tyne Road as you climb up over Becket Mountain and cross the Appalachian Trail. After going back downhill, the road becomes Yokum Pond Road, though it may not be marked. After passing the southern tip of Buckley Dunton Lake, watch for a large multivehicle garage on the left and a road going off to the left just before it. This turnoff is 2.5 miles from Route 20 and marked with a sign "Buckley Dunton Reservoir–Day Use Only." Turn here, and drive 0.5 mile to the boat access just before the dam. There is parking on both sides of this dead-end road.

Camping is permitted at the state forest campground on the west side of the forest, which you can reach by driving back around to East Lee and turning north on East Street, then following signs to the state forest campground. The campground is open from mid-May to Columbus Day and has fifty campsites that are available on a first-come, first-served basis. For more information, contact October Mountain State Forest, Woodland Road, Lee, MA 01238; 413-243-1778.

Mauserts Pond

Clarksburg, MA

This small pond in Clarksburg State Park, just south of the Vermont border in northwestern Massachusetts, is a great spot for family camping, hiking, and paddling. It won't take much more than an hour to explore the shoreline by canoe, but that will leave plenty of time to explore some of this heavily wooded 3200-acre park by foot. Boating is limited to carry-in boats, with access by the beach and picnic area at the east end. Even when the park is closed (the relatively short season ends Labor Day weekend), you can park your car at the main gate and portage a canoe in on the paved park road—a two-wheeled portage cart works great here!

The pond's shoreline is dominated by red maple, though you will also see black cherry, white birch, gray birch, white pine, and hemlock. Close to shore are highbush blueberry, winterberry with bright red berries in the autumn, sheep laurel, and American yew (*Taxus canadensis*), a quite unusual creeping shrub that seldom gets taller than about three feet and has red berries in the late summer. Along the northern shore of the pond are a number of marshy areas, with cattail, burr reeds, grasses, and active beaver lodges. You can squeeze your way a short distance up several of the inlet creeks and along a narrow channel that snakes behind the spit of land extending into the pond from the northern shore (this island is a good spot to see the yew).

The bottom of the pond is generally sandy, with some rocks to watch out for along the shore. Keep an eye out for freshwater mussel shells as you paddle along; some of the thin-walled shells are over five inches long. In the shallow water near shore and in the inlets are floating water shield and bullhead lily, and underwater you will see the quite common but fascinating carnivorous bladderworts (for more on this unusual plant see the section on Paradise Pond—pages 59–61).

GETTING THERE: From Route 2 (the Mohawk Trail), take Route 8 North near North Adams. Continue on Route 8 for 3.0 miles, then turn left on Middle Road, following signs to Clarksburg State Park. The park entrance is on the right after another 0.2 mile. After passing the contact station, the boat access is to the right by the beach. A number of hiking trails extend around the pond and through the area wood-

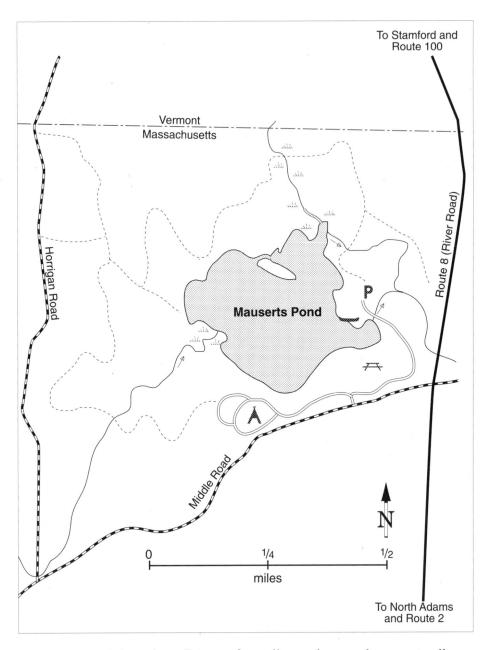

To Stamford and
Route 100

Vermont
Massachusetts

Route 8 (River Road)

Horrigan Road

Mauserts Pond

P

Middle Road

N

0   1/4   1/2

miles

To North Adams
and Route 2

lands. Clarksburg State Forest a few miles to the west has more trails and access to a gorgeous section of the Appalachian Trail. For information, contact Clarksburg State Park, Middle Road, Clarksburg, MA 01247; 413-664-8345 or 413-663-6312.

 # Connecticut

Quaddick Reservoir
Thompson, CT

In the northeastern corner of Connecticut, very close to the Rhode Island border, lies the long, narrow Quaddick Reservoir. The 467-acre reservoir is divided roughly into thirds. Those seeking solitude can pretty much forget about the two southern sections, especially on a nice summer weekend; they are heavily developed and can be very crowded with motorboats. The northern section of the reservoir, however, is wonderful—one of my favorite paddling spots in northeastern Connecticut.

The shallow water in this northern section is thick with vegetation: both floating water lilies and submerged bladderworts, fanwort, and coontail. The underwater vegetation keeps most speedboats out of here, though you will see lots of bass-fishing boats on a nice weekend. This is also a great place for water birds, especially mallards, black ducks, wood ducks, and great blue herons. The shallow coves and the far northern end—known as Stump Pond—provide the richest bird habitats. Surrounding this end of the reservoir are thick woods of white pine and mixed deciduous trees with such shrubs as sweet pepperbush, highbush blueberry, and sweet gale along the shoreline. In the shallow coves and inlets you will also see cattail, bulrush, burr reed, and various grasses. There is likely to be duck hunting here in the fall.

About the only drawback to Quaddick Reservoir—besides the motorboats that venture into the northern section (too bad the bridge isn't lower!)—is the noise from Thompson Motor Speedway. The auto racing track backs right up to the marsh surrounding Stump Pond, and the noise from it is very apparent when a race is going on. I even noticed a blue

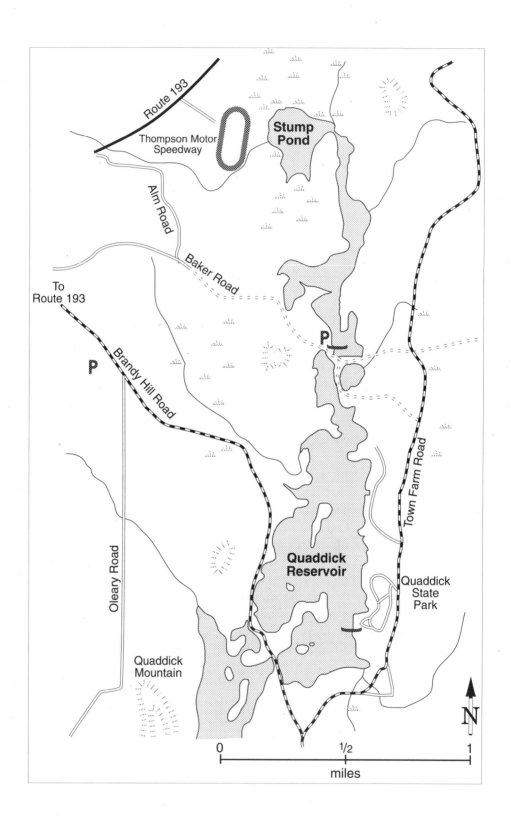

Route 193

Thompson Motor
Speedway

Stump
Pond

Alm Road

Baker Road

To
Route 193

P

Brandy Hill Road

P

Oleary Road

Quaddick
Reservoir

Town Farm Road

Quaddick
State
Park

Quaddick
Mountain

N

0   1/2   1
miles

haze of either exhaust or smoke hovering over the raceway as I paddled on a Sunday afternoon. Paddling here by yourself, listening to the methodical dipping of your paddle into water, or watching wood ducks circle low over the marsh, it is easy to reflect on the contrasts between your activity and that of the several thousand auto racing spectators a few hundred yards away. It is a sad commentary that so many more people choose to spend their time watching car races than out enjoying nature. I wonder what those wood ducks think about our species....You will do well to avoid paddling here when races are going on.

Quaddick Reservoir is well known for its excellent fishing. Large-mouth bass, smallmouth bass, calico bass, chain pickerel, yellow perch, bullhead catfish (hornpout), and sunfish are all caught here. Some of the bass are trophy size.

GETTING THERE: Take Interstate 395 to Exit 99 and turn onto Route 200 East to Thompson (approximately 0.7 mile). Turn left in Thompson on Route 193 north and drive 1.5 miles. Turn right onto Brandy Hill Road, and after 0.3 mile bear left onto Baker Road. After 1.4 miles on Baker Road, which is paved initially but turns to dirt, you will reach a timber bridge crossing the channel of water connecting the two northern sections of the reservoir. There is room for ten to fifteen

The north end of Quaddick Reservoir is wild and marshy. If the Thompson Motor Speedway is not being used, a paddle here should be quiet and relaxing.

cars along the road before the bridge, and a carry-in access is on the left side of the road just before the bridge.

The main boat ramp for Quaddick Reservoir is on the eastern side of the middle section of the reservoir. To reach this boat launch from the intersection of Routes 200 and 193 in Thompson, drive east on Quaddick Road (the continuation of Route 200) for 2.6 miles, and turn left following signs to Quaddick State Park. After 1.4 miles, you will turn left into the park; follow signs to the boat access. During weekends and holidays, there is a day-use fee, and you sometimes have to park your car several hundred yards from the boat launch. There are flush toilets here during the summer, with pit toilets available out of season. While I much prefer the more northern access point for canoes, I suppose there is something to be said for the idea of launching here just to help you appreciate the northern section of the reservoir more—after dealing with all the motorboats, water-skiers, and parking hassles.

There is no camping at Quaddick State Park, but the park does have picnic areas, hiking trails, swimming, drinking water, and concessions. The closest camping area on public land is the George Washington Management Area in Rhode Island (see section on Bowdish Reservoir). For more information on Quaddick Reservoir, contact the Connecticut Department of Environmental Protection, Office of State Parks and Recreation, 165 Capitol Avenue, Hartford, CT; 203-566-2304.

Mashapaug Lake and Bigelow Pond
Union, CT

Mashapaug Lake in northeastern Connecticut is a large (three-hundred-
-acre) natural lake with deep coves, rocky shores, and beautiful surrounding hemlock and white pine woods. The south end of the lake is
in Bigelow Hollow State Park. You will find a very nice picnic area
here with picnic tables on needle-carpeted ground overlooking the
lake's blue water. The trails along here wind between ancient stands of
laurel, and the light filtering through the canopy of hemlock, pine, and
oak seems just right to support a wide array of wildflowers. Most of the
eastern shore of the lake is within the eight-thousand-acre Nipmuck
State Forest, with the land rising more steeply from the water's edge. In
some areas, huge slabs of stone extend down into the water. There are
trails through here, but they are farther in, away from the water.

When I visited in 1992 (both in May and October) the water level
seemed lower than normal. With a generally rocky, fairly exposed
shoreline and a sandy bottom, the lake can feel somewhat sterile; I saw
very little in the way of floating or underwater vegetation as I paddled
around the shoreline.

While the south end of Mashapaug is undeveloped except for the
picnic area, there is moderate development along the western shore and
north end. Along some portions of the shoreline and on the islands
there is evidence of considerable erosion, leading me to suspect that the
10 MPH boating speed limit posted at the boat access either isn't followed or is a recent development. On several of the islands, there were
even barriers erected to slow this damage. Other than development at
the north end, the major drawback is road noise from I-84, which is just
a half-mile away at the closest point.

Mashapaug Lake is well known for its bass fishing: both largemouth and smallmouth. In fact, the state-record largemouth bass (a
twelve-pound, fourteen-ounce lunker) was caught here in 1961. Chain
pickerel, yellow perch, brown trout, and rainbow trout are also caught
in Mashapaug.

Also in Bigelow Hollow State Park is the very small but very
attractive Bigelow Pond. This nineteen-acre pond is undeveloped and
quite shallow, with lots of floating vegetation and many sphagnum
moss–covered hillocks where tree stumps have long since rotted away.
Look for sundew amid the sphagnum moss in these areas. In early
October I was surprised to see quite a few nodding ladies' tresses

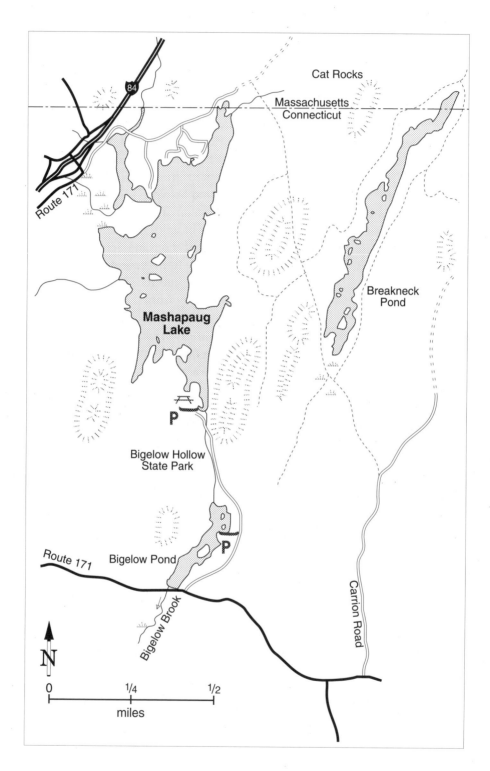

Cat Rocks

Massachusetts
Connecticut

Route 171

84

Breakneck
Pond

**Mashapaug
Lake**

P

Bigelow Hollow
State Park

Bigelow Pond

P

Route 171

Bigelow Brook

Carrion Road

N

0   1/4   1/2

miles

(*Spiranthes cernua*), a small white orchid occasionally found in boggy areas. Along the shoreline here you will see lots of blueberry, sweet pepperbush, and laurel, along with hemlock and white pine growing farther from the water's edge. In the shallow coves you will see some floating water plants, including fragrant water lily, bullhead lily, and water shield. I saw evidence of beavers, but not a lodge. There are a few wood-duck boxes, but I doubt there is enough protective cover for wood ducks to nest here on a regular basis. Biologically, Bigelow Pond feels much richer than Mashapaug Lake, but it is very small. There are lots of picnic tables around the pond, accessible by a well-used trail. The pond is fished for largemouth bass.

In Nipmuck State Forest, a mile or so to the east of Mashapaug Lake (as the crow flies), there is another body of water: Breakneck Pond. I believe this long, narrow pond is reachable only by hiking trail, and would require a very long carry to get a canoe in, but from the maps it looks as if the paddling would be tremendous. I'm hoping to give it a try one of these days.

GETTING THERE: To reach Mashapaug Lake and Bigelow Pond, take Route 84 to Exit 74, just south of the Massachusetts-Connecticut line. Follow signs for Route 171 South toward Union, Connecticut. After turning onto 171, drive south for 2.2 miles and then turn left, staying on 171 where Route 190 continues straight (there is a sign for Bigelow Hollow State Park at this turn). Continue on 171 for another 1.4 miles and turn left into Bigelow Hollow State Park. The access to Bigelow Pond is on the left after 0.3 miles, and the access to Mashapaug Lake is 1.1 miles down this park road at the end. There is plenty of room for parking at both boat access points. Mashapaug Lake is open to all boating, though there is a 10 MPH boating speed limit. Bigelow Pond is restricted to non-gasoline-powered boats.

For more information on Bigelow Hollow State Park and Nipmuck State Forest, contact the Connecticut Department of Environmental Protection, Office of State Parks and Recreation, 165 Capitol Avenue, Hartford, CT 06106; 203-566-2304.

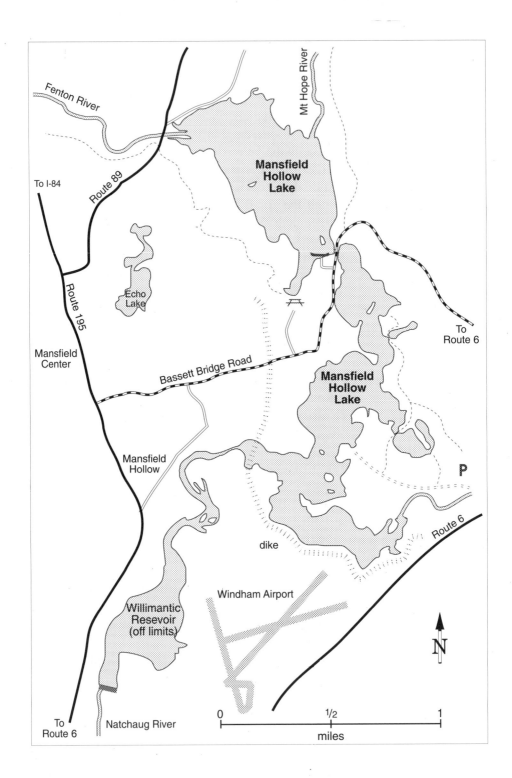

Mansfield Hollow Lake

Mansfield, CT

By southern New England standards, Mansfield Hollow Lake (or Naubesatuck Lake, as it is sometimes known) is big: 450 acres. The lake is divided roughly in half by the Bassett Bridge Road causeway (there no longer is a real bridge). The lake was created in 1952 when the U.S. Army Corps of Engineers, in response to devastating flooding of Willimantic in 1936, built a dam on the Natchaug River and a series of dikes to contain the lake. The primary function of the dam is flood control, though it also serves as a secondary water supply. A run-of-the-river hydropower electricity generation plant may be built at the dam sometime in the future.

Like many Corps of Engineers flood-control reservoirs in the Northeast, the water level of Mansfield Hollow Lake fluctuates. Usually after Columbus Day, the Corps drops the water level by about four feet to provide greater flood-control capacity during spring floods. As a result, the place has a somewhat exposed and sterile feel to it. Little floating vegetation gets established in the shallow water, and even the shrubs that frequently populate lake shorelines and like to keep their feet wet are less evident here. If the water level is down when you visit, there will be a wide, exposed gravelly shoreline around the entire perimeter. On the positive side, though, the lake is totally undeveloped, and the Corps has established an 8 MPH limit for boats, so you won't have to deal with water-skiers, jet-skis, and speedboats.

The southern section of Mansfield Hollow Lake, below the Bassett Bridge, is generally narrower with more coves and islands to explore. From the boat access, you can paddle through one of two large steel culverts into this section of the lake (the culverts are at different heights because of the varying water levels). Near the north end of this lower section, on the east side, is a small cove or pond connected by a small channel. Though small, this pond feels very remote and quiet—it is especially nice on a windy day. A larger pond farther to the south and east is not accessible by canoe without a carry. As you paddle into the southern end of the lake, the massive dike to the south looks a bit like the Great Wall of China as it looms over the lake. The primary inlet into the lake, the Natchaug River, flows in at the southeastern tip and is canoeable for a short distance upriver before rapids make paddling difficult (for more on downriver canoeing here, refer to the *AMC River Guide: Massachusetts/Connecticut/Rhode Island*).

Mansfield Hollow Lake is large and a great place to paddle if you want some real exercise. The dam and dike are quite visible on the southern section of the lake.

The northern section of the lake is wider with fewer twisting coves to explore, but it has a somewhat more natural feel to it, particularly at the north end. There are two inlets to the lake here: Mount Hope River, which comes in from the north; and Fenton River, which comes in from the northwest. You can paddle up the Mount Hope River inlet just a few hundred yards before your way is blocked by rapid water and rocks; there is a beaver lodge right at this point. Farther to the west, you can paddle under Route 89 and up the Fenton River much farther. I've paddled about a half-mile up here and found the paddling very easy on the slow-moving, meandering channel. The lower portion of the Fenton River here is backed up by the Mansfield Hollow Dam, so when the lake level is down, the river level is too. When I paddled here the banks along the lower Fenton River were exposed and muddy—not terribly attractive. There are beaver lodges along here and the banks are home to numerous muskrats; in the early morning hours or late afternoon you are likely to see both beaver and muskrat.

Most of the shoreline of the Mansfield Hollow Lake is wooded, with white pine and red oak the dominant species. You will also see white oak, shagbark hickory, pitch pine, red maple, gray birch, alder, aspen, elm, willow, and various shrubs, including sweet gale, sweet fern, blueberry, red-osier dogwood, and winterberry. In a few small pockets of marsh you will see Phragmites (common reed) and grasses. In early October here I saw an osprey, red-tailed hawk, mallards, black duck, red-breasted merganser, kingfishers, and quite a few eastern blue-birds. Fishing is popular here for warm-water species, especially large-mouth bass. Smallmouth bass are often caught in the three tributary rivers. Because the lake serves as a secondary water supply, swimming is not permitted.

GETTING THERE: Mansfield Hollow Lake is about equidistant from Interstates 84 and 395 in northeastern Connecticut. From Route 84, get off at Exit 68 and take Route 195 South through Mansfield Four Corners and Storrs to Mansfield Center. After passing the turnoff for Route 89 North, continue on 195 for another 0.5 mile and turn left onto Bassett Bridge Road, following a sign for Mansfield Hollow State Park. The boat ramp and large parking area are on the left 1.4 miles down Bassett Bridge Road. If you are driving from the Hartford area, take Routes 384 and 6 East (eventually a four-lane highway is to be completed all the way to Willimantic). Get off Route 6 onto Route 195 North, drive another 2.0 miles, and turn right onto Bassett Bridge Road. Follow directions as above. If driving west from Route 395, get off at Exit 92 and follow Route 6 West through Brooklyn and Clarks Corner. The turnoff for Bassett Bridge Road will be on the right in North Windham, 1.6 miles after passing the turnoff for Route 198 North. Follow Bassett Bridge Road for 2.1 miles (passing Mansfield Hollow Lake on both sides), and the boat access will be on the right.

For more information, contact the U.S. Army Corps of Engineers, West Thompson Lake Office, RFD 1, North Grosvenor Dale, CT 06255; 203-923-2982.

Muskrat
Chubby Fellow of the Cattail Marsh

Toward dusk on our marshy ponds and estuaries as you paddle past tall stands of cattails and phragmites, watch for a V of ripples moving across the still water. If the source of this activity is relatively small, chances are it's a muskrat. In the water, a muskrat can be distinguished from its larger cousin, the beaver, by the way it swims. All you will see of the beaver is the fairly large broad head—never the tail except when they slap it down in a warning. With a muskrat you can see the narrow tail snaking rapidly from side to side behind it and sometimes arching out of the water. Muskrats are also more likely to be seen in daytime than beavers, though both are chiefly nocturnal. While generally wary, muskrats sometimes seem oblivious to their surroundings. I have actually had one bump into my canoe when I silently crossed its path; with a startled jerk the little fellow dove to the safety of its underwater lodge entrance.

The muskrat, *Ondatra zibethicus,* is in the order Rodentia along with beavers, but it is much more closely related to voles, rats, certain mice, and lemmings that belong to the family Cricetidae. Its common name derives from the strong musky scent emitted from glands in its groin during breeding season. Adult muskrats are about a foot long, plus another eight to ten inches for the tail, and they weigh two to four pounds. Males and females can be distinguished only by close examination; from a canoe they look identical.

Muskrats are adept swimmers, using both their hind feet and their vertically flattened, scaly tail for propulsion. They can remain underwater for up to fifteen minutes, covering a distance up to 150 feet. Like beavers, their mouths are adapted for use underwater—the lips are split behind the four incisors so that they can cut stems and roots without swallowing water. The primary diet of muskrats is cattail, along with other common marsh plants such as bulrush, water lily, pickerel weed, arrowhead, and swamp loosestrife. They may supplement this vegetarian diet with mussels, crayfish, snails, tadpoles, and other aquatic animals, particularly during the winter months when vegetation is scarce. Being ever wary of predators, muskrats usually dig or cut their food and take it to a safer place to eat it, such as a specially constructed feeding platform or, in the winter, on top of ice—they will cut a hole in the ice and push piles of food up where they can watch for danger while eating. They are most active feeding at night, but can be seen during the daytime as well. Unlike beavers, they rarely venture more than 200 yards for feeding.

Muskrats build two types of houses: dens or lodges, depending on local conditions. Dens are dug in the bank of a pond or river and always have their entrances below water level. On some of our reservoirs and ponds with fluctuating water levels, these underwater entrances may be exposed at certain times of year. Muskrats tunnel with their front paws. Tunnels and dens can be used for many generations and develop into elaborate labyrinths. Tunnels up to 200 yards long have been found, and those 50 yards long are not uncommon. These tunnels can damage earthen dams, levies, and dikes. Individual nesting chambers are typically six by eight inches and lined with shredded plant material.

Lodges are built in shallow open water or marsh—places where bank dens cannot be built. These mound lodges look rather like small beaver lodges, but are built of vegetation and mud instead of sticks and mud. Material for the lodges is collected from the immediate vicinity— usually from a radius of just ten feet. Some muskrat lodges are as large as six feet high and eight feet across at the base. An underwater entrance and tunnel connects to the chamber, which in a typical lodge is about a foot in diameter. Unlike beaver lodges—which are constructed with integral cavities—muskrat lodges are built solid then tunneled out later.

While muskrat lodges do not afford very good protection from predators during the warmer months, once the mud freezes in the winter they become impenetrable fortresses. Some, in fact, are used only in the winter months, when a large lodge may house as many as eight or nine muskrats. Most lodges only last for a year, then collapse as the vegetation rots, but some are added to and used for two or more successive years. In addition to lodges, muskrats build feeding platforms from the same materials; these smaller structures provide safe places to eat collected food.

Muskrats are prolific. Females typically have two or three litters in a single season and may have even more. They can become pregnant again just a few days after giving birth. In the South, muskrats breed year-round. After a gestation period of about thirty days, four to six nearly hairless, blind kits are born in the den or lodge. They open their eyes after two weeks, begin swimming in their third week, and are totally independent after four or five weeks. In fact, if the mother has another litter at that time, she will forcibly evict the youngsters, even injuring them in some cases to drive them away. Rapid population growth, however, can lead to stress, competition for food, territory battles, and illness. Sometimes entire muskrat populations are wiped out by disease. Very commonly, only a third of muskrat young survive into their first winter.

While muskrats may congregate together in lodges in the winter—probably for reasons of warmth—they disperse in spring. Some individuals may travel as far as twenty miles overland looking for new wetland territory. During April and May it is not unusual to see muskrat road kills for this reason.

Muskrats have long been trapped for their soft fur, but their prolific reproduction and lower visibility has protected them from serious risk of extinction. (Beavers were hunted almost to extinction in the late 1800s.) They are hardy animals that seem able to survive, even prosper, in suburban and urban areas—wherever a bit of cattail marsh can be found.

Pine Acres Pond
Hampton, CT

Pine Acres Pond is about as different from nearby Mansfield Hollow Lake as you can get. The 133-acre pond is extremely shallow and much of it is thick with stumps from the trees that were growing here when the area was flooded in 1933. The deepest point is eight feet, with an average depth of just four feet. This certainly isn't a place to come for exercise, but after tiring yourself out over at Mansfield Hollow Lake, you may want to come here for some quiet solitude and wildlife observation. Gasoline-powered motorboats are prohibited from Pine Acres Pond.

Pine Acres has a wild and almost mystical feel to it. Paddling in the northern end of the pond you have to weave your way around literally thousands of stumps and fallen trees. Originally, this was a cedar swamp, but the Atlantic white cedars had long been cut for railroad ties, posts, and shingles by the time the pond was created (the cedars were cut during winter months when horses could be brought out on the ice). Some of the small-diameter stumps broken off just beneath the surface seem quite sharp—this is probably not a place you should bring your handmade birch bark canoe. Many are virtually invisible; you almost have to "feel" your way along, periodically backing up after getting hung up on an underwater snag. But that's all right. It keeps your pace very slow and methodical, increasing your chances of seeing some interesting wildlife. There are a number of beaver lodges around the pond, and you're quite likely to see wood ducks, great blue herons, and kingfishers. By hiking on some of the nearby trails, such as the Natchaug Trail, which runs along the southern end of the pond, you will also see lots of woodland species.

Red maple is the dominant shoreline tree, so in the autumn the pond is ablaze with red. Other trees and shrubs growing around the pond include white pine, red pine, red oak, gray birch, black birch, yellow birch, white ash, spruce, sweet pepperbush, blueberry, winterberry, and a few rhododendrons at the southern tip. The aquatic vegetation is thick: fragrant water lily, bullhead lily, and water shield on the surface, and bladderwort creating thick mats of vegetation underwater. These conditions provide good habitat for largemouth bass, yellow perch, and chain pickerel. The farther north you paddle on Pine Acres Pond, the more difficult the paddling, as the open water gradually merges into swamp. Keep an eye out for acid-loving sundews and cranberry, both of which are found here.

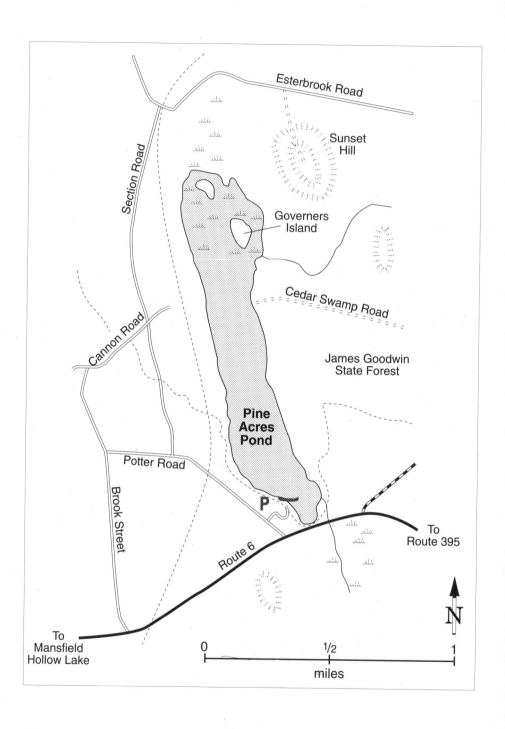

Pine Acres Pond is in the James L. Goodwin State Forest. Originally farmland in the 1800s, this 1800-acre tract was one of Connecticut's first scientifically managed tree farms. James Goodwin began managing it for forest productivity in 1913, in a period when little thought was given to sustainable forestry. Goodwin was a pioneer in forestry; he gave this land to the state in 1964 to demonstrate how wise forest management can serve timber, wildlife, and recreation needs concurrently.

GETTING THERE: From Interstate 395, get off at Exit 92 and take Route 6 West toward Brooklyn. Stay on Route 6 for 11.7 miles, passing Brooklyn and crossing Routes 169 and 97. Then turn right onto Potter Road. (Potter Road is 1.4 miles past the intersection of Route 6 and Route 97.) The parking area for the Goodwin Conservation Center will be on the right about a tenth of a mile from Route 6. Turn right onto a gravel road here and drive about 100 yards downhill to reach the boat launch, where there is parking for six to ten cars. If there isn't room to park at the water, unload and drive back up to Potter Road, where there is additional parking.

If you are driving here from the west (or from Mansfield Hollow Lake), take Route 6 East. Potter Road will be on the left 3.0 miles past the turnoff for Route 198 North. For more information on Pine Acres Pond or hiking trails in the James L Goodwin State Forest and Natchaug State Forest, contact the Goodwin Conservation Center, 23 Potter Road, North Windham, CT 06256; 203-455-9534.

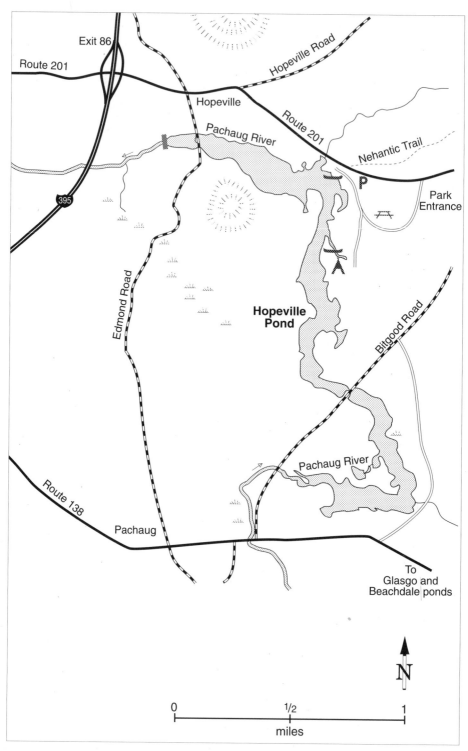

Exit 86

Route 201

Hopeville Road

Hopeville

Route 201

Nehantic Trail

Pachaug River

P

Park
Entrance

395

Edmond Road

**Hopeville
Pond**

Bitgood Road

Pachaug River

Route 138

Pachaug

To
Glasgo and
Beachdale ponds

N

0   1/2   1

miles

Hopeville Pond

Griswold, CT

Hopeville Pond is a widened three-mile section of the Pachaug River in Griswold, Connecticut, offering very pleasant, relaxing paddling. Hopeville Pond State Park was formerly the site of a wool mill that used water power from the Pachaug River. The area was purchased by the federal government in 1930 and managed for about thirty years by the Civilian Conservation Corps (CCC) until transferred to the state in 1959. Today, the 150-acre pond offers fine waterside family camping, hiking, swimming, and boating. Water-skiing is prohibited, and motor-boats are limited to 8 MPH, so you won't have to contend with speed-boats. Sharing the watershed of the Pachaug, this state park is joined also to Pachaug State Forest (see sections on Glasgo Pond, Beachdale Pond, and Green Falls Pond) by fourteen-mile Nehantic footpath, connecting the northeast side of Hopeville Pond with Green Falls Pond in Voluntown, over low hilly terrain. A canoeing-hiking round-trip, or shorter day alternative stretching-of-the-legs, is possible here.

Hopeville Pond winds through woodland, farmland, and areas with light cottage development between a dam at the north end, close to Interstate 395, and a section of river connecting to Pachaug Pond at the south end. The much larger and more developed Pachaug Pond can be reached by canoe by continuing upstream on the Pachaug River at the south end of Hopeville Pond, and carrying around the dam. Near the center of the pond on the eastern side just south of the park is an enclave of small cottages obviously built quite a few years ago on limited budgets, but very well cared for. I found these a refreshing change from the very large summer homes people seem compelled to build today.

Like other bodies of water in this part of the state, Hopeville Pond is shallow and its water is stained a deep reddish brown by the natural tannins. You will see lots of painted turtles along here, as well as great blue herons, kingfishers, black ducks, mallards, and, if you're lucky, wood ducks. Several male wood ducks in full breeding plumage landed right in front of my boat near the south end of the pond where I had paused under the cover of a tree. They were there for just a few seconds before they saw me and immediately took to the air with their high-pitched distress call. I also saw signs of beaver here and a lodge at the south end where the pond narrows to a river channel.

GETTING THERE: Hopeville Pond is very easy to find. Get off Interstate 395 at Exit 86, and take Route 201 East, following signs for Hopeville Pond State Park. Stay on Route 201, which forks to the right after about 0.5 mile (where Hopeville Road goes off to the left); the park entrance is on the right 1.0 mile past the fork. The actual boat ramp for Hopeville Pond is in the camping area, where parking is limited, but you can also launch a boat from the recreation area, though it requires a carry of about 100 feet down from the parking area. If the camping area is closed, you have to launch from this area. Check at the contact station when you first enter the park (if it is open) to find out where you should launch your boat. During the summer there is a day-use fee to enter the park.

You can camp at Hopeville Pond State Park, though the season of operation is limited. Campsites are fairly open and close to the water. There are two swimming beaches in the park with nice sand. Camping is also available across the pond from the state park at Campers World of Connecticut (P.O. Box 333, Jewett City, CT 06351; 203-376-2340). This campground has 100 sites and is mostly geared toward long-term RV camping. For more information on the pond and camping at the state facility, contact Hopeville Pond State Park, 193 Roode Road, Jewett City, CT 06351; 203-376-2920.

Glasgo Pond
Griswold, CT

Glasgo Pond is one of the narrow winding ponds in and around Connecticut's extensive Pachaug State Forest at the eastern edge of the state (see also sections on Beachdale Pond and Hopeville Pond). Glasgo has some development on it, particularly at the western tip near the dam and in the northern section into Doaneville Pond. But the development doesn't seem to dominate Glasgo Pond as it does on many of the region's other lakes and ponds. The total area of Glasgo Pond is 184 acres.

If you want to get away from the bass-fishing boats and houses, paddle east from the boat launch and squeeze under the Route 165 bridge (you have to lie back pretty far in your canoe). This southeastern extension of the pond is a real treat. Other than the moderate noise from Route 165, this section feels like a northern wilderness area—you almost expect to hear the wail of a loon, though this species has been absent from Connecticut's inland waterways for many years. This section of Glasgo Pond is almost totally within Pachaug State Forest—a sprawling twenty-three-thousand-acre tract of land (the largest area of public land in southern New England). It is ringed with red maple, white pine, and scarlet oak, with patches of cedar and tamarack along the northeastern shore and somewhat farther from the water. There is dense growth of a wide variety of shrubs right at the shore: sweet gale, sweet pepperbush, alder, mountain laurel, blueberry, winterberry. If you look carefully on the tussocks of sphagnum moss you will find the tiny-leafed vines and large fruits of wild cranberry. I also saw some nodding ladies' tresses, a late-blooming white-flowered orchid found in boggy areas. Beneath the water's surface are thick mats of fanwort and bladderwort that provide cover for the largemouth bass and pickerel caught here.

The far end of this little pond is sprinkled with small boggy islands. Exploring around these islands you are likely to startle a wood duck or two from their cover. This bird never ceases to amaze me with its sheer beauty. It is a wonder that this most beautiful of our waterfowl is found more widely on the lakes and ponds in southern New England than almost any other species. If you're quiet and patient and have binoculars, you should be able to get a good look at this very timid cavity-nesting duck. (For more on the wood duck, see the *AMC Quiet Water Canoe Guide: New Hampshire/Vermont.*) Along with wood

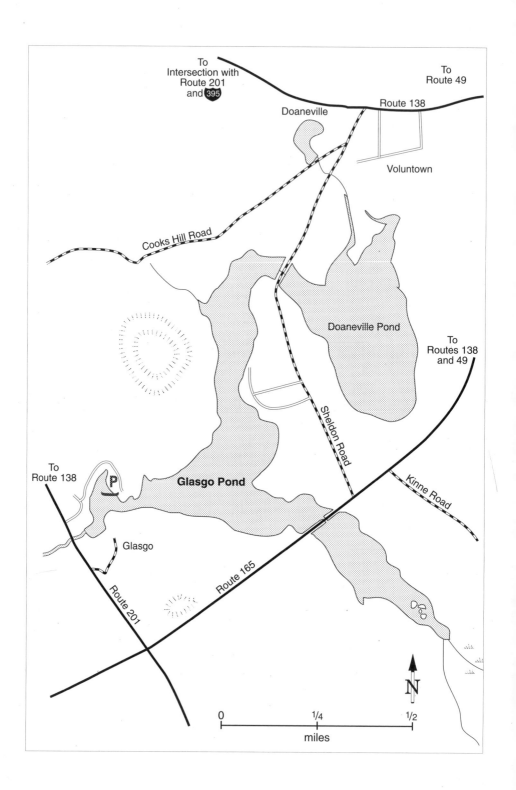

ducks, I saw kingfishers, black ducks, and a pied-billed grebe here, the last being a very small and quite reclusive ducklike bird occasionally seen in the area. At the far southeast end, the islands seem to merge together, forming a marshy area of bulrush, burr reeds, and grasses. You can hear the gurgle of water flowing over a beaver dam here, though it's hard to get close enough to see the beavers' handiwork.

Back out on the main Glasgo Pond, you can paddle north, passing houses on both sides, and then under the Sheldon Road bridge into Doaneville Pond. This bridge is high enough for motorboats to pass through, and for the quiet water paddler, it is a far cry from the extension of Glasgo Pond to the southeast. The relatively round Doaneville Pond has a small trailer park at the northwest end and perhaps ten or fifteen houses scattered along the shore. Most of the shoreline is heavily wooded with white pine and various deciduous species.

GETTING THERE: To reach Glasgo Pond get off Interstate 395 at Exit 85 and take Route 138 East toward Pachaug and Doaneville. Drive about 3.9 miles on 138, then turn right onto Route 201 South. Stay on 201 for 1.8 miles, then turn left onto an unmarked road with a "No Outlet" sign (if you reach Route 165, you have gone about 0.3 mile too far). A few hundred yards after turning onto this road, you will see a boat launch symbol pointing to the right. Turn right on the gravel access road here, and drive 0.2 mile around a little nub of Glasgo Pond to get to the parking area and boat ramp. There is parking space for twenty to thirty cars.

Camping is available a short distance away at Pachaug State Forest in several camping areas. To reach the state forest headquarters, drive back to Route 201 and turn left (south). After 0.4 mile, turn left onto Route 165. Stay on 165 for 2.4 miles (you will pass over the eastern end of Glasgo Pond, then 49 South will go off to the right, and you will join 138), then turn left onto Route 49 North. The state forest entrance will be on the left in 0.8 mile. Follow signs to the headquarters and camping areas. For more information on Pachaug State Forest, see the Beachdale Pond section.

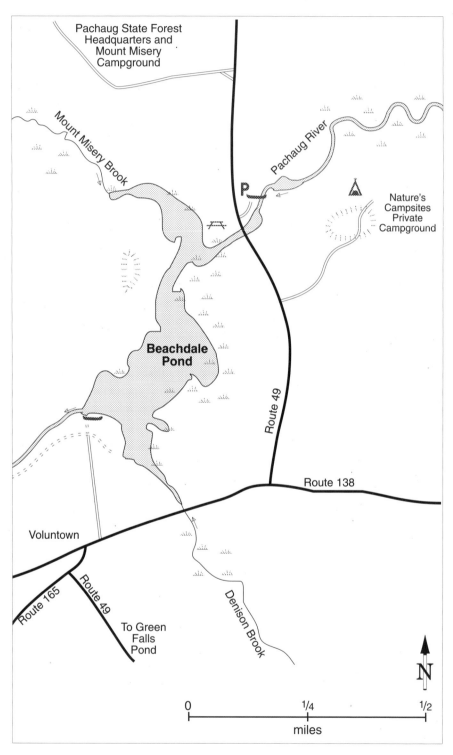

Pachaug State Forest
Headquarters and
Mount Misery
Campground

Mount Misery Brook

Pachaug River

P

Nature's
Campsites
Private
Campground

**Beachdale
Pond**

Route 49

Route 138

Voluntown

Route 165

Route 49

To Green
Falls
Pond

Denison Brook

N

0   1/4   1/2
miles

Beachdale Pond
Voluntown, CT

Though small (forty-six acres), Beachdale Pond is definitely worth visiting for a few hours of quiet paddling. And you can actually spend a lot more than a few hours by paddling up the Pachaug River or either of two other inlet brooks. The pond is very shallow, with extensive marshy vegetation. Watch for painted turtles hiding amid the arrowhead, pickerel weed, water lilies, and grasses. Road noise from Routes 49 and 138 will, to some extent, compete with the songbirds along here, but I didn't find the roads too intrusive.

Canoeing into the northernmost extension of the pond, the paddling gets somewhat more difficult, as you need to maneuver around partially submerged logs, hummocks of grass and sphagnum moss, and the occasional boulder lurking just beneath the surface of the water. Gradually, as you paddle farther north and west, though, Mount Misery Brook defines itself from the surrounding marsh. This winding channel offers plenty of exploration, especially for someone interested in wildlife observation. I'm not sure how far up Mount Misery Brook you can paddle, but I went for a good half-mile or so before I had to retreat from an advancing thunderstorm.

At the southern tip of Beachdale Pond, where Denison Brook comes in, you can also explore the slow-moving sinewy channel for some distance—after passing under the highway overpass—but I found this brook somewhat less interesting than Mount Misery Brook. It is less attractive, with muddy shorelines and some trash strewn along the shores. When I paddled here in mid-July you could paddle under the highway easily, but the water was quite shallow; had the water level been much lower it would have been difficult not to scrape bottom.

The southwestern end of Beachdale Pond is the only developed portion. There are a handful of homes along here, including a house right next to the dam and outlet (where there is a carry-in boat access point with room for about a half-dozen cars to park).

The primary boat launch area is on the Pachaug River, just east of Route 49. Next to the boat launch is a wheelchair access for anglers. Primary fish species caught here are largemouth bass and yellow perch, though the pond is also apparently stocked with trout. In addition to paddling under the Route 49 bridge into Beachdale Pond, you can also paddle upriver from here. Like Mount Misery Brook, the Pachaug River slowly meanders through marshy country—ideal habitat for all sorts of fauna and flora (including the extremely healthy poison ivy that overhangs the banks in places, reaching out to greet the unaware paddler). Not far up the Pachaug River you will pass a private campground (Nature's Campsites) that offers quite pleasant camping. Driving through this campground, I was surprised to see campsites with some separation to them and even grass growing on them. (In general, I have almost given up on private campgrounds in favor of state and federal campgrounds because the private ones usually squeeze the sites so close together, but this one is a lot better than most.) There are a few campsites right on the river, but most are farther back and wooded. Tent sites were $16 per night in 1992. Canoe rentals are available. For camping information, contact the Lazourack Family, Nature's Campsites, Route 49N, Voluntown, CT 06384; 203-376-4203.

Most of Beachdale Pond is located in Pachaug State Forest, which is the largest state forest in southern New England. From the first land purchase in 1928, the forest now covers some twenty-four thousand acres in six towns. Appropriately, the word "Pachaug" is derived from a Native American word meaning bend or turn in the river. This entire area was inhabited by Pequot, Narraganset, and Mohegan tribes prior to the arrival of Europeans. During the latter half of the seventeenth century, a combined force of the colonists and the Mohegans defeated both the Narragansets and Pequots, and in 1700 a six-mile-square tract of land was granted to the Mohegan war veterans. Eventually, the central

Located in Pachaug State Forest, Beachdale Pond is shallow and marshy. From here you can explore upstream on the Pachaug River and two other inlet brooks.

portion of this tract became "Volunteer's Town," and it was incorporated as Voluntown in 1721.

Pachaug State Forest offers several different camping areas. The Mount Misery camping area, with twenty-two campsites, is about 1.3 miles from the Route 49 Beachdale Pond boat access point (water, fireplaces, and pit toilets provided, and sites are available on a first-come, first-served basis). More remote but in the same general area is the Frog Hollow Horse Camp, which requires reservations in advance. And about five miles away (via Route 49 South) is Green Falls Pond and camping area (see section on Green Falls Pond).

There are numerous hiking and mountain-biking trails in the various sections of Pachaug State Forest. Quite close to Beachdale Pond is a wonderful rhododendron sanctuary—an unusual isolated stand of ancient rhododendrons and white cedar. There is a short loop trail through this sanctuary, that you should try to make time for, especially if you're visiting in early or mid-July, when the rhododendrons are usually in bloom. For more information on Beachdale Pond and hiking or biking in Pachaug State Forest, contact the Pachaug State Forest, RFD 1, Voluntown, CT 06384; 203-376-4075.

GETTING THERE: Beachdale Pond is easily accessible off Route 395 in eastern Connecticut. Get off at Exit 85 and drive east on Route 138. You will cross Route 201 after approximately 4.0 miles. Routes 165 and 49 come in from the south after 6.1 miles (stay on Route 138 East). Six-and-one-half miles from Route 395 turn left onto Route 49 North. You will see the entrance to the Beachdale Pond boat access on the right, just after crossing the bridge over the Pachaug River, 0.6 mile from Route 138/165. The road to the Mount Misery camping area and rhododendron sanctuary is on the other side of Route 49, just north of the boat access.

Green Falls Pond
Voluntown, CT

Green Falls Pond is one of the most remote bodies of water included in this guide. Though small (just forty-seven acres), it is a real treasure, ideal for a morning or afternoon of quiet paddling, and a super spot for family camping. Like Beachdale Pond and part of Glasgo Pond (see pages 123–129), Green Falls Pond is located in the sprawling Pachaug State Forest of southeastern Connecticut. Be aware, however, that although Green Falls Pond is off the beaten path, it does receive heavy visitation—particularly on nice summer weekends. Gasoline-powered motorboats are prohibited from the pond, further improving the pond in the eyes of quiet water paddlers.

The woods are beautiful around Green Falls Pond, with a tall canopy of red oak, chestnut oak, white oak, sugar maple, yellow birch, hemlock, sassafras, and shagbark hickory shading a fairly open leaf-carpeted understory of mountain laurel, flowering dogwood, and a wide variety of spring wildflowers. The shoreline is rocky and lined with blueberry, mountain laurel, and other shrubs, with plenty of places to pull up on the shore for a rest, walk in the woods, or picnic. There are a few islands on the pond and a tall dam at the southern tip. Quite a few trails weave through this portion of Pachaug State Forest, including the Nehantic and Narragansett trails. From the south end of the pond by the dam, you can walk downstream through a deep gorge with majestic hemlock trees rising well over 100 feet.

GETTING THERE: To reach Green Falls Pond from Interstate 395, get off at Exit 85 and drive east on Route 138. Stay on 138 for approximately 8.5 miles (138 makes a number of turns), then turn right onto a gravel road, following a sign for Green Falls Recreation Area. This turn is 1.0 mile past the fork where 165 splits off to the left and 138 to the right. Follow this gravel road for 0.8 mile and bear left into the Green Falls Recreation Area. (During weekends and holidays there is a day-use fee.) You will reach a small parking/picnic area near the pond in 1.5 miles, and the boat access is another 0.1 mile farther along.

There are eighteen campsites near Green Falls Pond (but not right on the water) that are open from the third Saturday in April through the end of September. If you want to camp after that date, camping is available in the Mount Misery Campground in the state forest through the end of December. Pachaug State Forest is also one of the few areas in Connecticut where backpacking is permitted, with special shelters and

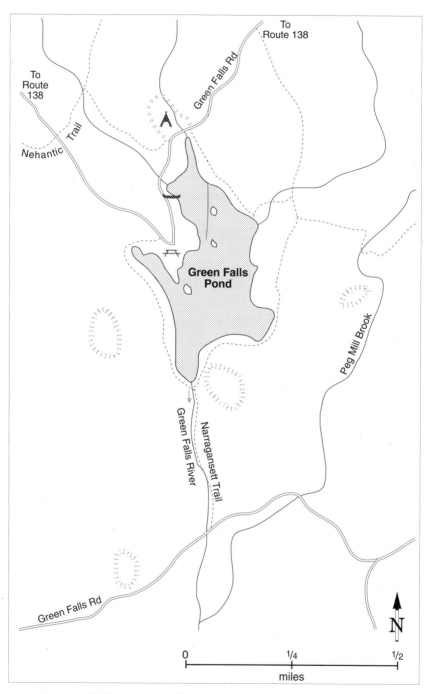

campsites available along trails that are for backpackers only (advance registration is required). For information on Green Falls and camping in the forest, contact Pachaug State Forest Headquarters, RFD 1, Voluntown, CT 06384; 203-376-4075.

Lake of Isles
North Stonington, CT

Lake of Isles is a great canoeing spot, with a highly varied shoreline, clean water, sandy bottom, huge granite boulders along the shore, several attractive islands, and no development except Boy Scout structures that are no longer in use. How long it will remain such a quiet spot is unknown, however. The Boy Scouts of Hartford, who own the surrounding land, have closed down their camp and in 1992 were trying to sell the property. According to area residents, the Pequot Native Americans are seeking to buy the land. If the Pequots choose to protect the area in its natural state and discourage the use of motorboats on the lake, the change in ownership could be great. But that is not at all certain. If the land is folded into the Pequot's reservation land, public access could be restricted, or, they might choose to develop the land. The Mashantucket Pequots recently built a large gambling casino in North Stonington that is proving to be highly successful financially, and they are planning a huge hotel complex. If they choose to develop the entire area around Lake of Isles, it would be a loss to all of us. Before you drive a long way to paddle here, I'd suggest calling the state to make sure the public access is still open.

The surrounding woodlands are comprised almost entirely of deciduous trees, including white and red oak, red maple, sassafras, yellow and gray birch, elm, American chestnut, white ash, beech, and black gum. Along the shoreline are lots of blueberry bushes, swamp honeysuckle, alder, and other shrubs. There is quite a bit of floating pond vegetation close to shore and in the marshy easternmost cove of the lake. Near the northern end of the lake, on the western side, you can paddle through a culvert connecting the two sides of the peninsula. Fish species caught here include largemouth bass, pickerel, yellow perch, black crappie, and sunfish.

GETTING THERE: Lake of Isles is not far off from Route 2 midway between Norwich, CT, and Westerly, RI. Driving east from Norwich, turn left off Route 2 onto Wattson Road 0.7 mile past the intersection with Route 164 (there should be a sign here for Lake of Isles). Drive north on Wattson Road for 0.6 mile, and then turn right on Lake of Isles Road (again there should be a sign). Lake of Isles Road turns to dirt after about a half-mile, and reaches a parking area near the boat launch after a total of 1.2 miles. If you are driving the other way on Route 2 from Westerly, RI or I-95 (Exit 92), turn right on Wattson Road 1.8

To
Wattson Road
and Route 2

Lake of Isles Road

P

Lake of Isles

N

0   1/4   1/2

miles

miles after the intersection with Route 214, and follow directions as above. There is parking at the launch area for about twenty cars.

The state lists an 8 MPH speed limit for motorboats on the lake, and a sign at the lake lists 6 MPH. Camping is not permitted on or around the lake. As mentioned above, the public access to Lake of Isles could change. To find out about public access, contact the Connecticut Bureau of Outdoor Recreation, State Parks Division, 165 Capitol Avenue, Hartford, CT 06106; 203-566-2304.

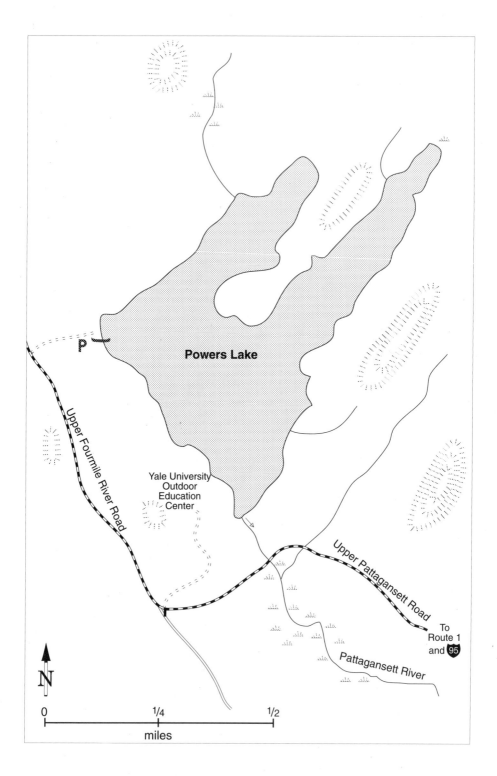

Powers Lake

Upper Fourmile River Road

P

Yale University
Outdoor
Education
Center

Upper Pattagansett Road

To
Route 1
and 95

Pattagansett River

N

| 0 | 1/4 | 1/2 |

miles

Powers Lake
East Lyme, CT

Powers Lake was a real surprise for me: a quite large (153-acre) lake just a few miles off I-95 in southern Connecticut that is totally undeveloped except for a retreat facility for Yale University! The paddling is great, the woodland flora varied, and the wildlife abundant. I was surprised at the diversity of deciduous trees along the shoreline: four different species of oak (red, white, scarlet, and chestnut), American chestnut, sassafras, yellow birch, red maple, tulip tree, hickory, black gum, beech, and southern white cedar. The immediate shoreline is thick with laurel, blueberry, alder, and other shrubs. While much of the shore is impenetrable, there are some large granite slabs providing access to shore for a picnic lunch or break from paddling.

The lake is shaped like a horseshoe with two long fingers extending to the northeast—which makes it seem larger than it is. The longer finger ends up in a beautiful marshy area that you can explore by canoe, though vegetation pretty well blocks your progress by midsummer. In the spring, before the various water lilies make their way to the surface, paddling in here would be much easier. In this part of the lake, look for delicate sundew plants on hummocks of grass and sphagnum moss. I saw two different species of this curious insectivorous plant (round-leaved sundew, *Drosera rotundifolia,* and spatulate-leaved sundew, *D. intermedia*). Most exciting, however, was the reptile life around the lake. I saw a number of northern water snakes, lots of painted turtles, a stinkpot turtle, and a quite rare spotted turtle (*Clemmys guttata*).

Except for the state-owned boat access, the entire surrounding area (some 2000 acres) is owned by Yale University. The camp and recreation area at the southwest end of the lake is used by Yale students, faculty, and associated groups for retreats, picnics, and general outdoor recreation (swimming, canoeing, rowing, volleyball, etc.). To use this area, you must be affiliated with Yale in some way.

GETTING THERE: Get off I-95 at Exit 74 and drive north on Route 161. After 0.4 mile, turn left onto Route 1 South (Post Road). Stay on Route 1 for just 0.5 mile and turn right onto Pattagansett Road, which passes along the north end of Pattagansett Lake. Continue on Pattagansett Road for 2.7 miles, then bear right onto Upper Fourmile River Road (or Whistletown Road) by the entrance to the Yale University

While very close to major population centers, Powers Lake is undeveloped. The northeastern end of the lake is marshy and the surface covered with vegetation.

Outdoor Education Center. Continue on this road for 0.6 mile, and turn right into the public boat access (when I visited the sign to this access was missing). There is plenty of parking space at the launch area, and an 8 MPH limit on boats should help discourage water-skiers and most of the larger boats. Water-skiers and jet-skiers tend to stick to Pattagansett Lake just to the south. Powers Lake would seem an ideal place to prohibit gasoline-powered motorboats altogether, and encourage quiet, low-impact paddling and rowing—especially given the presence of threatened spotted turtles.

Uncas Pond (Hog Pond)
Lyme, CT

Located in Nehantic State Forest, Uncas Pond is a gem. Though small (69 acres), the pond is mostly undeveloped (there are a few houses on the southeastern side), the water is clean, and gasoline-powered motorboats are prohibited, keeping the area pleasantly quiet—just right for paddling.

The pond is named for Chief Uncas of the Pequot Nation. The name "Uncas" recalls different images, depending upon who is writing, and from what vantage point. James Fenimore Cooper's *Last of the Mohicans* transplants this chief into the forests of upper New York. To his native rivals—the Niantics, the Narragansets—and even to his adopted Pequots, his name, "Fox," conjured up a circling forager who would strike when opportunity came. Indeed he did. The son of Mohegan Chief Owenoco, Uncas joined the more powerful Pequots after marrying a daughter of their chief, Sassacus, but rebelled several times against his father-in-law's rule. Banished to the Narragansets, he subdued them. Uncas allied himself to the English settlers in their successful war against King Philip's coalition of Native American nations in 1675. A monument to Uncas in nearby Norwich honors this friendship.

Uncas Pond is nestled into the hills of Nehantic State Forest and offers a very pleasant morning or afternoon of paddling—without motorboats.

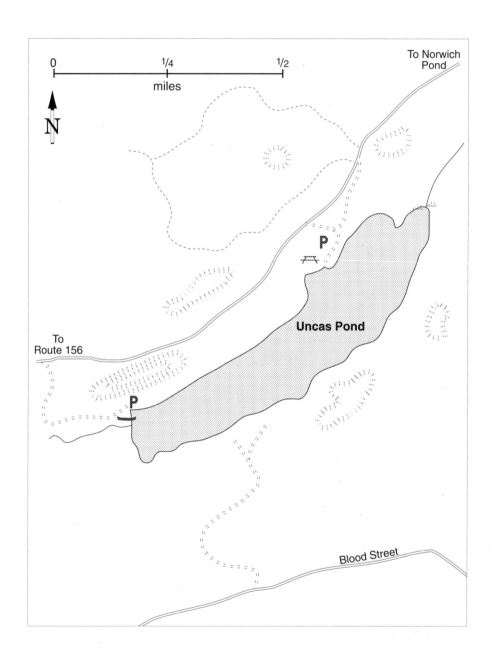

To Norwich
Pond

0   1/4   1/2

miles

N

To
Route 156

P

Uncas Pond

P

Blood Street

I was struck by the tremendous diversity of trees and shrubs growing around the pond, almost all of which were deciduous. You will see white oak, red oak, scarlet oak, black gum, red maple, sugar maple, beech, gray birch, yellow birch, sassafras, American chestnut (sprouts from trees killed by the chestnut blight), a few hemlock, alder, laurel, and swamp honeysuckle (a type of azalea). The shoreline is very densely grown with laurel. In fact, in some areas, you can't even see the actual shore, let alone get out and walk along the bank. Around most of the pond, the land rises steeply from the water's edge.

Most of Uncas Pond has a sandy bottom. If you look carefully through the somewhat brackish water, you may find freshwater mussels. Close to shore there is a narrow band of vegetation: pickerel weed, fragrant water lily, water shield, pondweed, and bullhead lily. At the northeast end is a small marshy area where the floating vegetation is thicker.

Nehantic State Forest offers some pleasant hiking and a nice picnic area near the north end of the pond, reachable either by canoe or by car, via the road to Norwich Pond—some picnic sites are right by the water. There is also a public boat access onto Norwich Pond (and I've paddled here) but it is smaller, rounder, and feels more developed with houses along most of the eastern side. From the boat access on Uncas Pond, a trail extends along the north side of the pond through a beautiful area of mammoth boulders, thick carpets of ferns, huge laurels, and feathery flowering dogwood trees. Fish caught in Uncas include trout, largemouth bass, pickerel, yellow perch, and sunfish.

GETTING THERE: Take Interstate 95 to Exit 70 (Old Lyme) and head north on Route 156 toward Hamburg. Drive 3.7 miles, and turn right on a rough dirt road into Nehantic State Forest. Follow this road for 1.2 miles, and take the right fork toward Uncas Pond. You will reach the parking area and boat launch in another 0.3 mile. There is no camping in Nehantic State Forest. For more information, contact the Connecticut Bureau of State Parks and Forests, 156 Capitol Avenue, Hartford, CT 06106; 203-566-2304.

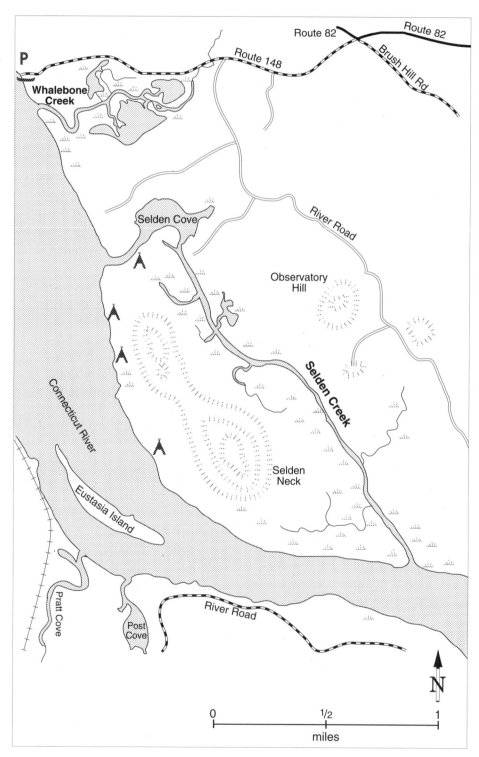

P

Route 82   Route 82

Route 148   Brush Hill Rd

Whalebone Creek

River Road

Selden Cove

Observatory Hill

Selden Creek

Connecticut River

Selden Neck

Eustasia Island

Pratt Cove

Post Cove

River Road

N

0   1/2   1

miles

Selden Creek and Whalebone Creek
Lyme, CT

I remember the first time I paddled down the southern section of the Connecticut River in the early eighties. There was a strong wind blowing up the river and our paddle down from Middletown had been arduous. At the Chester-Hadlyme Ferry we were to meet several other canoeists, including an uncle of mine who had paddled in this area for years. Heading south from here, with my uncle's guidance, we quickly left behind the whitecaps and strength-sapping wind to find the river's calm side channels along the eastern shore. We poked our way down to Old Lyme on these channels, able to enjoy the natural surroundings rather than having to concentrate solely on our paddling. Described here is one of these protected channels—Selden Creek—as well as a side-trip up Whalebone Creek.

The inlet to Whalebone Creek is just a short distance downriver from the parking lot by the Chester-Hadlyme Ferry. This creek is one of the most pristine tidal freshwater marshes you will find anywhere in Connecticut. One might wonder how an area can be tidal and fresh water at the same time, but that's the case here. The rising and falling Atlantic tide affects the water level on the Connecticut River as far up as Hartford, but the river current is too strong to permit movement of salt water very far upstream. The water that fills Whalebone Creek as the tide rises comes mostly from the Connecticut River, not from the sea. A short way south the fresh and salt water mix to create brackish water conditions, and by Great Island and Griswold Point, the salt-marsh ecosystem dominates.

There are two signal lights at the entrance to Whalebone Creek. Paddling into the creek you pass a tall cliff on the left festooned with wild grape and other vines. In the early morning light I watched a raccoon scurry up the rock face, peering down at me with obvious annoyance. Farther along on the left is a heavily wooded hillside. On the other side of the creek is marsh, dotted here and there with trees and shrubs adapted to the ever-changing water level.

Farther in on Whalebone Creek, wild rice (*Zizania aquatica*) is the dominant plant—and a very interesting one at that. Wild rice is not actually very closely related to cultivated rice, except that both are grasses. Wild rice reaches eight to ten feet in height, with round hollow stems up to an inch in diameter at the base, and long wide leaves up to four feet long and as much as two inches wide where they branch off the main stem. The stems almost look like bamboo. Flowers and seeds are borne at the tops of the stalks. If you are paddling here in late summer or early fall you can get an idea of how Native Americans harvest this grain in Minnesota: carefully bend one of the tall stems over into your boat and shake it to release the sheathed seeds. In the thick wild rice marshes of Minnesota the Native Americans literally fill their canoes as they harvest the grain. These seeds are then threshed and winnowed to get at the delicious brown or black grain.

Along with wild rice, you will see bulrush, saltwater cordgrass, pickerel weed, and a host of other marsh plants. You are also sure to see birds—lots of them. Even in early autumn, the place seemed alive with redwing blackbirds, marsh wrens, swallows, kingfishers, black ducks, wood ducks, great blue herons, Canada geese, and a few mute swans. At high tide—the preferred time to paddle here—you can explore quite far into Whalebone Creek, with its winding channels and pools of open water. In fact, you have to watch your course, as you can almost get lost in the mazelike marsh. If confused, note the direction of water flow under your canoe. By knowing whether the tide is coming in or going out, you can pretty easily find your way back to the main creek channel. At low tide, paddling here is far more restricted and less attractive.

Selden Creek

Back out on the Connecticut River and about two-thirds of a mile south on the same side is the inlet to Selden Creek. This channel of water extends around a tall island hill known as Selden Neck and back to the Connecticut River a couple of miles south. This is one of southern New England's true gems when it comes to quiet paddling and canoe camping. There is a 6 MPH speed limit on Selden Creek, so about the only motorboats you will see here are used for fishing. If you can avoid weekends, there will be few if any boats in here. (I had the unfortunate experience to find myself in the middle of a bass tournament here on my most recent visit, which upset the tranquillity considerably!) As with Whalebone Creek, the water in Selden Creek is fresh or only slightly brackish. Wild rice is common along the shores, though not as abundant and lush as it is in Whalebone Creek.

There are lots of small side creeks to explore along here if the tide is high enough. In one of these I was fascinated to watch schools of small fish—alewife perhaps—"skipping" along the surface of the water. The one-to-two-inch fish literally skip along the surface of the shallow water using their strong tails in an apparently defensive response to some disturbance, such as a paddler. In some cases, a fish will overthrust and end

*Whalebone Creek and
Selden Creek have large
stands of feathery wild rice,
some of which reaches a
height of ten feet.*

up flopping back and forth getting nowhere, but most seem to skip along for a foot or two at a time. The physics of this are remarkable.

When you get to the southern access onto the Connecticut River, you can either turn around and paddle back up Selden Creek, or have a go at paddling up the river. While I generally prefer loops (i.e., returning to the ferry via the river), I urge extreme caution if paddling on the main river here. Particularly on weekends, this section of the Connecticut River is heavily used by speeding pleasure boats and cabin cruisers, many of which throw out a very large wake. Oddly, even the huge tug-drawn barges and oil tankers that passed me here (at quite a good clip, I might add) seemed to generate smaller wakes than the cabin cruisers and speedboats, so be aware that wakes aren't always proportional to the size of the boat producing them. Also realize that the wake of a second boat can amplify the wake of a boat that just passed by, and that the water will be far rougher where cliffs drop down into the water (where there is a beach, the wave's energy is dissipated as the wave washes up, but when a wave hits a rock face in deep water the wave's energy is reflected back, creating very choppy water). This situation occurs near the northern end of Selden Neck, between the Spring Ledge and Hogback campsites. I was nearly swamped paddling along here when several boats passing by the steep shoreline generated a huge curling wave three feet tall. I took on a couple of gallons of water and beat a hasty retreat to a small sandy cove on shore to dump the water from my boat. If you do paddle along here, you *must wear* your PFDs, especially if you are not a good swimmer, and make sure your gear is packaged to keep dry.

Primitive canoe camping is permitted at Selden Neck State Park, which covers the entire Selden Neck island. There are four different access points to Selden Neck, as shown on the map. One is reached from Selden Creek; the others from the Connecticut River. My favorite is Quarry Knob—the farthest south—where you camp on a knoll overlooking the river and have easy access to the 226-foot rocky peak of Selden Neck. These campsites are designed for people paddling down the Connecticut River. Stays are limited to one night; registration and payment of a fee ($4 per person per night in 1992) is required. I was amazed to find literally no trash around the campsites—evidence that canoe campers really do carry out what they carry in. For camping information, contact Gillette Castle State Park (address below).

GETTING THERE: The most dramatic way to reach the parking area and boat access is to take Route 148 East from Route 9 (Exit 6) and cross on the Chester-Hadlyme Ferry. After getting off the ferry, turn into the parking area immediately to the left. There is parking space for about twenty cars here and an unimproved ramp. The ferry fee in 1992 was $4 one-way for a car and passengers. If you don't want to take the ferry or are concerned that it might not be operating you can get off Route 9 at Exit 7 and take Route 82 East, crossing the Connecticut by bridge in East Haddam. Where Route 151 turns off to the left, 82 turns south; stay on 82 toward Hadlyme. At the T-intersection where 82 turns left, turn right on Route 148 and follow signs to the Chester-Hadlyme Ferry.

The parking area is at the southern end of Gillette Castle State Park. Rental canoes are available here from the U-Paddle Service, though you usually have to call ahead and arrange for someone to be there (203-739-9791). While in the area, you might want to take a side trip to Gillette Castle, a fascinating stone mansion built between 1914 and 1919 by the eccentric actor William Gillette (who became famous for his portrayal of Sherlock Holmes on stage). The house and property were purchased by the state in 1943 to become Gillette Castle State Park, which is immensely popular, with well over 100,000 visitors annually. There is no charge to enter the park, but a fee is charged for touring the castle. For information on the park, or to obtain a camping permit for Selden Neck, write to Gillette Castle State Park, East Haddam, CT 06423; or call 203-526-2336.

Moodus Reservoir

East Haddam, CT

Moodus is an interesting place. The name comes from the Pequot Indian word "machimoodus" meaning "land of noises." Loud booms heard in the area have mystified residents for hundreds (and probably thousands) of years. A deep fault line is thought to be the cause of these booms, which a resident tells me sound like sonic booms. The tremors generally cannot be felt—only heard. For the paddler on Moodus Reservoir, these tremors should have no impact (although neither the author nor AMC can guarantee that a huge chasm won't suddenly open up while you're paddling, emptying the reservoir and swallowing you and your canoe).

The reservoir provides some excellent canoeing, particularly on a calm spring day when the shorelines are alive with nesting songbirds and spectacular wood ducks in the marshy coves are hiding from all but the quietest paddler. One could easily spend a day on this shallow 450-acre reservoir exploring the many long sinewy coves and watching for painted turtles amid the floating pond vegetation.

The reservoir is divided into two sections. Don't bother with the smaller section, northwest of the East Haddam–Colchester Turnpike

The east end of Moodus Reservoir is extremely shallow and marshy. Hundreds of swallows nest in the standing dead trees here.

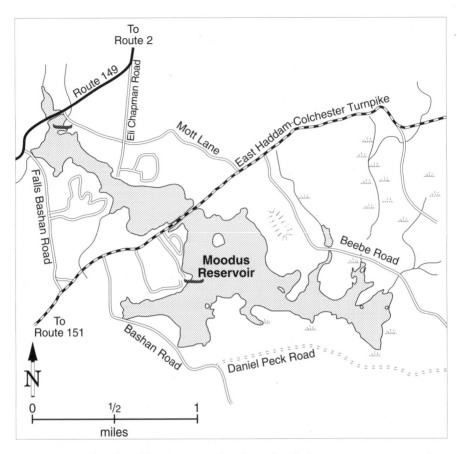

causeway; the shoreline is more developed and the water more crowded with water-skiers and motorboats than the larger section southeast of
the causeway. The causeway bridge is too close to the water to permit
paddling under (and believe me I'll paddle under any bridge as long as
the top of the canoe clears it). At first I was disappointed that you can't
paddle from one side to the other, but it's really to our advantage, since
it keeps most motorboats in the smaller section of the reservoir, where
the boat ramp is larger and more parking space is provided.

In the marshy coves keep an eye out for wood ducks, green
herons, great blue herons, and painted turtles. You are also likely to see
hundreds of tree swallows, which inhabit the standing dead trees in the
eastern end of the reservoir and feed on flying insects above the water's
surface. There are a number of duck-hunting blinds in the coves on the
northeastern end of the reservoir, so you would do well to keep away
during duck-hunting season. The trees around the reservoir are typical
of this part of Connecticut: red oak, white oak, sassafras, yellow and

gray birch, scarlet oak, red maple, beech, and a few white pine. There are surprisingly few conifers around Moodus Reservoir and most other lakes and ponds in this part of the state. Along the shores you will also see laurel, highbush blueberry, and swamp honeysuckle (a late-blooming azalea with long, sticky white flowers that have the same trumpet-like shape as honeysuckle flowers). As for fish, the primary species caught are largemouth bass—including trophy-sized specimens—and yellow perch.

GETTING THERE: If coming from the south or west, take Route 9 to Exit 7 (Route 82). Drive 4.9 miles on Route 82 East, crossing Route 154 and the Connecticut River, and turn left onto Route 151 North, heading toward the town of Moodus. Drive 1.2 miles on 151, then turn right onto the East Haddam–Colchester Turnpike. (This turn is just past a cemetery on the left and the East Haddam Town Hall on the right.) In 1.8 miles you will reach a stop sign where Falls Bashen Road goes off to the left; continue straight here. Turn right (uphill) onto an unmarked road 2.6 miles from Route 151 (0.7 mile past the stop sign at Falls Bashen Road). Follow this road for 0.2 mile to the boat access. There is parking for about eight cars here.

If you are driving from the east or north via Route 2, get off at Exit 18 and turn onto Route 16 West. Take Route 16 to Route 149 South. After 1.6 miles on Route 149, bear left onto Eli Chapman Road. Drive downhill for about 0.5 mile and turn left onto Mott Lane (by turning right on Mott Lane here you would reach the boat launch area for the northwestern section of the reservoir). Mott Lane dead-ends on the East Haddam–Colchester Turnpike after 0.9 mile. Turn right. You will cross over Moodus Reservoir on the causeway in 0.5 mile and reach the access road into the boat launch 0.6 mile from Mott Lane. Turn left (uphill) and drive 0.2 mile to reach the boat launch area.

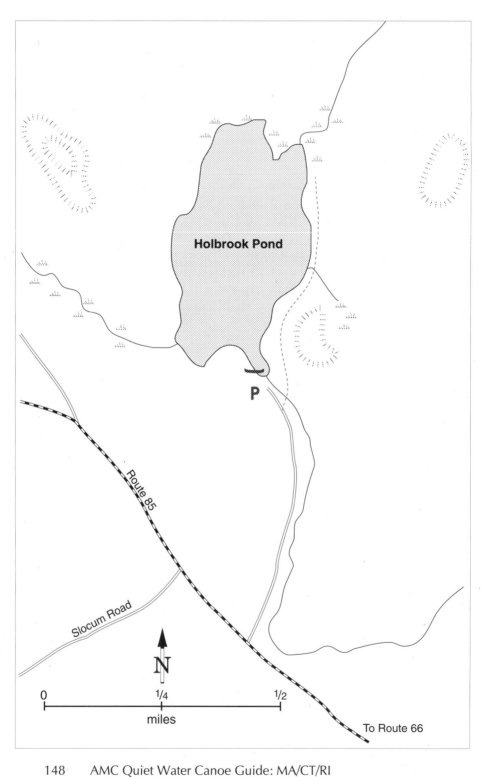

Holbrook Pond

Route 85

Slocum Road

P

N

0   1/4   1/2

miles

To Route 66

Holbrook Pond
Hebron, CT

Located in east-central Connecticut, Holbrook Pond is not remarkable, but it is a very nice roundish pond offering a pleasant morning or afternoon of paddling, fishing, hiking, and wildlife observation. There is no development whatsoever around its shallow seventy-three acre and it lies in a northern segment of the Salmon River State Forest.

The pond somehow has a "dirty" feel to it—dead and dying trees along the shoreline, tangled vines growing up over fallen trees, thick muck near the shores that oozes forth a stench of anaerobic decomposition as you stir the water with your paddle. Thick stands of shrubs in the shallow water, principally buttonbush, make paddling close to shore difficult. But this feel is misleading. The water is actually very pure, as evidenced by the extensive colonies of the byrozoan *Pectinatella*. Bryozoa live in colonies. Each unit, or zooid, of the colony has a rim of tentacles with tiny hairs, or cilia, that sweep the water for the microscopic algae, protozoa, and diatoms, that comprise their diet. Of the fourteen species of bryozoa found in fresh water, *Pectinatella* is the most dramatic. The colonies form large gelatinous masses on submerged branches and rocks—from a few inches to a couple of feet under water. I saw many hundreds of these colonies in Holbrook Pond during a visit in mid-July—more than I have seen in any other body of water. Some were as large as watermelons, but most were fist-sized. Bryozoa can only live in water that is very clean, so when you see these animals, you can be assured that the water is not significantly polluted. Look for these as you paddle around the pond, especially along the northeastern shoreline.

I saw wood ducks here, and quite a few wood-duck nesting boxes scattered along the shoreline. I also saw a few duck-hunting blinds, so you may want to paddle elsewhere during the fall duck-hunting season. Because the pond is shallow, there is considerable floating vegetation, including fragrant water lily, bullhead lily, water shield, and pondweed, with pickerel weed found closer to shore, especially near the outlet dam. Amid all this vegetation are largemouth bass, black crappie, and yellow perch.

GETTING THERE: To reach Holbrook Pond from the Hartford area, take Route 2 to Exit 13 and turn onto Route 66 East. Stay on 66 for 5.2 miles to Hebron, then turn left onto Route 85 North. The road into the

One of my frequent canoeing companions looking forward to a paddle around Holbrook Pond.

boat launch will be on the right 0.7 mile from Route 66. Follow the boat access road for another 0.7 mile and you will reach the pond and plenty of parking space. (If you are driving from the south or east, you can get off Route 2 in Colchester and drive north on Route 85. After crossing Route 66, continue another 0.7 mile; the boat access road will be on the right.) If you want to do some hiking, there is a trail extending around at least a portion of the pond. The trail starts at a smaller parking area that you reach just before getting to the main parking area and boat launch. For information, contact the Connecticut Bureau of Outdoor Recreation, State Parks Division, 165 Capitol Avenue, Hartford, CT 06106; 203-566-2304. Camping is not permitted at Holbrook Pond.

Pattaconk Reservoir
Chester, CT

Hidden away in the Cockaponset State Forest in south-central Connecticut is the Pattaconk Reservoir, a small but stunning body of water offering wonderful paddling. The fifty-six-acre reservoir is undeveloped except for a few picnic tables near the south end and hidden lean-tos for group camping at the north end. In a part of the state known more for tidal river canoeing, Pattaconk is a refreshing alternative with a real "mountain pond" feel to it.

The surrounding woods are comprised almost entirely of deciduous trees: four different oak species (red, white, chestnut, and scarlet), three birch species (gray, black, and yellow), red maple, sassafras, beech, shagbark hickory, black gum, American chestnut, and tulip tree. I was surprised to see so few white pines—a species that dominates many of our lake and pond shorelines. Growing densely along the shore—and overhanging the water in many cases—are laurel, highbush blueberry, and sweet pepperbush. Because of these shrubs, there aren't too many places where you can easily get out onto the shore, but there are some, and once you get past the immediate shoreline, the woods are quite open and great for walking.

In the water is some floating vegetation (fragrant water lily, pondweed, water shield, and bullhead lily), but there seemed to be little in the way of submerged vegetation. The water seems clean and the bottom generally sandy. The shoreline is dotted with occasional boulders. Largemouth bass, yellow perch, and sunfish are the fish most commonly caught here.

While the lean-tos at the north end are available only for youth group camping (scouting groups, for example), there should be no problem using the picnic tables and fireplaces for picnic lunches or even early suppers if you are out for a late afternoon paddle. This is also a small enough pond that if you work in the area, you might want to bring your canoe along and go out for a relaxing paddle either on your way to work or during an extended lunch break. You'd be surprised how much more productive an hour or so of paddling can make your day at the office! There are a number of nice hiking trails and old dirt roads in and around Cockaponset State Forest, including some accessible from Pattaconk Reservoir.

GETTING THERE: To reach Pattaconk Reservoir, take Route 9 to Exit 6. Then drive west on Route 148 toward Durham for about 1.5 miles to Cedar Lake Road. Turn right here and drive another 1.5 miles to the entrance to the Pattaconk Lake State Recreation Area on the left.

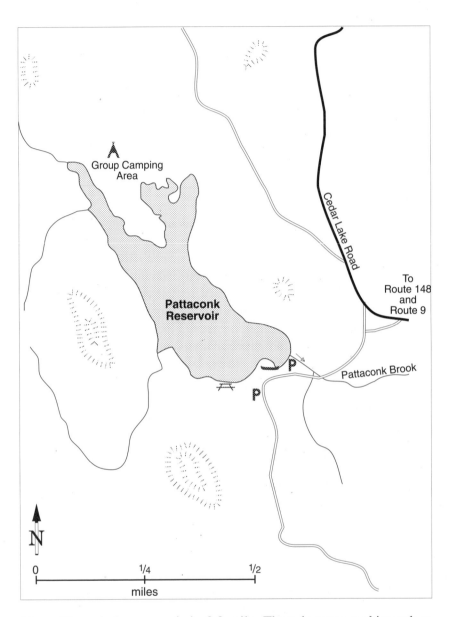

Group Camping
Area

Cedar Lake Road

To
Route 148
and
Route 9

Pattaconk
Reservoir

Pattaconk Brook

P

P

N

| 0 | 1/4 | 1/2 |

miles

You will reach the reservoir in 0.3 mile. There is some parking when you first get to the reservoir, and a lot more farther up the road on both the right and left. You have to carry your canoe about 100 feet to the water and launch from the bank.

For information on trails and group camping here, contact the Connecticut Department of Environmental Protection, Office of State Parks and Recreation, 165 Capitol Avenue, Hartford, CT; 203-566-2304, and ask for information on Cockaponset State Forest.

East River
Guilford and Madison, CT

East River, which forms the boundary between Guilford and Madison, Connecticut, in its lower stretches, provides superb tidal salt-marsh paddling. From the state boat launch on Grass Island near Guilford Harbor, the East River extends about five miles inland in a fairly wide, gently winding channel, with lots of small tributary streams to explore. Near the boat launch, Neck River bears off to the right but heads into a more populated area—you will do better to stay on the main river. One could easily spend a full day exploring this water system, observing the many changes with the rising and falling tide. At high tide you ride high in the canoe and can look out over the broad expanses of *Spartina patens* (salt-meadow grass). You will probably see herons and egrets standing in the grass fishing for small crabs and fish in the network of water-filled drainage ditches extending through the marsh. As the tide falls, you and your canoe drop down. The horizon disappears behind the high sod banks clad with mussels and alive with fiddler crabs and other generally hidden creatures of the salt marsh.

Spartina alterniflora *is the dominant grass species along the East River. Cedar and oak trees are seen on the higher banks along the river.*

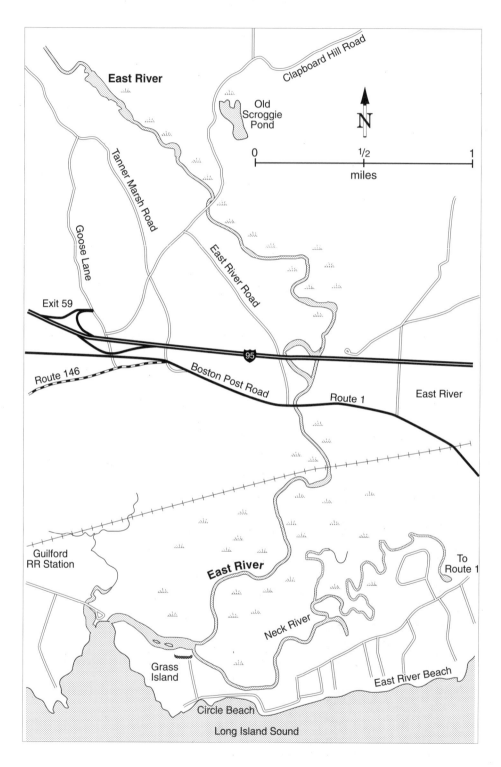

East River

Old Scroggie Pond

Clapboard Hill Road

N

0   1/2   1

miles

Tanner Marsh Road

Goose Lane

East River Road

Exit 59

95

Route 146

Boston Post Road

Route 1

East River

Guilford
RR Station

East River

To
Route 1

Neck River

Grass
Island

East River Beach

Circle Beach

Long Island Sound

The drainage ditches you see here and throughout our coastal salt marshes were dug in the 1930s and 1940s in an effort to eliminate pools of standing water that mosquitoes breed in. The effort was only marginally successful, though it put hundreds of people to work during the Great Depression. At high tide you can squeeze your canoe into some of these long, straight ditches, getting away from the main tidal river current and permitting close examination of salt-marsh flora and fauna (for more on the salt-marsh ecosystem, see pages 157–161).

From the state boat launch paddling upstream on the main channel of the East River, you will pass under a number of bridges. The first one you reach, about a mile-and-a-half from the boat ramp, is the Amtrak railroad line; you are very likely to see several trains pass by on this heavily traveled northeast corridor route. About a quarter-mile past that is the Route 1 bridge, where you can beach your canoe and walk up to one of the stores along the highway for a snack. If the tide is coming in, make sure your canoe is on high enough ground or well tied. (You can also launch a boat at this location, though parking is very limited.) Just a short distance past the Route 1 bridge, you pass under the I-95 bridge. Highway noise from I-95 is one of the more serious drawbacks to this otherwise wonderful stretch of river.

A short distance north of I-95 the land on both sides of the river is protected by the Connecticut Audubon Society. This tract is known as the Guilford Salt Meadow Sanctuary. At high tide, there are numerous small inlet streams alont the East River where you are likely to see lots of birdlife, including ospreys, marsh hawks, herons, and egrets. There are also some sections of high ground along here with red oak, white oak, sassafras, sumac, cedar, flowering dogwood, and a few black gum trees. You might want to explore some of these areas, but be fore-warned, there's lots of poison ivy, and this is a prime area for deer ticks that may carry Lyme disease. As you paddle farther upriver the noise from I-95 slowly fades away and you feel more and more alone. The few houses you will see along here are mostly old and in keeping with the salt-marsh environment.

If you time your visit right, you can paddle upriver from the boat access as the tide is coming in, enjoy paddling around the salt marsh near high tide, then paddle back down after the tide turns—so you're paddling with the current most if not all the time (river canoeing where you can always be paddling with the current and end up where you started!). If you are scheduling a visit, be aware that high tide several miles up East River will be quite a bit later than high tide at the coast. The tide at the coast is about twenty minutes before Bridgeport. With the current as gentle as it is on the East River, however, the wind is likely to be more of a factor than tidal current. By visiting in the early morning hours or in the early evening, you might be able to avoid the typical afternoon wind.

If you enjoy fishing, you can go after such species as winter flounder, fluke (summer flounder), striped bass, bluefish, scup (porgies), Atlantic mackerel, blackfish, menhaden, American eel, and snapper blues. Check with an area fishing-supply store to find out which lures or bait are most productive with these saltwater fish if you're used to freshwater fishing.

GETTING THERE: From Exit 59 on I-95, follow signs to Route 1 East. Drive 2.1 miles on Route 1, then turn right onto Neck Road. Bear right after a few hundred yards, then continue driving generally southwest, following boat launch signs. You will make a number of turns heading down Neck Road (most are pretty well marked) and reach the boat launch after 2.1 miles. If you make a wrong turn you can't get too far off track since Neck Road takes you out a rather narrow peninsula between the salt marsh and Long Island Sound. (The houses at the end of Neck Road stick up like sore thumbs as they await their fate with the next big hurricane or beach erosion.) There is plenty of parking at the boat launch.

As mentioned above, it is also possible to launch a canoe where Route 1 crosses the East River. If you are driving east on Route 1, a rough dirt road leads down to the right just after crossing the river. Be careful; the drop-off is quite steep. There is little room for parking at this access point, but by launching here you can avoid the windiest section of East River by Long Island Sound.

The Salt Marsh
Where River and Sea Meet

The salt-marsh ecosystem is one of the most unusual you will encounter on your paddling excursions. It is an ecosystem of tremendous productivity yet one so stressful on its inhabitants—plants especially—that very few can prosper. The stress comes from constant change. The incoming tide floods the marsh, saturating the peaty marsh soil with water. As the tide recedes, the marsh is exposed and on a hot, breezy, sunny day, its surface may actually dry out. The relative rise and fall of the tide varies daily, with extremes at the semi-

monthly "spring" tides that correspond to the full and new moons.

Even more significant than the constantly fluctuating water level in determining what can survive here is the water's changing salinity. As the tide comes in and sea water surges into the marsh, the salinity increases, reaching a peak at high tide. As the tide drops, so too does the salinity, reaching a minimum at low tide when incoming fresh water from the river or inlet streams flushes out or at least dilutes the sea water. Salinity conditions can vary markedly in different portions of a salt marsh—from nearly pure fresh water at one end, to salinity nearly matching that of the ocean at the opening to the sea. These salinity conditions are controlled by such factors as the volume of fresh water flowing into the marsh, the tidal differential along that section of coastline, and the size and configuration of the connection to the sea.

For plants of the salt marsh, the periodic flooding and salinity fluctuations have a tremendous impact. So specialized are the conditions that just two species of grass—*Spartina alterniflora* (saltwater cordgrass) and *S. patens* (salt-meadow grass)—dominate this ecosystem. These *Spartinas* comprise a natural monoculture—one of the few natural monocultures we can find—as far as the eye can see in our larger salt marshes. The inherent instability of monocultures has apparently not been a problem, as the *Spartina* marshes are thousands of years old, without evidence of disease or significant die-off.

Spartina alterniflora occupies the lower ground, where the twice-daily flooding inundates it with salt water. In ideal conditions, *S. alterniflora* will reach a height of ten feet, though it is more commonly less than half that height. *S. patens* is the species of the high marsh—the firmer land that is flooded only irregularly, at spring tides and during storms. Growing up to two feet tall, but often much less, this is the species that generations of coastal

New England farmers harvested as feed for their livestock (an acre of salt marsh produces twice as much hay as the best dry-land hayfields). *S. patens* is recognizable by the broad "cowlicks" that form on the marsh as swaths of the grass get matted down. A lower section of the stem is quite flexible as a defense against the forces of waves and strong current.

Another species able to withstand the rigors of the salt marsh is glasswort (genus *Salicornia*), an odd upright succulent plant with swollen jointed stems whose name, according to some sources, derives from its one-time use in making glass (the ash left from burning the plant is very high in sodium carbonate, an ingredient in glass). Amid the *S. patens* you may also see the delicate flowers of sea lavender (*Limonium nashii*), a plant that has long been collected for dried flower arrangements. (In fact, pressure from collectors has reduced sea lavender abundance considerably; picking the plant should be avoided.) There are other plants here—seaside goldenrod with thick fleshy leaves, sea aster, sea plantain, and sea purslane among them—but the number of species able to withstand this rigorous environment is remarkably small.

So complex are the mechanisms used by plants to adapt to high and constantly changing salinity levels that this could be the subject of an entire college course—integrating chemistry, physics, and plant physiology. Living organisms have to maintain a fairly precise balance of fluid and dissolved substances in their cells. When the concentrations of dissolved minerals and other substances are different, water wants to flow from the less concentrated to the more concentrated to equalize this "osmotic pressure." If the cells of a plant are more dilute than sea water—as is the case with most plants—the water in their cells will try to flow out through the cell membrane, drying and killing the plant cells. This is why most plants cannot survive life in the salt marsh. *Spartina* can survive through a complex series of evolutionary adaptations. [For an excellent discussion of the salt-marsh adaptations of *Spartina*, see the book *Life and Death of the Salt Marsh*, by John and Mildred Teal (Ballantine Books, 1969)].

In the less saline extensions of many of our salt-water marshes you may see wild rice and other less salt-tolerant species. On tidal rivers, sea water can only penetrate upriver a certain distance before the fresh water dilutes it to such an extent that freshwater plants and animals can survive. Paddling up these rivers, you can watch the progression of species—and species diversity—as you paddle farther and farther inland. How rapidly the salt water is diluted as you paddle upriver depends on the volume of fresh water flowing in the river. As the salinity drops, freshwater

species such as wild rice appear. On a large river like the Connecticut, salt water cannot penetrate far upstream—even though the river is "tidal" for many miles upstream (as the tide comes in, the rising sea water slows down the flow of the river, and the water level rises).

Animal life in the salt marsh is also fascinating. Unlike plants, most—but not all—of the animals here can move about to adapt to the rising and falling water levels. Most mollusks and invertebrates either bury themselves deep in the muck to survive the changing conditions, or swim in the current, like the fish that live or spawn here. Mussels and barnacles, however, attach themselves tightly to rocks, pilings, or other solid objects, and so cannot move about. To survive the twice-daily drying at low tide, these mollusks must close up tightly. Some of the fish that inhabit the salt marsh can regulate the osmotic balance of their bodily fluids to adjust to the changing salinity of the water. Some lower invertebrates actually bloat up in lower-salinity water, then shrink as the salinity increases.

The fiddler crab (so called for its one very large front claw that gives it the appearance of a little fiddler) has several adaptations to salt-marsh life. In addition to the gills that all crabs have, fiddler crabs have a primitive lung, enabling them to breathe air as long as they keep the lung moist. They can also survive without oxygen for long periods of time when they tunnel down into the oxygen-deficient mud. Fiddler crabs also enjoy a remarkable salt-and-water regulation system that enables them to maintain constant osmotic equilibrium both in diluted sea water, and in water more concentrated than sea water, as is found in briny tidal ponds that have evaporated over a period of days or weeks.

The salt marsh is rich in birds, which need to adapt less to the environment. At times of low tide, you can see dozens of wading birds and sandpipers feeding on the insect larvae and crustaceans in the exposed mud flats. Clapper rails and marsh wrens nest amid the *Spartina.* Marsh hawks weave back and forth low over the marsh in search of mice, and ospreys scan the deeper water for fish from much higher up. Snowy egrets, great egrets, little green herons, and great blue herons can be seen by themselves or in small groups, stepping daintily along the marsh in search of small fish and other prey. During spring and fall migrations, salt marshes are favorite stopping-over points for many duck species. Raccoons and an occasional river otter are also seen by the lucky early-morning paddler on our salt marshes.

Insects also play an important role in the salt marsh, and efforts to control insects—chiefly mosquitoes—have been the cause of some of the most significant human impact on this ecosystem.

In the 1930s, vast areas of salt marsh were drained by the Civilian Conservation Corps. Evidence of this only moderately successful effort to eliminate standing water in the high salt marsh can still be seen clearly today throughout the salt marshes on southern New England. The long straight ditches a few feet wide that reach into the marsh from the open water—some of which you can actually paddle into a short ways at high tide—are these mosquito-control ditches. Some have now almost disappeared after more than fifty years, but most are remarkably distinct.

Many commercially important fish and shellfish species depend on the salt-marsh ecosystem. Oysters, scallops, various clams, blue crabs, shrimp, bluefish, flounder, and striped bass are among the shellfish and fish found here. In fact, a full two-thirds of the eastern U.S. commercial fish and shellfish catch depends on the salt marsh for at least some phase of its life cycle.

It is the incoming rivers and streams, for the most part, that carry nutrients into the salt marsh to support this productivity—not nutrients generated within the marsh. In the salt marsh, the inflowing fresh water spreads out and deposits its sediment, rich with minerals and nutrients. Unfortunately, this same inflowing water carries pollutants as well. All too often you will see posted signs warning of polluted water that is off-limits to shellfishing. But the salt

Along with the more common Spartina alterniflora *and* S. patens, *you may also see the more dramatic* S. cyno- suroides, *or big cordgrass, along tidal rivers.*

marsh plays a vitally important role in breaking down many of these pollutants. It is like a giant sewage treatment plant in its ability to purify water and extract toxins—but the organisms that help purify the water become toxic in the process. The long-lasting pesticide DDT, used from the late 1940s until the early 1970s was heavily concentrated in salt-marsh organisms, from crustaceans and fish, up the food chain to ospreys (and other predators). By the time DDT was finally banned, the osprey had almost vanished from New England's salt marshes.

Salt-marsh ecosystems are vitally important to us, both economically and biologically. Hundreds of thousands of acres of coastal salt marsh have been lost to development during the past hundred years, and the relatively small remnants of these once-vast stretches of salt marsh from Maine to Florida are still threatened by development and pollution. The best way to appreciate just how exciting and important these resources are is to paddle on them—to feel the tidal current under your boat, and watch the *Spartina* waving in the breeze.

It is up to us—those who appreciate the unique beauty of the salt marsh and who understand the fragile nature of this ecosystem—to guarantee that additional salt-marsh acreage will not be lost to development and pollution. Learn about the salt-marsh environments in your area and talk to local planning officials to find out how you can help protect these places.

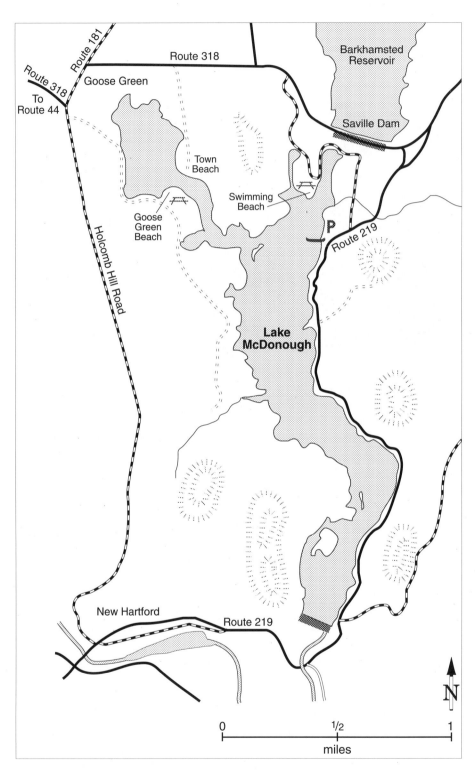

Route 181

Route 318

Route 318

To
Route 44

Goose Green

Barkhamsted
Reservoir

Saville Dam

Town
Beach

Swimming
Beach

Holcomb Hill Road

Goose
Green
Beach

P

Route 219

Lake
McDonough

New Hartford

Route 219

N

| 0 | 1/2 | 1 |

miles

Lake McDonough
Barkhamsted, CT

Just to the south of Barkhamsted Reservoir, which supplies drinking water to the Hartford area, is Lake McDonough. Like Barkhamsted, Lake McDonough is also maintained by the Hartford Metropolitan District, but it is not a public drinking-water supply, and canoeing is permitted. Even though you have to pay both to get into the recreational area and to launch a boat (for a total of $6.50 in 1992), the canoeing is very pleasant—in part, perhaps, because the cost keeps the crowds away.

While there is no development anywhere on the large lake, some sections are nicer than others. I found the section extending to the northwest to be most enjoyable. Motorboats are restricted from this part of the lake, and you are further from highways here (Route 219 extends along the north-south axis of the lake). The shores of this part of the lake are grassy, the water very clean, and the bottom generally sandy. Surprisingly, there is no floating vegetation anywhere on the lake, though it is certainly shallow enough. I suspect that the Metropolitan District lowers the water level each fall to discourage vegetation from getting established. With so little natural vegetation, the lake seems somewhat sterile. I didn't see a turtle anywhere on the lake, and I only saw a few birds, including a family of Canada geese. The one beaver lodge I saw appeared old and long abandoned. An aqueduct carrying fresh water to Hartford extends almost the entire length of the lake, buried at the bottom.

The larger portion of the lake extending south from the launching area has a few very nice islands that provide great picnic spots. The west shore, with its many coves and small inlets to explore, is a lot more interesting than the east shore, along which Route 219 passes. Even on a beautiful sunny Saturday afternoon in mid-August, there only seemed to be fifteen or twenty motorboats on the lake, plus maybe a dozen canoes and rowboats. Fishing is popular here, for such species as largemouth bass, yellow perch, and pickerel.

GETTING THERE: From the end of Route 8 in Winsted, turn right onto Route 44 East. Drive 3.1 miles and turn left onto Route 318. Stay on 318 for 3.0 mile, (follow road signs carefully, as there are a few turns). After crossing over the Saville Dam (you get a great view over both Lake McDonough and Barkhamsted Reservoir), take the first right, then another almost immediate right onto Route 219. After turning onto Route 219, drive 0.4 mile and turn right into the Lake McDonough Recreation Area (you will see a sign indicating boat launch at this turn). After passing the gatehouse, you will turn left toward the boathouse, where you can park and launch your boat. As mentioned, there is a fee both to enter the recreation area and to launch a boat.

If you continue straight instead of turning left after the gatehouse, you will pass in front of the Saville Dam, with an impressive fountain and mammoth doors leading into the face of the dam (tours of this dam are offered periodically) and eventually reach a parking area and swimming beach. This is a nice family beach with lifeguards and plenty of sand. There is another swimming area—the Goose Green Beach—open to visitors and accessible either by car or canoe in the northwest extension of the lake. (A third beach across the cove from Goose Green Beach is open only to residents of Barkhamsted and New Hartford.) A short distance past the fountain on the road to the main beach you will find a trail up to the top of the dam, passing an area known as the Rock Gardens. There are toilet facilities at the boathouse, both beach areas, and at the south end of the lake, across Route 219.

The Lake McDonough Recreation Area is open from the third Saturday in April through Labor Day, and on weekends through September. Boat launching on Lake McDonough is permitted only at the Metropolitan District Commission boat launch. Boating hours are 10 AM to 8 PM weekdays and 8 AM to 8 PM on Saturdays, Sundays, and holidays. Rowboats and paddleboats are available for rent at the boathouse, but not canoes—though you can launch your own boat here. Motorboats are limited to 10 MPH on the lake. For more information, contact the Metropolitan District Commission, 39 Beach Rock Road, Pleasant Valley, CT 06063; 203-379-0916.

Burr Pond

Torrington, CT

Burr Pond is a great spot for a family outing. Those who want to explore the pond by canoe can do so while others hike or enjoy the beach at Burr Pond State Park. For paddlers, there is a boat access at the north end of the pond, right on Burr Mountain Road. Paddling down along the eastern shore from here you will pass the park facilities, including lots of picnic tables nestled in the woods by the shoreline, a small sandy swimming beach, restrooms, and a concession stand. You will see picnic areas all the way around to the dam and outlet. From here on, though, the shoreline is undeveloped. Except on a sunny weekend, you should be able to get away from most of the activity—especially if you plan your visit relatively early in the morning.

The shoreline is generally rocky, with large slabs of rock extending into the water in some places, providing sunny picnic or rest spots. Keep an eye out for the many boulders lurking just beneath the surface, or your canoe will add to their accumulated layers of paint! Trees are predominantly deciduous—red oak, white oak, beech, red maple, white birch, black birch, gray birch, alder, and a few tulip trees—along with white pine and hemlock. During late July and August your paddling along here is likely to be seriously slowed down by the blueberry bushes and their copious fruit. There are a couple of very nice islands on the pond that are well worth a visit. At the extreme southern tip note the waterlogged stumps of a few huge trees that still remain from the creation of the pond almost 150 years ago. Their great spreading root systems are clearly visible under the water and provide protective cover for fish.

Along with paddling here, you might want to do some hiking. A good trail extends all the way around the eighty-eight-acre pond. At the south end, the trail passes a lookout point at Big Rock Cave. On the west shore, near the large island that you can just barely squeeze a canoe around, you may see the Buttrick Memorial Tablet. Philip Buttrick, secretary of Connecticut's Forest and Park Service from 1924 to 1929, helped to plan this preserve and two other unspoiled areas as state forest reserves—immediately west and north from this pond, and he chose this point for his ashes to be spread. Near the pond's outlet, just outside the park is another plaque marking the location of the first condensed-milk factory, in 1857, a few years after Milo Burr built a dam across the confluence of several mountain streams to create the

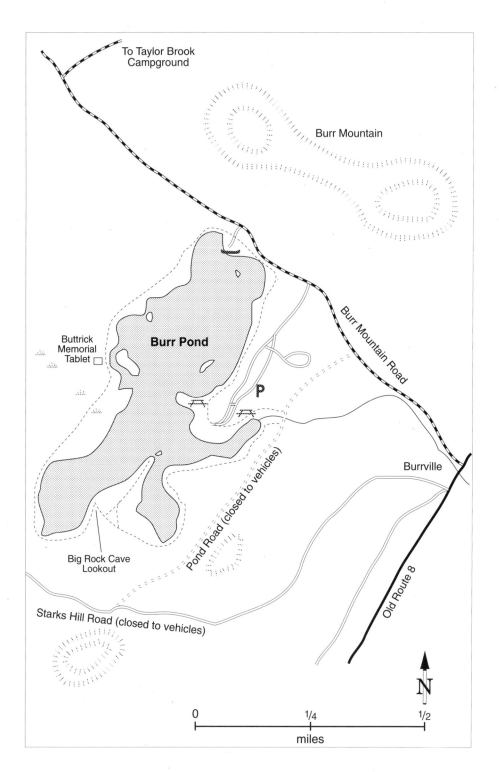

To Taylor Brook
Campground

Burr Mountain

Burr Pond

Buttrick
Memorial
Tablet

Burr Mountain Road

P

Burrville

Big Rock Cave
Lookout

Pond Road (closed to vehicles)

Old Route 8

Starks Hill Road (closed to vehicles)

N

0   1/4   1/2

miles

pond. Inventor and surveyor Gail Borden discovered the process of milk preservation by evaporation and condensation, and here set up the first successful plant for producing and marketing it. Borden's Condensed Milk still bears his name. In 1861, the company relocated to Wassaic, NY, to serve an expanding market including Union troops at the outbreak of the Civil War. The original plant here was destroyed by fire in 1877.

GETTING THERE: To reach Burr Pond, get off Route 8 at Exit 46 and drive east about 0.2 mile to Old Route 8. Take Old Route 8 south for 1.0 mile, then turn right onto Burr Mountain Road (there are signs to Burr Pond State Park). You will reach the entrance to Burr Pond State Park after 0.5 mile, and the public boat access on the left 0.2 mile past the park entrance. There is a fee to get into the park, but you can launch a boat for free at the boat access. Canoes and paddleboats are available for rent in the park.

There is no camping at Burr Pond State Park, but you can camp at the state-run Taylor Brook Campground about two miles away. From the boat access, continue up Burr Mountain Road for another 0.9 mile. Turn right, following the signs for camping, drive another 0.8 mile, then turn left. The entrance to the campground will be on the left after another 0.1 mile. In 1992 campsites were $10 per night. Campers here can get into Burr Pond State Park without paying an additional fee (there is also a trail connecting the two facilities). For more information, contact Burr Pond State Park, 385 Burr Mountain Road, Torrington, CT 06787; 203-482-1817. The campground office phone number is 203-379-0172.

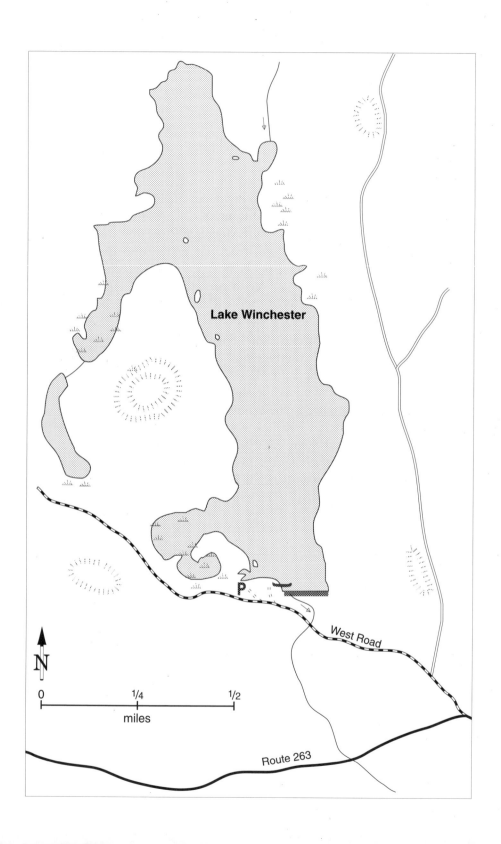

Lake Winchester

N

0   1/4   1/2
miles

West Road

Route 263

Lake Winchester
Winchester, CT

Located in northwestern Connecticut, Lake Winchester is a real beauty. The 229-acre lake is almost totally undeveloped and offers a highly varied shoreline to explore—in short, a great spot for a day of canoeing and one of my favorite paddling spots in this part of the state.

From the boat access at the south end, a deep marshy cove extends around to the west. The floating vegetation is pretty thick here by midsummer—water shield primarily, along with fragrant water lily and bullhead lily. You can't paddle into the very tip of this cove (except in early spring, perhaps) because of the dense vegetation. Toward evening or early in the morning, this is a great spot to watch beavers, which have a lodge on the northern shore of the cove. Another deep inlet farther up the lake extends to the southwest. Like the more southern cove, this is heavily vegetated, particularly at the tip, but it's very much worth exploration. There are a couple of beaver lodges in here as well.

Much of the shoreline around Lake Winchester is open and inviting. While the shrubs are generally thick right at the water, here and there are places where you can disembark and get through the bushes into the woods. Large pine and hemlock trees provide a thick carpet of needles. Amid these conifers are red oak, black birch, gray birch, beech, and red maple. In the spring, you'll see lots of wildflowers here—pink lady's slippers, trillium, and Solomon's seal to mention just a few. You'll also see quite a bit of mountain laurel, both right along the shore and into the woods. When in full bloom, these woods are spectacular. Then in the late summer, you should be able to find plenty of highbush blueberries along the shore—nothing beats picking berries from a canoe!

In general, the water seems very clean. I saw a few freshwater mussels, and the fishing is considered good for largemouth bass, pickerel, yellow perch, and calico bass. An eight-horsepower limit on the lake, plus a lot of old tree stumps either protruding out of the water or lurking just beneath, keeps motorboating to a minimum, so Lake Winchester should be pretty quiet.

GETTING THERE: To reach Lake Winchester, take Route 8 to the end in Winsted. At the end of the exit ramp, turn onto Route 44 West and drive 1.2 miles to Route 263. Turn left onto 263 (follow highway signs carefully, as 263 makes a few turns) and drive for 4.4 miles, staying on 263 as you pass through Winchester Center. Four-tenths of a mile past Winchester Center (4.4 miles from Route 44), 263 bears to the left, but you should continue straight on West Road. Drive another 0.6 mile and you will come to the Lake Winchester boat access and parking area on the right. The boat launch is reached first. You can unload your boat here, then drive just a bit farther up West Road to a large parking area.

If you are driving down Route 272 from Norfolk or Massachusetts, continue past South Norfolk and turn left onto Route 263 East. Drive 1.8 miles on 263 and take a sharp left onto West Road. The boat access will be on the right after another 0.6 mile. There is an outhouse at the parking area. Camping is not permitted around the lake, but nearby camping is available near Burr Pond (see pages 165–167).

Wood Creek Pond

Norfolk, CT

Located near the northwestern tip of Connecticut, Wood Creek Pond is an out-of-the-way body of water offering a very pleasant morning or afternoon of paddling. It is a shallow, heavily vegetated pond that extends about a mile from south to north. The few houses on Wood Creek Pond are set well back from the shoreline and do not detract from the solitude. I did see some land-clearing activity in 1992, however, which might be the first signs of more substantial development to take place here.

Both the far south end and far north end of the pond are marshy. Near the launch point at the south end you may see nesting Canada geese. If the geese have young, notice the adults' defensive posturing if you approach too close. They often ruffle the feathers in their necks to look bigger and more forbidding to any would-be aggressors. As you paddle north, the ground rises fairly steeply from the shore and is heavily wooded with mountain laurel, red maple, and other deciduous trees interspersed with hemlock and white pine.

Very shallow and thick with vegetation, Wood Creek Pond provides hours of exploration and discovery for the quiet paddler.

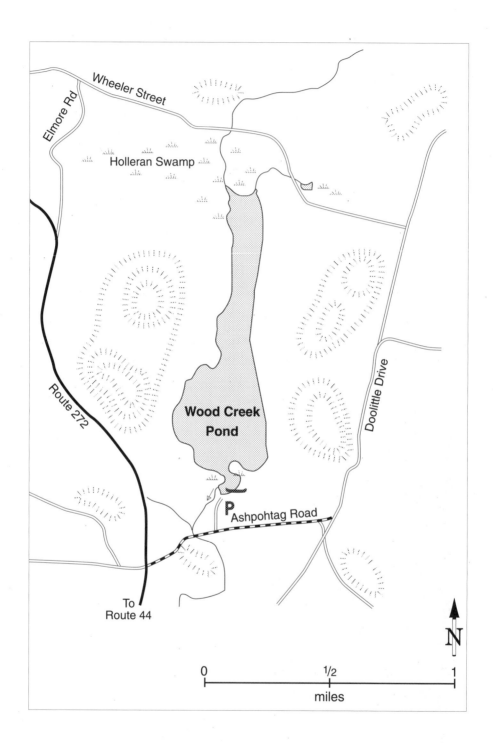

Wheeler Street

Elmore Rd

Holleran Swamp

Route 272

Wood Creek
Pond

Doolittle Drive

P

Ashpohtag Road

To
Route 44

N

0   1/2   1
miles

The surface vegetation can get quite thick; indeed paddling can get pretty tough near the north end by midsummer. You'll see fragrant water lily, water shield, pondweed, and bullhead lily. If you're paddling when the bullhead lily is in bloom, take a few minutes to look at this fascinating flower. The yellow "petals" on the waxy yellow flowers are actually sepals; the true petals are smaller and look more like stamens. In the center of the flower is a wide pistil with yellow cap and reddish sides. One marvels at the evolutionary forces that produced such a unique flower.

The north end of the pond is so shallow as to be almost uncanoeable, with thick soupy muck a few inches beneath the surface made up of decades of only partially decomposed vegetation on its way to becoming peat. If you stick your paddle in, methane and other gases bubble out with the distinctive odor of anaerobic digestion. You have to wind your way carefully around the stumps and submerged logs camouflaged in the soupy water. This part of the pond is much more accessible to the paddler in the early spring before new vegetation sprouts up and when the water level is at its highest. Keep an eye out for great blue herons and nesting songbirds here.

I noticed two beaver lodges on Wood Creek Pond, one on the west side and one on the east. In the shallow water you will see plenty of pumpkinseed sunfish. In places where the bottom is sandy look for the shallow bowl-shaped depressions they make for depositing eggs. The aggressive males stand guard over the eggs until they hatch, fanning them with their tails, then defending the young until they are large enough to survive on their own. These males show such perseverance in caring for their eggs that you can hover right over them in your canoe and watch them from inches away.

GETTING THERE: From the south or east, take Route 44 about ten miles west of Winsted, then turn right (north) onto Route 272 in Norfolk. (If you're coming from the west on 44, turn left onto 272 approximately seven miles from the intersection of Routes 7 and 44.) Drive 1.4 miles north on 272, then turn right onto Ashpohtag Road. Continue for 0.3 mile, and turn left into the Wood Creek Pond boat access. There is parking here for at least twenty cars.

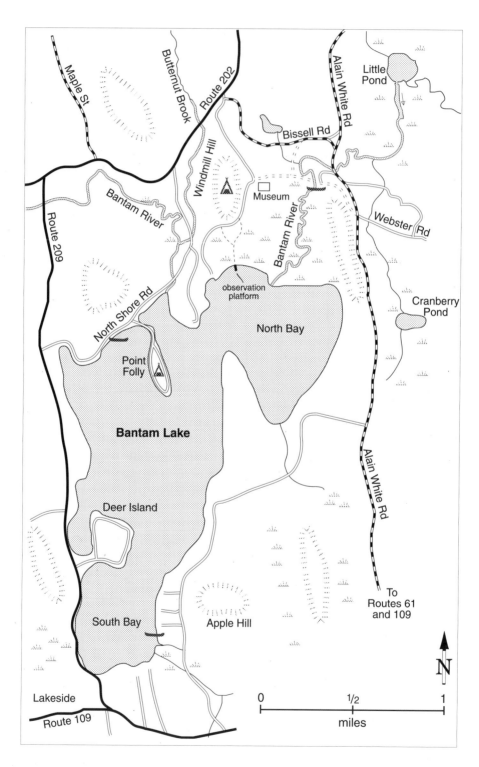

Maple St

Butternut Brook

Route 202

Alain White Rd

Little Pond

Bissell Rd

Windmill Hill

Museum

Bantam River

Webster Rd

Route 209

Bantam River

North Shore Rd

observation platform

North Bay

Cranberry Pond

Point Folly

Bantam Lake

Deer Island

Alain White Rd

Apple Hill

To Routes 61 and 109

South Bay

Lakeside
Route 109

0   1/2   1
miles

N

Bantam Lake/White Memorial Foundation
Litchfield, CT

Bantam Lake, at 933 acres, is the largest natural body of water in Connecticut. The two-mile-long lake is nearly a mile across at its widest point and has a maximum depth of twenty-five feet. Except for the north end, the lake is fairly heavily developed with summer cottages, and summer motorboat use is considerable. A public boat ramp at the southern end of the lake (on East Shore Road off Route 109) attracts boaters from a wide area. To avoid this congestion, I'd stick to the north end of the lake and the Bantam River, which enters and exits the lake here and provides superb quiet water paddling through an extensive tract of land owned and protected by the White Memorial Foundation.

The White Memorial Foundation is a remarkable institution that has created one of southern New England's finest wildlife sanctuaries. The four-thousand-acre sanctuary includes diverse ecosystems, ranging from upland hardwood forests, open fields, and pastures, to marshes, swamps, and open water. Some of the land is managed for forest productivity or wildlife habitat, while other areas are left totally natural and used for research on natural succession. More than thirty-five miles of trails and dirt roads (off-limits to motorized vehicles) take you through these areas. And you can explore the wetlands along the Bantam River by canoe. Motorboats are prohibited from the river, so you can expect to see only other canoeists here, along with lots of wildlife, including an occasional beaver.

The best access point on the Bantam River is about midway between the North Bay of Bantam Lake and Little Pond, by a bridge that is closed to vehicles. From here you can paddle upstream on the gently twisting river about one and one-half miles to Little Pond. There is a noticeable current, but it is slow enough to permit easy upstream paddling. The river passes through thick red maple swamp and marshland, the shores festooned with alder, willow, viburnum, dogwood, buttonbush, winterberry, cattail, bulrush, burr reed, pickerel weed, and grasses galore. You will see signs of beaver along here, and indeed, you may have to drag your canoe over a beaver dam; when I visited, there was one dam with about a four-inch rise that we were able to muscle our way over without getting out. Early in the morning or toward dusk you will probably see a few beavers working or swimming about.

As for birdlife, there are few places in inland Connecticut with as much diversity as is found here. Permanent summer residents that you are likely to see along the river include wood duck, mallard, black duck, blue-winged teal, hooded merganser, pied-billed grebe, Canada goose, mute swan, great blue heron, green heron, spotted sandpiper, belted kingfisher, and tree swallow. Including woodland species, a total of 115 birds are known to nest at the sanctuary, and 246 species have been seen here. The best times for birding are during the spring and fall migrations.

It should take you about an hour to paddle up to Little Pond from the put-in point, longer if you spend a lot of time observing the fauna and flora. Little Pond is small, shallow, weedy, and ringed with marsh. You may see people walking around the pond on a great trail that includes seventen hundred feet of elevated boardwalk—keeping hikers out of the mud and protecting the fragile marsh ecosystem. At Little Pond you can hear some road noise from Routes 202 and 63, which are both less than a mile away, but you still feel pretty much out in the wilds.

Paddling downstream from the access bridge, you will reach the North Bay of Bantam Lake in about a mile along the twisting river. In the morning hours, this section of the lake should be pretty quiet. Nearly the entire shoreline of North Bay is owned by the White Memorial Foundation, though there are some cottages leased by the foundation to summer residents. Paddling to the right when you enter the lake (west), you will pass some old concrete piers that seem very out of place jutting out into the lake and then ending. These once held a railroad spur that was used for ice harvesting. Some of these piers now hold a bird observation platform. The outlet from the lake is just around the short peninsula from this observation platform; you may want to explore along the outlet.

Farther along, you will see a longer peninsula of land extending out into the lake. This is Point Folly. On it is a campground managed by White Memorial Foundation with forty-seven campsites, mostly on the water. Unlike most private campgrounds, Point Folly Campground has lots of space between campsites, so you don't feel that you're camped in a parking lot. There is also a bird observation platform on Point Folly, and a boat-launching ramp on North Shore Road by the campground store. Campground residents can use the Litchfield Town Beach, which is located between the Bantam River inlet and outlet. This campground is open from mid-April until Columbus Day weekend; 1992 rates were a very reasonable $9.25 per night for tent sites and $10.75 for trailer sites. There are no hookups. There is another family campground in a wooded area of the sanctuary of Windmill Hill.

The Windmill Hill Campground has twenty sites, and the 1992 rates were $7 per night.

GETTING THERE: From Route 8, get off at Exit 42 and head west on Route 118. Drive 3.7 miles on 118, and bear right onto Route 254 toward Litchfield. In 1.1 miles you will reach the intersection of Routes 202 and 63 in Litchfield. Turn onto 202 West and drive 2.2 miles. Watch for Bissell Road turning off to the left (there is a sign here for the White Memorial Conservation Center). Turn left and stay to the left on the paved road (a gravel road goes off to the right toward the Conservation Center). Continue on Bissell Road for 0.8 mile, then bear right onto Alain White Road (shown on some maps as Whites Woods Road). Drive along Alain White Road for only about 0.2 mile, crossing over the Bantam River. Immediately after crossing the bridge, take a sharp right onto a small dirt road. Follow this for a little over 0.1 mile to a dead end at a bridge that has been closed. You can park your car along this road, and launch your canoe near the bridge. You have to carry down the bank, and you'll find a good spot just past the bridge (without crossing it), or just before it. If there isn't any space to park at this point, some people also launch canoes from the bridge where you crossed the river on Alain White Road.

While you are here, you should try to visit the small natural history museum (small admission fee charged for nonmembers) with excellent displays on the area wildlife. From the boat access described above, drive back to the paved road, turn left over the bridge, bear left onto Bissell Road, then take the first left onto a gravel road. You will pass along a bend of the river on your left, then turn right to get to the museum, parking area, restrooms, and other facilities. In the museum are a gift shop and bookstore, a nature library, and a bird feeding station. Other activities here include conferences and group retreats, picnicking, nature study courses, field trips, summer nature programs for children, and frequent lecture programs. The White Memorial Foundation is supported by membership. For information on membership, camping, or the foundation's wide-ranging education, conservation, research, or recreation programs, contact the White Memorial Foundation or Conservation Center, P.O. Box 368, Litchfield, CT 06759; 203-567-0857.

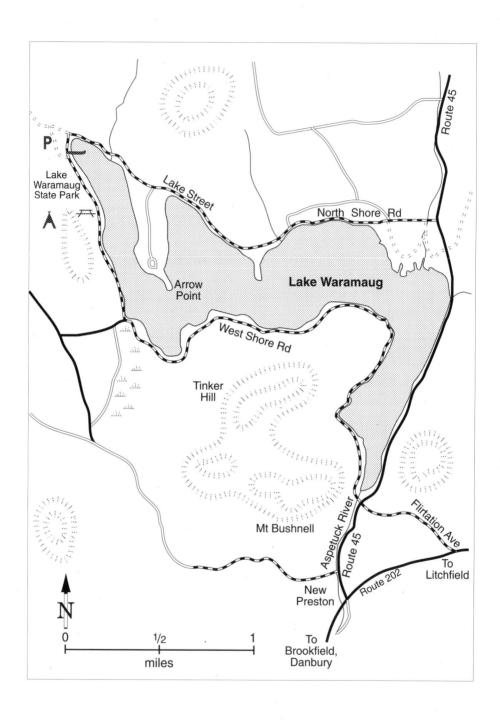

P

Lake Waramaug State Park

Lake Street

North Shore Rd

Arrow Point

Lake Waramaug

West Shore Rd

Tinker Hill

Aspetuck River

Route 45

Flirtation Ave

Route 45

Mt Bushnell

New Preston

Route 202

To Litchfield

To Brookfield, Danbury

Route 45

N

0   1/2   1
miles

Lake Waramaug
Washington, Warren, and Kent, CT

Situated in the foothills of the Berkshire Mountains in western Connecticut and surrounded by rolling farmland and picturesque Victorian-era houses, Lake Waramaug offers enjoyable and very scenic canoeing—particularly in the autumn when the rich fall colors attract photographers from far and wide. While Lake Waramaug has moderate motorboat use during nice summer weekends, the lack of a public boat ramp pretty well limits motorboat use to lakeside residents—quite unlike nearby Candlewood Lake, for example. Waramaug is a well-known destination for city dwellers seeking a weekend refuge in the country. Four inns situated around the lake offer lodging and dining in country elegance, with access to the water for patrons interested in canoeing. Those looking for more rustic lodging can camp at Lake Waramaug State Park.

The northwestern section of the 680-acre lake—extending from Lake Waramaug State Park down to Arrow Point—is the least developed part of the lake, though there is a picnic area here. During a sunny summer weekend the shoreline can be crowded with picnickers. Most of the shoreline is wooded and dotted with houses, many of which are large and elegant. You will see some huge old chestnut oaks here, along with sugar maple, red maple, red oak, white birch, beech, hemlock, and a few black gum (which turns a brilliant red in late summer or early fall). Your eyes will also be drawn to the open fields overlooking the lake from the south and west. Some of this is farmland and some a golf course.

Along with motorboat use, the lake is popular for rowing and sailing: in May Lake Waramaug is the site of the Women's National Rowing Regatta. Area prep schools also use the lake for rowing practice. If you want some exercise, this is a great place for some distance paddling—a warm-up canoe trip around the eight-mile-plus perimeter before breakfast will give you a hearty appetite!

I was surprised to find the water quite cloudy when I visited in the autumn, and I question how nice the swimming is at the state park. Portions of the lake are very thick with underwater vegetation, primarily a species of pondweed with long rippling leaves (*Potamogetin spp.*). The bottom is generally sandy and the shoreline rocky.

GETTING THERE: Lake Waramaug is off the beaten path and a little hard to get to. From Danbury and New York, you can take Interstate 84 to Exit 7 and drive north on Route 7/202. When the four-lane highway ends, continue north on 202 through New Milford and all the way up to New Preston (202 makes a few turns; follow the signs). In New Preston, bear left onto Route 45 North. (The distance from Route 84 to New Preston is about twenty miles.) Continuing north on Route 45, you will come to a fork at the south end of Lake Waramaug (0.5 mile from Route 202). You can bear left onto West Shore Road here or continue straight, driving along the lake on Route 45 for another 1.6 miles, then turn left on North Shore Road. West Shore Road is narrower, so the signs to Lake Waramaug State Park direct you to the North Shore route. With either road, you will follow the lake around to the northwestern end, where you will see the entrance to Lake Waramaug State Park. (On West Shore Road the distance to the park entrance is 3.8 miles; on North Shore Road, the distance is 2.3 miles, not including the stretch along Route 45.) From the parking area at Lake Waramaug State Park you have to carry your canoe across the road and launch from the shore; there is no ramp or parking by the water.

There are eighty-eight campsites at Lake Waramaug State Park, overlooking—but not on—the lake. Some sites are open and some wooded. For information on the park and camping, write to Lake Waramaug State Park, 30 Lake Waramaug Road, New Preston, CT 06777; 203-868-2592. Those looking for more elegant accommodations can stay at one of the four inns located on the lake: Birches Inn (203-868-0229); the Inn on Lake Waramaug (203-868-0563); Boulders Inn (203-868-0541); or Hopkins Inn (203-868-7295). Connected with Hopkins Inn is the Hopkins Vineyard, which offers wine tasting and self-guided vineyard tours. When you aren't canoeing or sampling wine at the Hopkins Vineyard, you might want to visit some of the small antique and craft shops in the restored milltown of New Preston, just south of the lake.

Squantz Pond
New Fairfield, CT

Squantz Pond adjoins and appears to be an extension of Candlewood Lake—Connecticut's largest lake at over 5400 acres and with seventy-two miles of shoreline. But it is not. The two are divided by Route 39, and there is no connection between them. In fact, the 288-acre Squantz Pond already existed at the time Candlewood Lake was created in the 1930s (more about Candlewood later). Though Squantz Pond could hardly be characterized as a quiet or remote body of water, it offers about the best canoeing in southwestern Connecticut. Indeed, if one can avoid busy summer weekends and stick to the western shore—instead of the heavily developed eastern side, Squantz is a very nice place. You might even get used to the noise from Route 39, which extends along its entire eastern shore.

Massive granite boulders line the undeveloped western shore of Squantz Pond. Hemlock trees sweep down over the water, mountain laurel is nestled amid the granite boulders—some of which are covered with polypody fern—and tall oaks and hickories provide a deep shady woodland just in from the shoreline. You can pull up almost anywhere along here, tie your canoe to a tree or rock, and enjoy a walk in the woods—there is an informal leaf-carpeted trail extending along most of the shoreline, rising above the steep rock faces in places—or enjoy a picnic lunch. You might also enjoy swimming from the shore here, but be aware that the water is murky and there are many hidden boulders. Diving or jumping in from the boulders is very dangerous. The western shoreline is in Pootatuck State Forest.

While most of Squantz Pond is fairly deep, the northern tip is shallow and marshy. I saw dozens of painted turtles in this small protected inlet, along with mallards and a handful of wood ducks amid some small patches of reeds and cattail. Don't get your hopes up too much, however. This is a very small pocket of marsh and not very far from houses, docks, and motorboats. If you enjoy paddling around marshy areas, see the section on Bantam Lake (about twenty miles away), which includes a wonderful inlet river that is teeming with wildlife.

While to some of us Squantz Pond will seem built up and crowded with motorboats, there are far more boats across Route 39 in Candlewood Lake. The two public launch points on Candlewood have parking for a total of six hundred cars with trailers, and there are thousands of motorboats at private docks and marinas. Intimidated by what has been

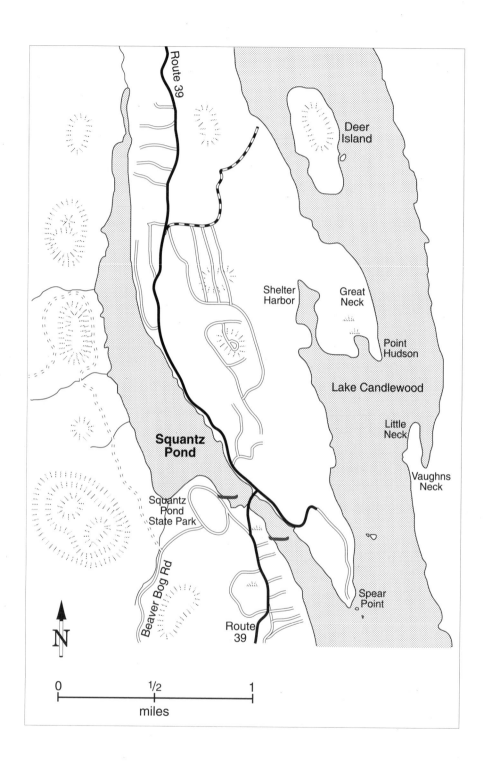

Route 39

Deer
Island

Shelter
Harbor

Great
Neck

Point
Hudson

Lake Candlewood

**Squantz
Pond**

Little
Neck

Vaughns
Neck

Squantz
Pond
State Park

Beaver Bog Rd

Route
39

Spear
Point

N

0   1/2   1
miles

described as the Long Island Expressway of lakes, I have not paddled on Candlewood, but can imagine that in just the right conditions and just the right time, it could be pleasant. It would have to be early in the morning, midweek, before Memorial Day or after Labor Day, and on a calm day. Most of Candlewood's long fingers extending to the north and south have considerable development along their shores. Some areas could be quite nice, though. For example, if you launch at the boat ramp on Squantz Cove—just a quarter-mile from the Squantz Pond access—paddle out around Spear Point and across to the western side of Vaughn's Neck, you will come to an undeveloped stretch of shoreline with a picnic area maintained by Connecticut Light and Power. Shelter Harbor and Point Hedden, across from Little Neck, also look inviting.

GETTING THERE: To reach Squantz Pond, take Interstate 84 to Exit 6 in Danbury, and drive north on Route 37 toward New Fairfield. Stay on 37 for 4.6 miles, then turn right onto Route 39. Follow 39 for 3.8 miles; the entrance to Squantz Pond State Park—where the boat launch is located—will be on the left. (Just before reaching Squantz Pond State Park you will pass the Squantz Cove boat access onto Candlewood Lake on the right.) Drive into Squantz Pond State Park, and stay to the right, following signs to the boat landing. There is space for about fifty cars here, fewer if they have trailers. There is a large picnic area in the park, along with restrooms, drinking water, concessions, and hiking trails. For information on Squantz Pond or the park, contact Squantz Pond State Park, 178 Shortwoods Road, New Fairfield, CT 06810; 203-797-4165.

# Rhode Island

Bowdish Reservoir
Glocester, RI

Bowdish Reservoir is an interesting spot. Unfortunately it is a lot less interesting than it apparently was at one time. Before flooding, the reservoir was a large bog. Today, the only remnants of the bog are a few floating sphagnum islands near the center of the reservoir. When the water level was raised, these mats broke loose from the bog and floated to the surface. They are anchored there by tree roots.

On these islands you can observe some quite rare bog plants that are usually seen much farther north. Among these species are black spruce (a conifer with extremely short needles), Atlantic white cedar, leatherleaf, bog laurel, bog rosemary, sundew, pitcher plant, and—rarest of all—a dwarf mistletoe that lacks roots and always grows in association with black spruce. Looking at older maps, I believe these islands are smaller than they were at one time, and I suspect they will disappear altogether eventually—perhaps the victim of motorboat wakes.

Bowdish Reservoir is a far cry from wilderness. The southwestern edge of the reservoir is fairly developed and bounded by heavily traveled Route 44. Even at the far eastern end, by the George Washington Management Area, you can still hear the cars and trucks. There is also a mammoth private campground extending along most of the northern shore of the pond. The Bowdish Lake Camping Area has to be one of the largest private campgrounds I've seen, with 450 sites along a sprawling network of roads. Like most private campgrounds, this one seems to be geared primarily toward trailer and RV camping; as you paddle along the shore, it seems a bit like a huge trailer park. (To its credit, though, the campground is somewhat more spread out than most, with quite a bit of space between the heavily wooded sites.)

The shores of Bowdish Reservoir are generally rocky. Huge slabs of granite extend down into the water in places, including near the boat launch at the eastern tip. The small island in the reservoir's southern extension appears to be mostly solid rock (unfortunately, this island is privately owned and has a house on it, so is not open to exploration). The forested land of the George Washington Management Area along the eastern end of the reservoir is readily accessible to hikers and picnickers—just find a break in the shoreline shrubs and land your canoe. There are also several very attractive trails through the surrounding oak/hemlock forest that you can reach from the parking area near the boat launch. Dominant species here are hemlock, three oaks (white, red, and scarlet), black birch, white pine, and mountain laurel. At the edge of the water you will also find lots of highbush blueberry and sweet pepperbush, which has very fragrant, late-blooming white flower spikes.

There is also quite a bit of vegetation in the reservoir itself. Underwater plants include water milfoil, fanwort, and bladderwort. Floating plants include water shield and bullhead lily.

Bowdish Reservoir is a fairly large body of water (226 acres) with an average depth of less than six feet and a maximum depth of eleven feet. In a strong wind, sizable waves can build up across the open water, so use caution paddling here. The reservoir is fished for warmwater species, including largemouth bass, yellow perch, chain pickerel, and bullhead catfish, though an overabundance of sunfish has apparently stunted growth of the more desirable game fish.

GETTING THERE: Bowdish Reservoir is located just north of Route 44 in northwestern Rhode Island. If driving west on Route 44, continue for 4.5 miles after passing the turnoff for Routes 100 and 102 North in Chepachet, and turn right into the George Washington Management Area. Continue on this road for about 0.3 mile and bear left toward the boat launch. There is room for a half-dozen cars to park right by the boat access, and space for more in the parking area above.

The George Washington Management Area has forty-three "primitive" tent and trailer campsites and two shelters in a wooded area overlooking Bowdish Reservoir. Rates in 1992 for the tent/trailer sites were $8 per night for Rhode Island residents, $12 for nonresidents. For more information, contact the George Washington Management Area, 2185

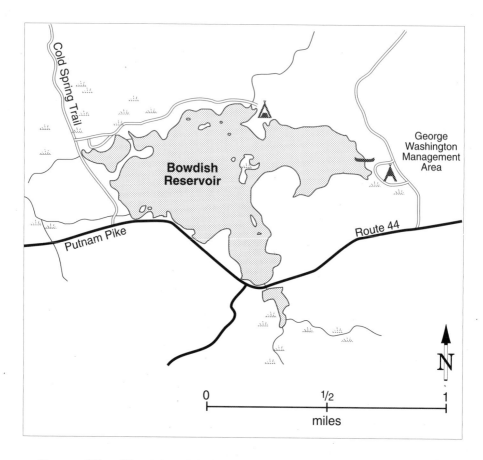

Putnam Pike, Chepachet, RI 02814; 401-568-2013. For information on the private campground on the north shore of the reservoir, contact Bowdish Lake Camping Area, P.O. Box 25, Chepachet, RI 02814; 401-683-0254. In 1992 wooded campsites here ranged in price from $14 to $25 per night, with somewhat lower rates for "field camping."

Eastern Painted Turtle
Quiet Water Companion

You won't have to spend very much time out paddling on our lakes and ponds before you spot your first painted turtle. But getting a really good look at one may be a little more difficult. The Eastern painted turtle, *Chrysemys picta,* is the most visible of our turtle species. (The much larger and more dramatic snapping turtle may actually be more common, but its bottom-dwelling habits keep it out of view most of the time.) On marshy ponds well suited to painted turtles, I have seen literally hundreds of them basking in the sun on half-submerged logs, grassy tussocks, or mud banks—always within easy reach of underwater safety. Painted turtles are very alert to danger; if you are talking as you paddle along, or if you have an aluminum canoe and bang the sides with your paddle, they may disappear from view long before you get close enough to have a good look. I've found that I see the largest numbers of painted turtles when I'm quietly paddling alone and taking my time.

The painted turtle has a smooth, fairly flat, gently arched top shell (carapace) that reaches a length of seven inches. The carapace is patterned and can be quite colorful, thus the name. Narrow lines of yellow separate the dark olive green or black scutes (the interlocking plates that were evolutionarily adapted from vertebrae to form the turtle's shell), and a wider red or orange band can usually be seen along the outer edge of the shell (although these colors may be hidden by a brownish deposit that sometimes forms on the shell). On the head and neck are distinctive yellow stripes. The bottom shell (plastron) is yellow and sometimes marked with dark blotches. Without examining painted turtles closely, it is difficult to tell the sexes apart; males are smaller than females, and have longer tails and longer front claws.

Painted turtles are found throughout much of the United States and range farther north than any other turtle species. There are four distinct subspecies of painted turtle, two of which can be found in southern New England. Our more common Eastern painted turtle (*Chrysemys picta picta*) can be distinguished because it is the only turtle in which the large scutes on the carapace are lined up in rows across the back (side to side). With the Midland painted turtle (*Chrysemys picta marginata*), also found in some parts of our region, these scutes alternate instead of running straight across. Unless you get close enough to get a really good look, or have binoculars, it may be hard to distinguish these subspecies.

The painted turtle diet consists of both plant and animal material.

From your canoe you may see them underwater, feeding on submerged vegetation and various crustaceans, tadpoles, snails, and insect larvae. But they don't seem to spend that much time feeding. Mostly you will see painted turtles basking in the sun. This habit is most often attributed to just that—absorbing the warm rays of the sun—but there is some evidence that the basking also helps to dislodge leeches that can attach themselves to turtles. You will sometimes see territorial disputes on prime logs or mud banks—especially if there are few basking locations on the pond—but you are just as likely to see the turtles stacked on top of one another several deep, in *Yertle the Turtle* fashion, seemingly oblivious to territorial concerns.

Painted turtles mate during the spring or summer, with most activity from late April through mid-June. If you see one or more turtles swimming around a stationary individual, the ones swimming are probably males courting a female. One to two months after mating, the female leaves the water to build a nest and deposit a clutch of eggs. Nests are usually made in open sloping sand or gravel banks or even lawns receiving lots of sunlight and not too far from water. The female will dig a shallow nest with her hind feet and deposit seven to nine (sometimes up to twenty) soft-shelled eggs. She may also build several false nests, perhaps in an effort to mislead the skunks, raccoons, and other predators that consume up to 90 percent of the turtle's eggs.

One of the most unique aspects of painted turtles has only recently been well understood: the ability of hatchlings to withstand freezing. Especially in more northern parts of their range, painted turtle young often overwinter in their underground nests after hatching in the fall. With the nest just a few inches deep, temperatures can drop well below freezing for periods of time. The hatchlings effectively "freeze" when the temperature drops low enough—with muscle activity, breathing, heartbeat, and blood flow totally stopping—yet they usually recover fully when the temperature rises. While most biological functions stop, some minimal brain activity continues, and only about half of their body fluids actually freeze solid. As the temperature drops below freezing, ice begins forming in the turtle's extremities and grows inward, but high concentrations of sugars in the blood work like antifreeze to keep the critical body core fluids from solidifying. While a few other reptiles and amphibians exhibit similar freezing adaptations, none are as well adapted as painted turtle hatchlings. After the first year, however, even painted turtles lose the ability to survive freezing.

In the pond, painted turtles hibernate at above-freezing temperatures in the bottom mud—an area almost devoid of oxygen. Though less unique among turtle species, the ability to hibernate underwater for periods up to three or four months without coming up for air is also fascinating. During periods of very low activity, many turtles and frogs can "breathe" (absorb oxygen and release carbon dioxide) directly through specialized membranes. But painted turtles, and closely related sliders, can survive in totally deoxygenated water for a period of several months. Indeed, these turtles have the greatest known tolerance for oxygen deprivation of any vertebrate in the animal kingdom, with an ability to survive in water totally devoid of oxygen for up to 150 days. Specialized biochemical adaptations make their survival possible. They store large reserves of the carbohydrate fuel glycogen, which can be broken down to produce energy without using oxygen (a process called glycolysis). Because lactic acid is produced during glycolysis, another adaptation is required: the release of calcium and magnesium from the turtle's shell to buffer the acid.

And you thought you were looking at just an ordinary pond dweller, didn't you! Instead, the painted turtle is a veritable treasure trove of fascinating and unique biological adaptations that enable it to survive the harsh conditions of New England and southern Canada.

If you are interested in turtles, you will enjoy *The Year of the Turtle: A Natural History* by David Carroll (Camden House Publishing, Charlotte, VT, 1991), a wonderful naturalist's account of forty years of turtle observation in New England.

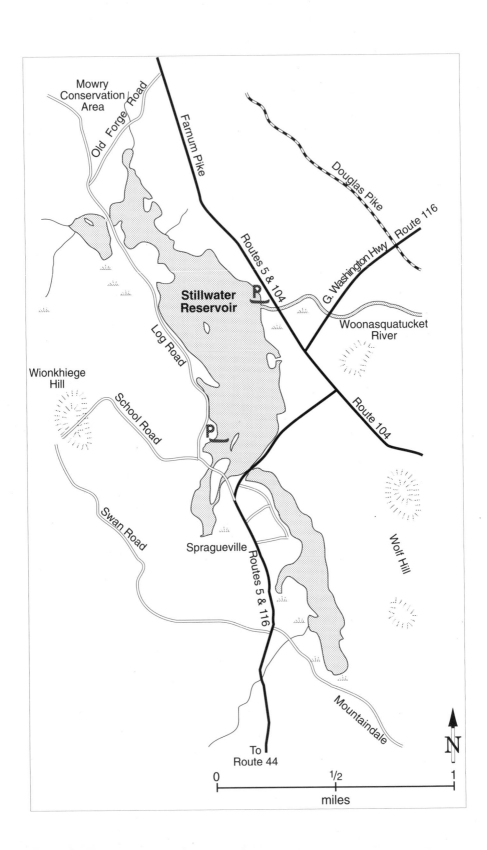

Mowry
Conservation
Area

Old Forge Road

Farnum Pike

Douglas Pike

G. Washington Hwy — Route 116

Routes 5 & 104

**Stillwater
Reservoir**

Woonasquatucket
River

Log Road

Wionkhiege
Hill

School Road

Route 104

Swan Road

Spragueville

Wolf Hill

Routes 5 & 116

Mountaindale

To
Route 44

N

0   1/2   1

miles

Stillwater Reservoir

Smithfield, RI

Stillwater Reservoir, also known as Woonasquatuck Reservoir and Stump Pond, is a very pleasant spot for a day of paddling. The 304-acre reservoir is shallow (average depth eleven feet; maximum fifteen feet), and some areas are quite weedy. Once heavily polluted and prone to severe summer drawdowns, Stillwater Reservoir has dramatically improved in recent years, following shutdown of several of the region's most polluting industrial facilities. Development is heavy in certain areas—including a new condominium development on the east shore of the main reservoir, a cluster of houses on the west shore three-quarters of the way up the lake, and lots of houses and condominiums along the west shore of the southern extension in Spragueville—but portions of the reservoir feel relatively remote and wild. A little-used road extends along much of the western shore, and traffic from Route 5/104 can be heard to the east. At the northern end on the eastern shore is an industrial development, but it is set well back and is pretty well hidden by trees.

During a morning paddle in mid-April I saw as many as fifty painted turtles, a snapping turtle (just its nose extending above water), a dozen or more mallard ducks, a few Canada geese, and a pair of gorgeous wood ducks. You'll find blueberries along the mossy banks in midsummer, and farther inland the area is heavily wooded, with red oak and white oak predominating. Red maple is common close to shore, and you'll see willows in some areas. For some reason, there has been a considerable dieback of red oak along the west shore—perhaps pollution. While it is a bit disconcerting to see all the dead treetops, it provides a veritable paradise for woodpeckers, which can be heard drumming around most of the reservoir. Fishing is popular here for warm-water species, including yellow perch, largemouth bass, bullhead, pickerel, and northern pike—though I suspect few of the fish are eaten.

If you feel adventurous, you might want to explore an isolated extension of the reservoir near the northern end on the west side. You can usually slip a canoe through the culvert that runs under Log Road to reach this area, but the culvert is narrow—probably too narrow for the largest canoes—and even in a small canoe, you have to lie down and pull yourself through. (Watch out for anglers fishing from the road.) You will see a narrow island in this part of the reservoir with an out-of-place stone wall running down the center of it—evidence that the reservoir did not always exist. At the northern tip of the main reservoir is a tiny segment of water reachable by paddling under a wooden bridge. Though very shallow and weedy in summer, this area is thick with painted turtles.

You can (just barely) paddle under the Route 5/116 overpass into the southern extension of the reservoir, but it's not really worth the effort. You have to lie down in your canoe to get under two large pipes that extend below the bridge, and the shoreline south of the bridge has very heavy development along it. There is also a large quarry at the south end, marring the natural landscape.

GETTING THERE: From Providence or the south, Stillwater Reservoir can be reached from Route 44. Driving west on 44, pass I-295 and turn right onto Route 5 North. From the point at which Route 116 joins Route 5 from the south (a little over a mile from Route 44), continue another 1.2 miles and make a shallow left onto Log Road. Drive 0.3 mile (passing the fire department) and bear right at the fork (staying on Log Road). You will reach a parking area and boat ramp on the right in another 0.1 mile. There is an overflow parking area just past the main area, also on the right. There is room for thirty to fifty cars in these two parking areas.

There is another access point to the reservoir that is suitable for carry-in boats, this one on the east side and farther north—on Route 5 and 104 just north of the reservoir outlet. This parking area is 0.5 mile north of the junction of Routes 5 and 104, and 0.3 mile north of the split of 116 and Routes 5/104. Driving north, the parking area is on the left. There is room for fifteen to twenty cars here. Note that this access point is closer to the best canoeing sections of the reservoir.

Near the north end of Stillwater Reservoir, on Old Forge Road, there is a beautiful picnic area and hiking trail. The Mowry Conservation Area, managed by the Smithfield Conservation Committee, is situated along a fast-flowing brook that flows around huge boulders, one of which overhangs the brook. From the Route 5/104 access, drive north and take your first left onto Old Forge Road. The Mowry Conservation Area will be on the right with parking on the left. From the main boat access on Log Road, drive north, crossing over the northwest extension of the reservoir, and take the right fork onto Old Forge Road. The conservation area is on the left shortly past the fork, with parking along the right side of the road.

Olney Pond
Lincoln, RI

Just minutes from downtown Providence, Olney Pond offers surprisingly good paddling. The heavily wooded shoreline is dotted with beautiful granite boulders, some striated with bands of quartz, or blazened with clusters of polypody fern. The 120-acre pond is undeveloped except for the recreational facilities of Lincoln Woods State Park—and herein lies the problem: Olney Pond is often extremely crowded with recreational users on weekends and sunny weekday afternoons. The road extending around the pond perimeter is used by hikers, bicyclists, roller skaters, and joggers, many of whom come from nearby offices for a break during the day. Being so close to Providence and so attractive, the heavy use isn't surprising, but you should be prepared for it. Also, Route 146 passes very close to the pond, so highway noise can be bothersome.

There is a particularly beautiful rocky cove at the extreme northern tip of the pond, where you need to wind your way carefully around huge boulders extending from the water. Red oak is the dominant tree species in the surrounding woods; other species include white oak, dogwood, white ash, hickory, and, close to shore, red maple. At a trail

Olney Pond, with huge granite boulders along its shores, is a real gem. Expect heavy recreational use, however, because Lincoln Woods State Park is very popular.

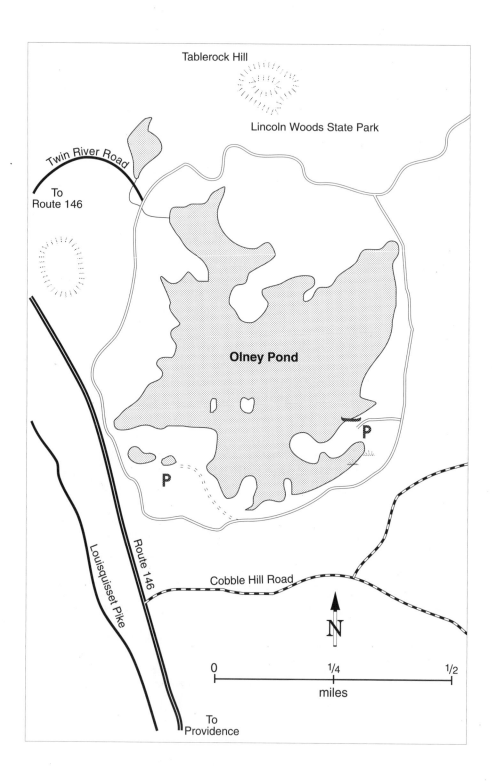

Tablerock Hill

Lincoln Woods State Park

Twin River Road

To
Route 146

Olney Pond

P

P

Louisquisset Pike

Route 146

Cobble Hill Road

N

0   1/4   1/2
miles

To
Providence

junction near the pond's northernmost cove you will notice a marker describing the Zachariah Allen Woodlot, planted in 1820. About a third of a mile from here, to the northwest on Quinsnicket Hill, Allen took ownership of a forty-acre worn-out, barren pasture and planted acorns and chestnuts in what was one of the earlier experiments in silvaculture. Today, more than 170 years later, you can visit that woodlot in the northwest corner of this state park. A marker by an old spring site describes this unusual businessman-botanist and his investment through planting acorns and chestnuts in plowed soil. Even before the area became a state park, city folks from nearby Providence visited the woodlot via steam-cars to Lonsdale or "electrics" from Pawtucket. The Quinsnicket Hill woods are full of ferns and wildflowers, including such uncommon species as maidenhair spleenwort and smooth yellow violet.

Motorboats are permitted on the pond, but there is a ten-horsepower limit, which precludes water-skiing and keeps out larger boats. Most of the boating here is for fishing. Even though the pond is shallow (maximum depth fifteen feet), it is stocked with trout and landlocked salmon, and fishing for these species is considered quite good—though the fishing pressure is quite high and the salmonids may be fished out fairly early in the season. There are also bluegill sunfish, pickerel, and largemouth bass in the pond.

GETTING THERE: Olney Pond is readily accessible a few minutes off Route 146, just north of Providence. Get off at the Twin River Road exit for Lincoln Woods (about four miles north of I-95), and follow signs to Lincoln Woods State Park, just to the east. The access road leads to a gatehouse (there is a day-use fee, with season passes available) and a loop that extends around the pond. The primary recreational areas and parking are to the right. Follow signs to the boat launch. The access road to the boat launch area is not open until fishing season begins. Lincoln Woods State Park also offers picnicking, swimming, game fields, numerous hiking trails, restrooms, and a concession stand.

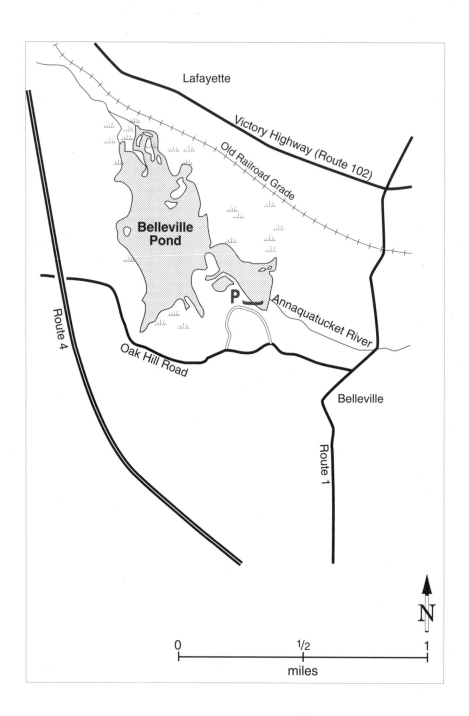

Lafayette

Victory Highway (Route 102)

Old Railroad Grade

**Belleville
Pond**

Annaquatucket River

Route 4

Oak Hill Road

Belleville

Route 1

P

0   1/2   1

miles

N

Belleville Pond

North Kingstown, RI

Belleville Pond has some of the best inland marsh habitat that I've seen. It is absolutely full of waterfowl, and its shoreline provides hours of quiet exploration. There is no development right on the pond, though a couple of houses are visible at the southwestern tip. The 159-acre pond, like many in Rhode Island, is very shallow, with a maximum depth of eight feet and an average depth of just five feet. The shallow water is highly productive biologically, which supports the waterfowl populations.

During an October visit—admittedly when both summer residents and migrants could have been present—I saw pied-billed grebes, mallards, black ducks, bufflehead, wood ducks, American coot, green-winged teal, cormorants, Canada geese, mute swans, great blue herons, and marsh wrens. During the warmer months, the pond is full of painted turtles. Marsh and aquatic plants here include cattail, phragmites, swamp loosestrife, bulrush, pickerel weed, bullhead lily, fragrant water lily, water shield, duckweed, fanwort, and bladderwort. The underwater vegetation (fanwort and bladderwort primarily) is dense in places, providing good habitat for such fish species as largemouth bass, chain pickerel, bullhead, yellow perch, golden shiners, and sunfish. A fish ladder at the outlet (Annaquatucket River, which flows three miles into Narragansett Bay) enables alewife to swim upstream into Belleville Pond to spawn, so this species is also present seasonally. Belleville Pond is considered one of the better largemouth bass ponds in the state.

At the north end of the pond, poorly defined, marshy islands abound. Quietly exploring around these islands and the increasingly narrow channels of open water between them as you near the north end, you are almost sure to see some birds. Be aware, though, that Belleville Pond is heavily used for duck hunting in the fall. You will see lots of duck-hunting blinds here. If you are considering a fall visit, be sure to check on the waterfowl hunting seasons, which are different each year (contact the Rhode Island Division of Fish and Wildlife, Oliver Stedman Government Center, 4808 Tower Hill Road, Wakefield, RI 02879; 401-789-3094). While most duck hunters are good outdoorsmen who truly care about the environment, I was disappointed here to see hundreds of empty shotgun shells strewn around the marsh and in the water by the blinds. And I saw one injured black duck, unable to fly and sure to face death with winter approaching.

Around the less marshy sections of the pond, deciduous trees dominate: red oak, white oak, red maple, aspen, gray birch, black gum, and scarlet oak. On the more solid sections of shoreline highbush blueberry, sweet pepperbush, and alder provide shelter and food for a wide variety of songbirds. You can hear the highway (Route 4) through the trees, but it doesn't detract too much from the solitude here.

GETTING THERE: If you are coming from the south, follow Route 1, and stay on 1 where it splits off from Route 4. Continue north for another 1.2 miles and turn left off Route 1 onto Oak Hill Road. After 0.3 mile, turn right on a dirt road. There is a sign here indicating Town of North Kingstown recreation land. The boat access is 0.2 mile down this road, near a ballfield. This road loops back to Oak Hill Road.

If you are driving from the north, take Route 4 South to Route 102 East. Drive 2.3 miles on 102 and turn right onto Route 1 South. Stay on Route 1 for 0.7 mile, and turn right onto Oak Hill Road. Then follow directions as described above. Camping is not permitted here.

Worden Pond and Great Swamp

South Kingstown, RI

Worden Pond and the rivers leading into and out of it provide some of the best canoeing in Rhode Island. There is a public boat-access point at the south end of Worden Pond, from which one can reach all the areas covered in this section. If you can arrange a drop-off and pickup, however, a better option is a one-way trip into Worden Pond on the Chipuxet River from Taylor's Landing (including exploration north into Thirty Acre and Hundred Acre ponds if you have the time), and then out of the pond on the Pawcatuck River to the Biscuit City Road access.

Thirty Acre Pond and Hundred Acre Pond

From Taylor's Landing on Route 138 in West Kingston you can make an enjoyable trip upstream on the Chipuxet River—depending on the water level—into Thirty Acre and Hundred Acre ponds. Paddling up the narrow river, you are likely to come to a beaver dam that you will have to drag your canoe over. (If this dam is not present, access up the narrow channel may be blocked by brush and low water.) Above the beaver dam is the widened section of the Chipuxet known as Thirty

If you paddle north on the Chipuxet River, you will probably have to drag your canoe over this beaver dam. Above the dam the river widens out, forming Thirty Acre Pond.

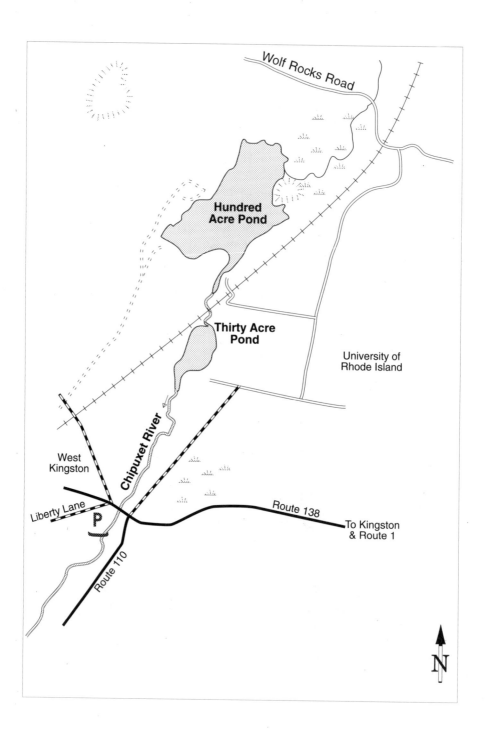

Acre Pond, a gorgeous pond rich in wildlife. The pond is surrounded largely by woodland and agricultural research fields owned by the University of Rhode Island—you may notice the irrigation pumps along the shore that are used for these fields. There is only one house on the pond, though you may also see (and hear) a small brick pump-house near the south end of Thirty Acre Pond where potable water is pumped from an underground aquifer (beneath the shallow pond) for the University. I saw a number of pied-billed grebes amid the pond's thick vegetation (water lilies, fanwort, pickerel weed, burr reeds, swamp loosestrife), as well as great blue herons, kingfishers, and painted turtles. You will see an occasional Amtrak train speeding past the pond at the north end.

At the north end of Thirty Acre Pond, you can paddle under the railroad bridge—a cavernous arched stone-and-concrete bridge—and a second much lower bridge that you have to duck under to get into Hundred Acre Pond (Watch for rocks under the railroad bridge at times of low water.) Though far more developed than Thirty Acre Pond, Hundred Acre Pond is still quite nice, at least on a quiet morning in the spring or fall. There are perhaps two dozen houses and cottages along here and mostly small boats (canoes and small motorboats), though I saw one large high-horsepower motorboat that seemed very out of place. You will see quite a bit of black gum along the perimeter. The less-developed eastern shore of Hundred Acre Pond is heavily grown in mountain laurel, highbush blueberry, and sweet pepperbush. The northern end of the pond is marshy, and you can follow the winding Chipuxet River on up through the dense swamp of red maple, cedar, alder, and swamp loosestrife that is full of songbirds. The canoeable channel narrows and the vegetation converges from the two sides until you are finally blocked from further progress near the Wolf Rocks Road. (The vegetation along this section of the Chipuxet may occasionally be pruned back, as some books refer to a put-in point on Wolf Rocks Road.) Paddling from Taylor's Landing up to here takes a couple of hours if you allow time for watching birds and perhaps dipping a fishing line into the water.

Chipuxet River into Worden Pond

The more common canoe route from Taylor's Landing is downstream into Worden Pond—a distance of about three miles (if the tight curves were straightened out). The river here is narrow and tightly twisting through the Great Swamp. The current is definitely noticeable, but not

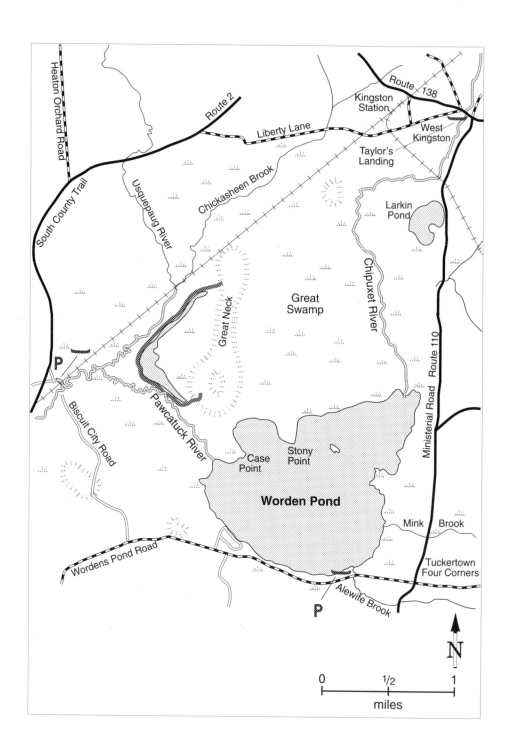

so strong that you couldn't paddle back against it if necessary. Paddling generally south, you pass through red maple swamp, with patches of cattail, bulrush, and phragmites on the oxbow curves and thick stands of such shrubs as sweet gale, dogwood, winterberry, and sweet pepperbush. Wild rice also grows sparingly along here—look for the tall delicate grass in the early fall when the tasty grain can be shaken from the fruiting heads.

Not too far from Taylor's Landing you will pass under an abandoned railroad trestle, and a little over halfway down to Worden Pond, you will pass under power transmission lines where you were once able to walk on elevated planking across the northern half of Great Swamp. When you reach Worden Pond, take note of the wind conditions. The thousand-acre pond can be quite treacherous if the wind is strong, especially since the wind comes typically from the south and builds up sizable waves across more than a mile of open water. If it is possible to schedule your trip so that you reach Worden Pond before 10 AM you will improve your chances of avoiding windy conditions.

There is some development along the eastern and southern shore of Worden Pond, and Worden's Pond Road passes along the south shore, so unless you are disembarking at the public boat landing at the south end, you will probably enjoy the northern shore more. You will pass a privately owned island on your left, used as a hunting and fishing camp, and then Stony Point on the right—which makes a great picnic stop. Stony Point is aptly named: large, seemingly out-of-place granite boulders extend into the pond. On the small rise here you will see beech, white oak, red oak, and sassafras, along with the more water-tolerant red maple and black gum found throughout Great Swamp.

The maximum depth of this natural basin is seven feet, and the average depth only four feet. There are extensive areas of bulrush growing in the shallow water, and if you enjoy fishing, you can go after largemouth bass, pickerel, northern pike, bullhead catfish, yellow perch, white perch, landlocked alewife, golden shiner, American eel, and smallmouth bass. It is a highly regarded spot for largemouth bass and pickerel. Surprisingly, the pond bottom is fairly firm and sandy along here instead of thick ooze as you might expect. In the cove west of Stony Point is a large seaplane hangar, oddly alone at the edge of the Pond. The hangar was built in the early 1960s and used by the federal Fish and Wildlife Service until 1973 or 1974. From a sandy access point just east of the hangar you can reach a network of trails crisscrossing Great Neck and extending along a dike built to maintain wildlife habitat in the swamp (see discussion below). Great Neck rises to a surprisingly high 182 feet.

It was here on Great Neck in 1675 that the Great Swamp Fight occurred—the turning point in King Philip's ill-fated rebellion against the English settlers. When the Pilgrims arrived in New England in 1620, they were befriended and kept alive by the Native Americans, who taught them how to plant corn and live off the New England landscape. Over the years, though, more and more settlers arrived in the New World, pushing the Native Americans onto smaller and smaller corners of remaining wilderness. As pressure built, Metacom, a Wampanoag chief dubbed King Philip of Pokanoket by the colonists, convinced the Narraganset and other tribes to resist the settlers. In 1675, Metacom's braves launched a series of bloody raids against the whites that became known as King Philip's War. Many settlements were attacked and some destroyed. Whites retaliated by attacking native settlements.

The first heavy snow of December was falling when colonial soldiers from Connecticut, Massachusetts, and Plymouth colonies set out on a march inland from the burned-out garrison at Pettaquamscutt, south of Wickford. Their goal was to destroy an enemy fortress somewhere in a vast swamp near Kingston. Opposing them were King Philip's raiders and a band of about one thousand Narragansett braves, squaws, and children who had gathered with their winter stores inside a freshly built fort. In the battle the Narragansett were slaughtered. It was the fiercest fight of King Philip's War.

If the wind is calm and the water clear as you paddle on Worden Pond, you may see evidence of more modern military operations. Sizable depressions are visible in the bottom of the pond, looking rather like oversized sunfish nesting sites. These are practice-bomb craters. From 1943 until the end of the Korean War, the pond was used for bombing practice. The military placed a mock battleship here that was used for target practice. So even if you see and hear an occasional motorboat, remember: it could be a lot worse!

Pawcatuck River from Worden Pond to Biscuit City Road

Continuing around the northern shore of Worden Pond from the seaplane hangar, you will round Case Point and then reach the Pawcatuck River outlet (this first stretch of river, until it joins the Usquepaug River, is sometimes referred to as the Charles River). The Pawcatuck is, if anything, even more tightly twisting than the Chipuxet, and this seems to be a denser, more magical part of the Great Swamp. Tall scarlet oak and red maple trees shade the river, and dense canopies of grape and greenbriar vines sweep down to the water's surface. Be aware, though, that one of the healthiest vines along this stretch of river is poison ivy: in some places poison ivy is draped over fallen trees so thickly that you can't avoid brushing against it as you paddle underneath, so if you are allergic to poison ivy, plan your attire appropriately. Depending on the amount of deadfall, you may also have to carry your canoe over or around an obstruction or two. Because of the tight curves along the Pawcatuck, you will do much better in a canoe without a keel.

About a mile from Worden Pond, you will see a built-up bank on the right and an obvious spot to pull up your canoe by some concrete abutments. This is the dike built to create the Great Swamp Waterfowl Impoundment, which provides nesting habitat for numerous waterfowl species. Climb the bank to the trail that extends along the dike and over to Great Neck. Birdwatching here is fantastic. In a mid-October trip we were treated to the rare sight of a peregrine falcon and its nearly successful efforts to catch a teal. You are much more likely to see osprey here—a relatively common though still exciting raptor that you will see dive for fish. Ospreys nest atop the power-line poles that cross the swamp here. Beneath this power line, you can walk out into the swamp for quite a distance on a plank boardwalk—the same one you saw if you paddled down from Taylor's Landing. When I visited in 1992, the section of boardwalk close to the dike was still in good shape, while farther north there were some breaks in it. Though it might be tempting to carry your canoe over the dike to explore the water on the east side, it's best to leave that area to the wildlife.

From the landing by the dike, the tightly twisting river continues west, passing under the power line and then joining with the Usquepaug River, which comes in from the northeast. If you wish, you can explore up along this river—it parallels the railroad tracks for about a mile, then turns north, crossing under the railroad bridge. If you bear to the left, continuing downstream at the rivers' confluence, you will get to the railroad tracks and Biscuit City Road landing in about three-quarters of a mile. Paddle along the tracks for a short distance and watch for a fork to the right (there is a sign nailed to a tree here indicating "Boat Landing"). Take this fork, paddle under the railroad tracks, and the landing will be just ahead. If you miss the fork, you will reach the Biscuit City Road bridge over the river. Turn around and watch for the fork to the left.

Worden Pond is a large, shallow pond. While it is usually idyllic in the early morning, strong winds can make paddling very difficult and even dangerous.

GETTING THERE: Taylor's Landing can be reached by taking Route 138 West from Route 1. Drive 5.2 miles on Route 138, go through the intersection with Route 110, cross over the Chipuxet River, and take an immediate left onto Liberty Lane, then another immediate left into the parking area for the Great Swamp Management Area. There is room for about a dozen cars here. The Biscuit City Road boat access is reached by taking Route 2 South from Route 138, driving 4.2 miles, then taking a shallow left onto the old Biscuit City Road (unmarked). The boat access is about 0.1 mile down this road. (Biscuit City Road used to cross the tracks right by the boat access, but the road is now blocked off and a new spur connects Route 2 with Biscuit City Road on the other side of the tracks.) There is parking space for about twenty cars at the landing.

The other access point to Worden Pond is on Worden's Pond Road. Take Route 110 to Tuckertown, then drive west on Worden's Pond Road for 0.5 mile. The access is on the right, with parking space for about fifteen cars. There are two private campgrounds on the south side of Worden Pond: Worden's Pond Family Campground (416A Worden's Pond Road, Wakefield, RI 02879; 401-789-9113, which has 200 campsites (75 for tents and 125 for trailers); and Card's Camp (1065 Worden's Pond Road, Wakefield, RI 02879; 401-783-7158, which has 275 campsites for trailer camping only. Neither of these campgrounds has sites directly on Worden Pond.

Tucker Pond
South Kingstown, RI

Tucker Pond, just to the south and east of Worden Pond in southern Rhode Island, has perhaps the most dramatic stand of rhododendron or rose bay (*Rhododendron maximum*) I have seen north of the southern Appalachians. Almost the entire shoreline of this 100-acre pond is covered with this largest member of the heath family—a group that includes mountain laurel, azalea, blueberry, cranberry, and leatherleaf. Though I haven't been here when the rhododendrons are in bloom (typically June), I can imagine that they are spectacular. On the steeper south and east sides of the pond, they extend up quite high on the banks, with taller white oak, black gum, and pitch pine extending above—as if those trees were growing in a sea of green.

There are about a dozen houses around the pond, but these do not seem terribly imposing, and the ten-horsepower limit for motorboats keeps boating activity to generally quiet fishing. The water seems clean, with a sandy or gravelly bottom. Because this is a natural kettle pond without a major inlet, the water level fluctuates with rainfall. In a dry year, the level may be down considerably. The hilly area extending from Tucker Pond for a few miles south is known as the Charlestown recessional moraine and was created when the last glacier receded ten to twelve thousand years ago. Tucker Pond and the collection of smaller kettle ponds to the south, in an area known as the Matunuck Hills, were formed from chunks of glacial ice left by the receding glacier. There are a number of Nature Conservancy properties around these smaller ponds, whose shoreline ecosystems are fragile and support a number of plant species quite rare in Rhode Island. As a result, public exploration of the other ponds is strongly discouraged; even on Tucker Pond, you should observe the vegetation from your canoe only.

Around much of the perimeter is a band of floating water plants where the water is shallow enough, but most of the pond is open water. Where the rhododendrons do not totally dominate the shoreline, there are highbush blueberry, sweet gale, sweet pepperbush, and red maple. There are a few marshy coves with swamp loosestrife, pickerel weed, and bulrush. There are several islands in the pond, including a large one (with a house fairly well hidden near the peak).

GETTING THERE: To reach Tucker Pond, take Route 110 south from Route 138 in West Kingston, or north from Route 1 in Perryville, to Tuckertown. Where Worden's Pond Road goes off to the west at the

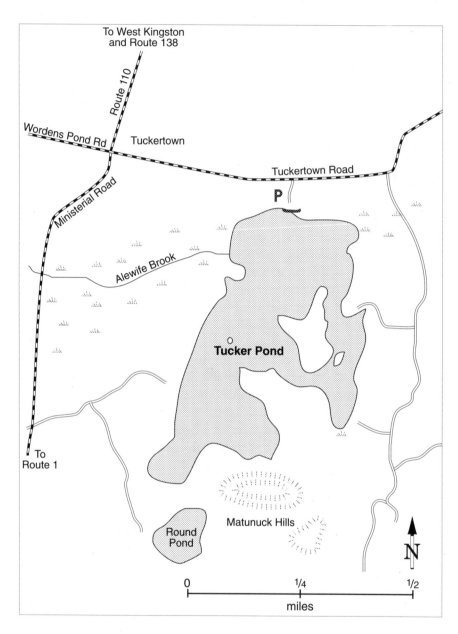

To West Kingston
and Route 138

Route 110

Wordens Pond Rd

Tuckertown

Tuckertown Road

Ministerial Road

P

Alewife Brook

Tucker Pond

To
Route 1

Matunuck Hills

Round
Pond

N

| 0 | 1/4 | 1/2 |

miles

blinking yellow light, turn east on Tuckertown Road. This will be a left turn if you are driving south on 110; right if you are driving north on 110. The state boat access is on the right in 0.5 mile. There is parking space for fifteen to twenty cars. For area camping possibilities, see the sections on Worden Pond, Watchaug Pond, or Ninigret Pond.

Alton Pond and Wood River
Hopkinton, RI

Alton Pond is a small but very pleasant pond that extends north from the town of Alton in southern Rhode Island. Starting from the state-maintained boat access just off Route 91 on the west side of the dam, you initially pass a number of houses—and quite a few people fishing from small powerboats on a nice day. But the farther north you paddle, the nicer it gets. In less than a mile from the boat access, the thirty-nine-acre pond narrows to a winding, deep channel: the Wood River. As you leave the pond, you seem to leave most of the boats and all but the most industrious fishing activity. In fact, I didn't see another soul for the next couple of hours as I leisurely paddled my way north to Woodville.

Alton is one of a string of old textile towns almost hidden along the Wood and Pawcatuck rivers in southern Rhode Island. In their day, these wool and cotton mills were the economic pillar of this area. Alton Pond was formed behind the power-producing dam installed by David L. Aldrich in 1860. His mill changed hands over the years, but is still used for textile production—though the product today is elastic webbing. And, just like a hundred years ago, fishing is the favorite activity on the quiet pond. Trout are stocked here, but Alton Pond is too shallow to sustain a breeding population. Other species include yellow perch, sunfish, largemouth bass, and pickerel. The main pond has considerable milfoil growth, but the main channel of the Wood River seems clear.

Along the Wood River, there are numerous oxbows, side channels, eddies, and hidden ponds, all of which are rich in wildlife. I saw several pairs of wood ducks (plus lots of nesting boxes), a green heron, mallards, and songbirds galore. Scattered piles of mussel shells along the shoreline were evidence of raccoon feasts. Much of the shoreline is marshy, with tussocks of grass extending out into the water. If you're quiet as you paddle along, you'll see literally hundreds of painted turtles on a sunny day, basking on floating logs or on these tussocks of grass. Along the shore are ancient blueberry bushes, black gum, red maple, and white pine. In stretches where the ground rises steeply from the water there are dense, lush stands of mountain laurel. With the river flowing so slowly, it is quite easy to lose the main channel and find yourself in one of the oxbow ponds, though by late spring most of these are fairly thick with vegetation.

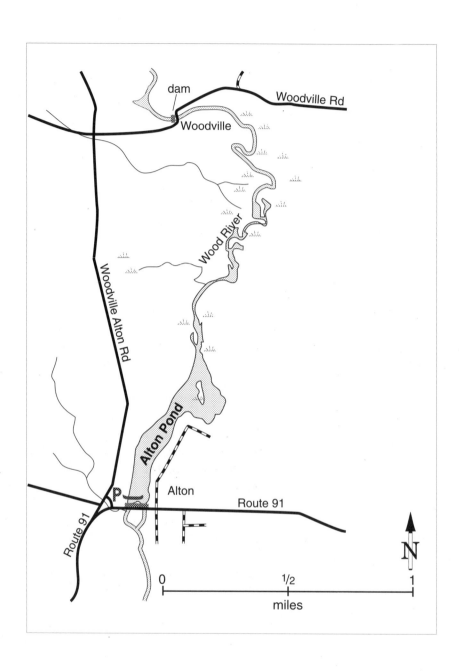

dam

Woodville Rd

Woodville

Wood River

Woodville Alton Rd

Alton Pond

Route 91

P

Alton

Route 91

Route 91

N

0   1/2   1
miles

While there seems to be a slight "industrial" smell to the river (much less than was once the case), it is beautiful along here, and it feels quite remote. One-and-a-half or two miles upstream, the channel forks. By paddling up the smaller left fork you quickly come to an old farm and mill building. The mill looks long-abandoned, but must have been quite impressive in its day. After the fork, the main channel curves around to the southeast before continuing on toward Woodville. Soon you reach a bridge where Woodville Road crosses the river, and a beautiful dam just beyond. It is here that water was diverted for the mill. At the dam is the ruins of a much older stone mill building. There is room for a few cars to pull over along the Woodville Road just across from a nursery and gift shop, Wood River Evergreens. For someone preferring a one-way paddle, this could provide a good drop-off point, though I don't mind paddling back the way I have come—there's always more to see on the return trip.

GETTING THERE: If you approach from the west on Route 91, drive to the village of Alton, approximately 1.4 miles west of the Hope Valley Road intersection at Wood River Junction. After passing Alton Pond on the right, drive another hundred yards or so and take a sharp right onto the Woodville Alton Road; then take a fairly immediate right into the Nathaniel S. Lewis Memorial Boat Landing (the landing and sign are readily visible from Route 91). There is room for about fifteen cars in the parking lot here. For more information on paddling the Wood River, refer to the *AMC River Guide: Massachusetts/Connecticut/Rhode Island.*

Watchaug Pond
Charlestown, RI

Located near the southern tip of Rhode Island, Watchaug Pond is a large body of water (573 acres) that, despite heavy recreational use, offers enjoyable canoeing, particularly for a family camping at Burlingame State Park. With 755 campsites, Burlingame is the largest camping area in the state and certainly one of the largest in New England. The campground is often filled to capacity during the summer months—and the chances of finding a campsite anywhere near the water are next to zero. So for me, Watchaug Pond is a place to visit either early or late in the season (the campground is open from April 15 through Columbus Day).

While paddling on the pond on a quite cool late afternoon in early May, I was surprised to see a half-dozen kids on jet-skis near the southeastern end, by the public boat-launch area. Heavy use at that end, along with some shoreline development on the east side of the pond, provide strong incentive to concentrate on the northern and western sections for your paddling. The marshy western end feels much more remote and wild. In fact, even as I heard the whining drone of jet-skis in the distance as dusk approached, I watched an otter near the outlet at the northwestern tip. It was a pleasant contrast. Although you rarely see otters in southern New England, you're likely to see this delightful mammal sooner or later if you spend much time paddling around the less-developed lakes, ponds, and rivers at dawn or dusk.

You can get away from most of the activity on Watchaug Pond by paddling down the Poquiant Brook, Watchaug's outlet, at the northwestern tip of the pond. I followed this quiet, meandering brook for at least a half-mile through thick marsh. On a windy day when Watchaug Pond is rough, escaping into this quiet, secluded area makes a lot of sense. You'll see lots of blueberry bushes along here, with cedar, black gum, and a wide assortment of marsh plants. Keep an eye out for wood ducks—I saw a few here. They are elusive, and you're most likely to see them disappearing over the treetops as you paddle near. I was also surprised to see a loon on this pond. It must have been a migrant on its way through, as there are no current records of loons nesting in Rhode Island.

Near the southern end of Watchaug is the Kimball Wildlife Refuge, owned and managed by the Audubon Society of Rhode Island. There are wonderful trails through the oak and laurel woodland here. Contact the Audubon Society to find out about their frequent natural programs here (Audubon Society of Rhode Island, 12 Sanderson Road,

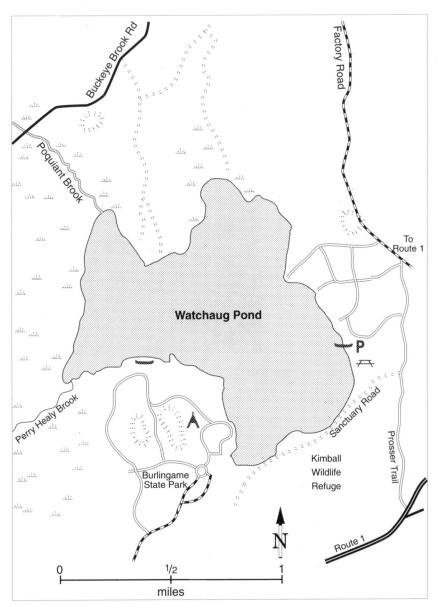

Buckeye Brook Rd

Factory Road

Poquiant Brook

To
Route 1

Watchaug Pond

P

Perry Healy Brook

Sanctuary Road

Prosser Trail

Burlingame
State Park

Kimball
Wildlife
Refuge

N

Route 1

```
0                    1/2                    1
|--------------------|--------------------|
                 miles
```

Smithfield, RI 02917; 401-231-6444).

Burlingame State Park manages the boat launch and picnic area on the southeastern tip of the pond, as well as the large camping area farther west. The camping facility offers canoe rentals by the day, half-day, and various other time periods up to a week. There is a day-use fee at the campground and at the picnic area during the primary summer season. For more information on camping or picnicking, write to Burlingame State Park, Division of Parks and Recreation, 2321 Hart-

The edge of Watchaug Pond just after dawn in early May. The best time to visit Watchaug is before school's out in the spring, or after Labor Day.

ford Avenue, Johnston, RI 02919; or call 401-322-7994 (-7337).

GETTING THERE: The Burlingame State Park camping area is easy to reach off Route 1. Coming from the west (driving on Route 1 North) drive 1.1 mile past the intersection of Route 1 and 216, turn left off Route 1, and follow clear signs to the Burlingame Camping Area, turning right twice to get into the park. If you are driving south on Route 95, take Route 3 South to 216 near the Connecticut border, and follow 216 south to Route 1. Turn onto Route 1 North, and follow the above directions. If driving down the coast on Route 1 South, watch for signs to the Burlingame Camping Area a few miles after passing the intersection with Routes 112 and 2. To reach the Burlingame Picnic Area and public boat access from the campground, take Route 1 North, 2.2 miles past the camping area access road, then make a U-turn on Route 1, following signs to the Burlingame Picnic Area—this will take you back on Route 1 South for 0.2 mile, then right onto Prosser Trail. After 0.7 mile, turn left into the Burlingame Picnic Area, again following clearly marked signs. You will reach the parking area shortly, and the boat launch is just a few hundred yards past it. Parking is limited at the boat launch area, so you may need to drive back to the picnic area and park there. By driving past the boat launch on Sanctuary Road, you will reach the Kimball Wildlife Refuge, mentioned above.

Ninigret Pond

Charlestown, RI

At seventeen hundred acres, Ninigret is Rhode Island's largest coastal pond. While portions of the pond are quite developed, it offers very enjoyable canoeing—in the right conditions—and superb wildlife observation opportunities. Be aware, though, that strong winds, tidal currents, and moderate motorboat traffic during summer weekends can present hazards for the paddler.

The eastern third of Ninigret Pond is quite heavily developed, while the western two-thirds are relatively wild, except for the extreme western end and some houses along the northwestern edge. Roughly centered on the pond and mostly on the northern shore is the Ninigret National Wildlife Refuge. Most of this four-hundred-acre refuge was once a United States Naval Reservation auxiliary landing field, which explains the extensive areas of pavement. Along with paddling here, you might want to hike around the old airfield and observe how nature is gradually reclaiming the miles of runway. More than 250 species of birds have been recorded here, with prime birding in the spring and fall. Be aware that the area is used for duck hunting; you should schedule a fall visit so as not to coincide with waterfowl-hunting seasons.

The northern and southern shores of Ninigret are quite different. Along the northern shore, the vegetation is primarily shrubby grassland with bayberry, blueberry, beach plum, shadbush, wild cherry, dogwood, cedar, and seaside goldenrod—an ecosystem that provides excellent bird habitat, especially as a stopover for migrating warblers. The marshier tidal coves and inlets have tall stands of Phragmites, with patches of *Spartina* occupying the lower sections that are regularly flooded.

Along the southern shore of the pond—on the inland side of the barrier beach—salt-marsh grass dominates the vegetation: *Spartina patens* and *S. alterniflora*. Mixed in the with the *Spartina* is sea lavender (*Limonium nashii*), a delicate plant with tiny lavender flowers resembling the baby's breath used by florists. It is commonly dried for use in wreaths and dried flower arrangements. In fact, so much sea lavender has been collected in some areas of the Northeast that it no longer adds its subtle lavender blush to the the salt marsh. Enjoy the plant where it is growing, and avoid the temptation to pick it. You will see scallop shells washed up, patches of eelgrass flowing with the tidal currents, and clumps of seaweed and sponge on rocks as you paddle the shallow pond. This is one of the best locations for catching winter flounder, and bluefish can be caught when they enter the pond to feed

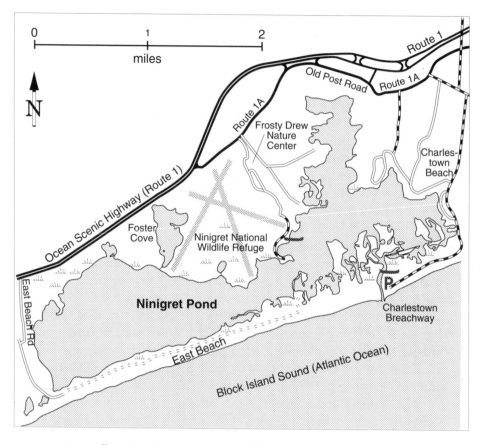

on young flounder in the summer. The pond also harbors soft-shell clams, quahog, Atlantic bay scallop, and oysters, all of which are harvested commercially .

You can beach your canoe in some places along the south shore of Ninigret Pond and walk across the dunes to East Beach to enjoy the crashing waves of the Atlantic Ocean. East Beach is accessible by foot or four-wheel-drive vehicle only, and parking at the end of East Beach Road is limited to keep the crowds down. The section of Ninigret's south shore that is part of the wildlife refuge is closed to the public to protect bird nesting. Least terns and piping plovers—both listed as endangered species—may nest on the barrier beach or dunes above the high-tide line, so be very careful not to disturb any nesting birds.

GETTING THERE: There are several ways to get into Ninigret Pond. One option is to drive into the Ninigret Wildlife Refuge on the north side of the pond, via Route 1A (Old Post Road). From Route 1, turn onto Route 1A just west of Charlestown (to turn off here you have to be on Route 1 North; if you are traveling on Route 1 South, follow signs for the U-turn onto 1 North). Follow signs to the Frosty Drew Nature Center and the East Entrance to Ninigret National Wildlife Refuge. From the parking area (on one of the old runways) you have to carry your canoe to the water on one of the trails).

To launch your canoe without a carry, drive to the Charlestown Breachway, where there is a public boat ramp and parking area (there is a hefty charge for parking). To reach this access point, take Route 1 to the turnoff for Charlestown Beach (again, if you are traveling on Route 1 South, you will have to make a U-turn after passing the exit). The northbound exit for Charlestown Beach puts you on Narrow Lane. Go through the lights and turn left onto 1A at the T, following signs for the beach. Continue on this road for 0.2 mile, and turn right just before a small store. After another 1.3 miles you will cross over a small channel of water at the eastern end of Ninigret Pond and the entrance to the Town Beach parking area, which is limited to Charlestown residents. Continue for another 1.0 mile to the state-run Charlestown Breachway Area. There is a boat launch and parking area here, as well as seventy-five "campsites" for trailers (really just parking spaces on the hard-packed sand). At this boat access, you have to deal with a fairly strong tidal current through the breachway (a man-made connection between Ninigret Pond and the ocean to permit constant flux of water in the pond, which helps the shellfishery). If you can schedule your visit so as to launch your canoe with the tide coming in and return as the tide is going out, you can avoid fighting the current, but because the breach-way is narrow, the tide in Ninigret Pond lags considerably behind the ocean tide. (The sea water can't flow in quickly enough to keep up with the rising tide, so even after the ocean tide turns and begins dropping, the water level in Ninigret is still lower and water continues to flow in through the breachway until the water levels equalize. How much the tide lags behind the ocean tide depends on the tidal differential, which in turn depends on the phase of the moon.)

For information on the Ninigret National Wildlife Refuge, contact Ninigret N.W.R., P.O. Box 307, Charlestown, RI 02813; 401-364-9124. For information on camping and the Ninigret Conservation Area, contact the Rhode Island Department of Environmental Management, Division of Parks and Recreation, 2321 Hartford Avenue, Johnstown, RI 02919; 401-322-0450. Camping is also available at Burlingame State Park just north of Route 1 from Ninigret Pond (see section on Watchaug Pond).

Alphabetical Listing of Lakes and Ponds

Connecticut

Massachusetts

Rhode Island

About the AMC

The Appalachian Mountain Club pursues a vigorous conservation agenda while encouraging responsible recreation, based on the philosophy that succcessful, long-term conservation depends upon firsthand experience of the natural environment. Our members have joined the AMC to pursue their interests in hiking, canoeing, skiing, walking, rock climbing, bicycling, camping, kayaking, and backpacking, and— at the same time—to help safeguard the environment in which these activities are possible.

Since it was founded in 1876, the Club has been at the forefront of the environmental protection movement. By cofounding several of New England's leading environmental organizations, and working in coalition with these and many more groups, the AMC has positively influenced legislation and public opinion.

Volunteers in each chapter lead hundreds of outdoor activities and excursions and offer introductory instruction in backcountry sports. The AMC education department offers members and the public a wide range of workshops, from introductory camping to the intensive Mountain Leadership School taught on the trails of the White Mountains.

The most recent efforts in the AMC conservation program include river protection, Northern Forest Lands policy, Sterling Forest (NY) preservation, and support for the Clean Air Act.

The AMC's research department focuses on the forces affecting the ecosystem, including ozone levels, acid rain and fog, climate change, rare flora and habitat protection, and air quality and visibility.

AMC Trails

The AMC trails program maintains over 1,400 miles of trail (including 350 miles of the Appalachian Trail) and more than 50 shelters in the Northeast. Through a coordinated effort of volunteers, seasonal crews, and program staff, the AMC contributes more than 10,000 hours of public service work each summer in the area from Washington, D.C. to Maine.

In addition to supporting our work by becoming an AMC member, hikers can donate time as volunteers. The club sponsors ten-day service projects throughout the United States, Adopt-a-Trail programs, trails day events, trail skills workshops, and chapter and camp volunteer projects.

The AMC has a longstanding connection to Acadia National Park. Working in cooperation with the National Park Service and Friends of Acadia, the AMC Trails Program provides many opportunities to preserve the park's resources. These include half-day volunteer projects for guests at AMC's Echo Lake Camp, ten-day service projects, week-long volunteer crews in the fall, and trails day events. For more information on these public service volunteer opportunities, contact the AMC Trails Program, Pinkham Notch Visitor Center, P.O. Box 298, Gorham NH 03581; 603-466-2721, www.outdoors.org.

The club operates eight alpine huts in the White Mountains that provide shelter, bunks and blankets, and hearty meals for hikers. Pinkham Notch Visitor Center, at the foot of Mt. Washington, is base camp to the adventurous and the ideal location for individuals and families new to outdoor recreation. Comfortable bunkrooms, mountain hospitality, and home-cooked, family-style meals make Pinkham Notch Visitor Center a fun and affordable choice for lodging. For reservations, call 603-466-2727.

At the AMC headquarters in Boston and at Pinkham Notch Visitor Center in New Hampshire, the bookstore and information center stock the entire line of AMC publications, as well as other trail and river guides, maps, reference materials, and the latest articles on conservation issues. Guidebooks and other AMC gifts are available by calling toll-free 800-262-4455 or visiting www.outdoors.org. Also available from the bookstore or by subscription is *Appalachia,* the country's oldest mountaineering and conservation journal.

ISBN 1-878239-19-8

6 52932 01295 0